Microsoft® Word 2000

Sherry Kinkoph

Sams is a Division of Macmillan Computer Publishing, USA
201 W. 103rd Street
Indianapolis, Indiana 46290

SAMS

Visually in Full Color

How to Use
Microsoft® Word 2000

International Standard Book Number: 0-672-31531-9

Library of Congress Catalog Card Number: **98-88329**

First Printing: April 1999

01   00   99   4   3   2   1

Interpretation of the printing code: The rightmost double-digit number is the year of the book's printing; the rightmost single-digit, the number of the book's printing. For example, a printing code of 99-1 shows that the first printing of the book occurred in 1999.

Printed in the United States of America. This book was produced digitally by Macmillan Computer Publishing and manufactured using computer-to-plate technology (a film-less process) by GAC, Indianapolis, Indiana.

Executive Editor
Jim Minatel

Acquisitions Editor
Renee Wilmeth

Development Editor
Jill Hayden

Managing Editor
Thomas F. Hayes

Project Editor
Mike La Bonne

Copy Editor
Pat Kinyon

Indexers
Larry Sweazy
Craig Small

Technical Editor
Debra Schnedler

Proofreader
Maribeth Echard

Book Designers
Nathan Clement
Ruth C. Lewis

Cover Designers
Aren Howell
Gary Adair

Production
Trina Wurst

Contents at a Glance

Contents

CONTENTS **V**

About the Author

Sherry Kinkoph has authored more than 30 computer books for Macmillan Publishing over the past six years. Her recent publications include *Easy Office 97 Small Business Edition, Sams Teach Yourself Quicken Deluxe 99 in 10 Minutes*, and *Using Microsoft Works Suite 99*.

Sherry started exploring computers in college and claims that she whipped out many a term paper by using a trusty 128KB Macintosh. Today, Sherry's still churning out words, but now they're in the form of books. And instead of using a Macintosh, she's moved on to a trusty PC. A native of the Midwest, Sherry currently resides in Fishers, IN, and continues in her quest to help users of all levels master ever-changing computer technologies. You can email Sherry at **skinkoph@inetdirect.net**.

Dedication

To my euchre club: **Alicia** and **Kevin Gray, Carmen** and **Dan Laudenschlager, Robin** and **Alan Oglesby**, and my favorite partner **Greg**—for all their support and silliness. May they be so impressed to have a book dedicated to them that they'll let me win the next tournament.

Acknowledgments

Special thanks to **Renee Wilmeth** for her excellent acquisitions work; to **Jill Hayden** for her fine development work; to **Pat Kinyon** for dotting the i's and crossing the t's; to **Mike La Bonne** for shepherding this book every step of the way until its final form; and to **Debra Schnedler** for checking the technical accuracy of the book. Finally, extra special thanks to the **production team** for assembling this visual masterpiece.

How to Use This Book

The Complete Visual Reference

Each chapter of this book is made up of a series of short, instructional tasks, designed to help you understand all the information that you need to get the most out of your computer hardware and software.

 Click: Click the left mouse button once.

 Double-click: Click the left mouse button twice in rapid succession.

 Right-click: Click the right mouse button once.

 Pointer Arrow: Highlights an item on the screen you need to point to or focus on in the step or task.

Selection: Highlights the area onscreen discussed in the step or task.

 Click-and-Type: Click once where indicated and begin typing to enter your text or data.

 Click & Drag

Release

How to Drag: Point to the starting place or object. Hold down the mouse button (right or left per instructions), move the mouse to the new location, and then release the button.

 Key icons: Clearly indicate which key combinations to use.

Each task includes a series of easy-to-understand steps designed to guide you through the procedure.

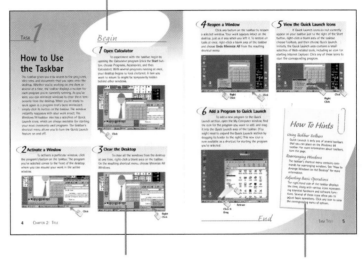

Each step is fully illustrated to show you how it looks onscreen.

Extra hints that tell you how to accomplish a goal are provided in most tasks.

Menus and items you click are shown in **bold**. Words in *italic* are defined in more detail in the glossary. Information you type is in a `special font`.

Continues

If you see this symbol, it means the task you're in continues on the next page.

Tell Us What You Think!

As the reader of this book, *you* are our most important critic and commentator. We value your opinion and want to know what we're doing right, what we could do better, what areas you'd like to see us publish in, and any other words of wisdom you're willing to pass our way.

As the Executive Editor for the General Desktop Applications team at Sams Publishing, I welcome your comments. You can fax, email, or write me directly to let me know what you did or didn't like about this book—as well as what we can do to make our books stronger.

Please note that I cannot help you with technical problems related to the topic of this book, and that due to the high volume of mail I receive, I might not be able to reply to every message.

When you write, please be sure to include this book's title and author as well as your name and phone or fax number. I will carefully review your comments and share them with the author and editors who worked on the book.

Fax:　　317-581-4770

Email:　`office_sams@mcp.com`

Mail:　　Executive Editor
　　　　　　General Desktop Applications
　　　　　　Sams Publishing
　　　　　　201 West 103rd Street
　　　　　　Indianapolis, IN 46290 USA

Introduction

*D*id you just buy a copy of the new and improved Word 2000, or did your office recently upgrade? Need to learn how to use Microsoft Word 2000, but don't have time to wade through an exhaustive tome to find out what you need to know? Are you a visual learner—like to see how to do things rather than read about them? If you answered yes to any of these questions, *How to Use Microsoft Word 2000* is the book for you.

This book is written and assembled especially for visual learners and users who want to get up and running fast with the new and improved Word software. In the pages to follow, you will learn how to use the basic features and functions of Word in an easy-to-understand, straightforward manner. You will learn

- ✓ How to create and save Word documents
- ✓ How to apply all kinds of formatting to make your documents professional-looking and readable
- ✓ How to use the new personalized menus
- ✓ How to work with the new toolbar functions
- ✓ How to work with templates and wizards
- ✓ How to use Word's proofing tools to help you polish your documents
- ✓ How to use Word's Internet features

Each topic is presented visually, step by step, so you can clearly see how to apply each feature and function to your own computer tasks. The illustrations show exactly what you will see on your own computer screen, making it easy to follow along.

You can choose to use the book as a tutorial, progressing through each section one task at a time, or as a reference, looking up specific features you want to learn about. There's no right or wrong way—use the method that best suits your own learning style.

In no time at all, you will have mastered all the basic tools needed to use Word for your own office or home needs. In addition, you will have gained the fundamental skills for working more productively on your computer. You can't find a better word processing program than Microsoft Word 2000, and you can't learn it more easily than with *How to Use Microsoft Word 2000*.

Task

How to Get Started with Word

Welcome to Microsoft Word, one of the most popular, best-selling word processing programs ever created. With it, you can create all manner of documents, including letters, memos, reports, flyers, manuscripts, newsletters, and more. When it comes to working with text, there's no match for Microsoft Word.

Whether you purchased Word as a standalone product, or whether you're using it as a part of a the Microsoft Office suite of programs, Word will probably become your most-used computer program. Its versatility and numerous features make it an essential part of your daily computing tasks. In this first chapter of the book, you will learn how to get up and running fast with Word and acclimate yourself with the various elements in the program window. The fundamental skills covered in this chapter will prepare you for working with Word's numerous tools and features covered in the chapters that follow. ●

How to Start and Exit Word

There are several different methods you can employ to start and exit Word. By far the most familiar way to open a program is to use the Start menu on the Windows 98 taskbar. You can also start Word by using a shortcut icon on the desktop, if available, or by double-clicking any Word file displayed in Windows Explorer or My Computer.

After you finish using Word, use one of several methods for closing the program window. Don't forget to save your work before exiting.

Begin

1 Open the Start Menu

Click the **Start** button on the Windows taskbar.

Click

2 Choose Programs

Click **Programs** to display the menu list.

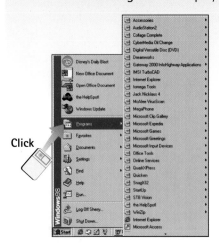

Click

3 Choose Microsoft Word

Click **Microsoft Word** from the Programs menu list.

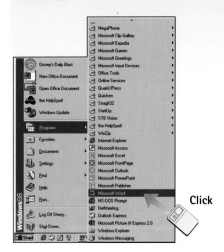

Click

4 The Program Window Opens

Immediately, Word opens into its own window with its name in the title bar.

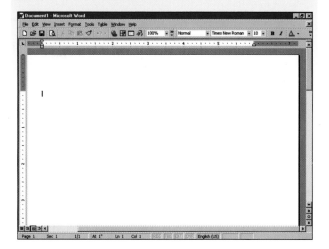

5 Quick Exit

The quickest way to close Word is to click the window's **Close** button, the button with an X in the upper-right corner of the window, or press **Alt+F4** on the keyboard.

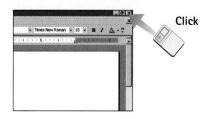

Click

6 Save Your Work

If you haven't saved your work yet, Word prompts you to do so before exiting. Click **Yes** to save, **No** to exit without saving, or **Cancel** to cancel the exit procedure. (To learn more about saving files, turn to Task 2, "How to Save Your Work," in Chapter 2.)

End

How-To Hints

Create a Shortcut Icon

You can easily create a shortcut icon for Word to access the program from the Windows desktop. Right-click a blank area of the desktop and select **New, Shortcut**. Use the **Browse** button to locate the executable file for the program, **WINWORD.EXE** (you'll find this file by opening the **Program Files** folder, opening **Microsoft Office**, and then opening the **Office** folders), and double-click it. Then click **Next** and give the shortcut a name you will easily recognize. Click **Finish** and the icon is added to the desktop. Next time you want to open the program, just double-click its shortcut icon.

Other Exit Routes

You can also close the Word program window by displaying the **File** menu and selecting **Exit**. Yet another way to exit is to click the **Control-menu icon** (the icon that looks like a tiny document with a big W at the far left end of the Title bar), select **Close**, or just double-click the icon itself.

How to Get Around the Word Window

When you first open Word, a blank document opens onscreen. The document is surrounded by tools you can use to help you enter and work with text and other items you place in the document. If you're new to Word, take a few moments and familiarize yourself with the window elements in this task.

Begin

1 The Program Window Controls

The program window opens along with a blank document window. Usually, both windows are maximized—the program window fills the whole screen, and the document window fills the program window. When the program window is maximized, a Restore button is displayed in the set of buttons in the upper-right corner of the window's screen.

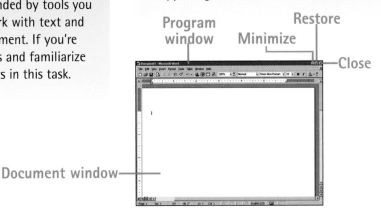

Program window · Minimize · Restore · Close

Document window

2 Maximize the Program Window

If your program window isn't maximized, click its **Maximize** button.

Maximize

3 Minimize the Program Window

To minimize the program window to a button on the Windows taskbar, click the **Minimize** button. To enlarge the window again, click the button on the taskbar representing the document with which you were working.

Minimized program window

4 View the Title Bar

The title bar tells you what is in the window. When the document window is maximized, it has to share the title bar with the program window, so the title bar contains the names of both the program (Microsoft Word) and the file. (Document1 is a temporary name for your document. When you save it for the first time, you will replace that name with a name you choose.)

Title bar

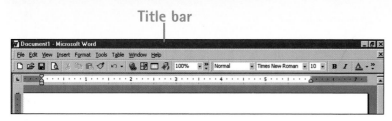

5 Use the Menu Bar

The Word menu bar contains menus, which in turn contain all the available Word commands. All the tasks you need to perform are available through menu commands. To use the menu commands, click the menu name to display the menu, and then click the command you want. (Learn more about Word's menus in Task 3, "How to Work with Personalized Menus.")

Menu bar

Continues

6 Use Toolbar Shortcuts

Word's toolbars contain shortcuts for frequently used commands. By default, the Standard and Formatting toolbars appear side by side when you first start the program, but there are many other toolbars you can use, as you'll learn in Task 4, "How to Work with Toolbars." To activate a toolbar button, click it.

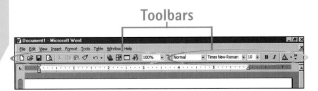

Toolbars

7 View the Ruler

The ruler shows you where your margins are, and it lets you set tabs and indents. Depending on what Word view you're using, you may see both the horizontal and vertical rulers. If you don't see the ruler, you can display it by opening the **View** menu and choosing **Ruler**.

Horizontal ruler

8 Utilize the Work Area

The typing area in a new document is the large blank space bordered by vertical and horizontal scroll bars. The *insertion point* (a vertical, blinking line, also known as the *cursor*) shows you where the next character you type will appear. When the mouse pointer is placed over the typing area, it resembles an I-beam.

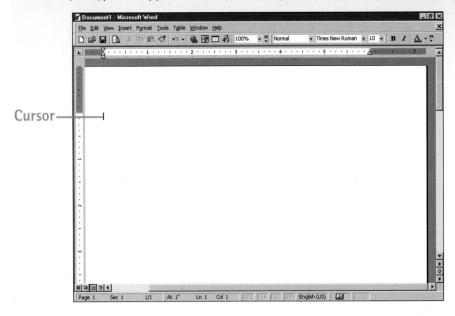

Cursor

9 Move Your View with Scrollbars

The vertical and horizontal scrollbars allow you to view different portions of your document. Use the arrows on the scrollbars to scroll in the appropriate direction or drag the scroll box. Use the **Previous Page** and **Next Page** buttons (at the bottom of the vertical scrollbar) to quickly jump from one part of your document to the next.

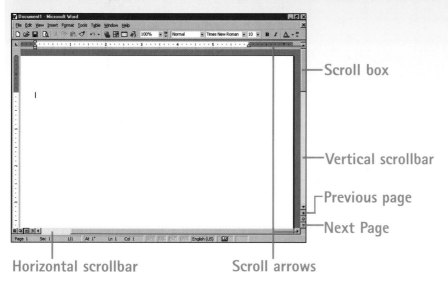

Scroll box

Vertical scrollbar

Previous page

Next Page

Horizontal scrollbar

Scroll arrows

10 View the Status Bar

The status bar, located along the bottom edge of your screen, indicates the current page number, the total number of pages, and the location of your insertion point on the page.

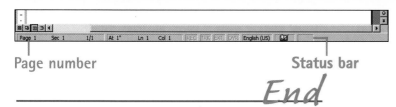

Page number

Status bar

End

How-To Hints

What Toolbars?

If you don't see the Standard or Formatting toolbar, or if you see other toolbars you would like to hide, open the **View** menu and select **Toolbars**. This displays a list of available toolbars. A check mark next to the toolbar name means the toolbar is displayed. Click a toolbar to select or deselect it for display.

No Scrollbars?

If either of your scrollbars or your status bar isn't showing, open the **Tools** menu and choose **Options**. Click the **View** tab; then, under the Show heading, click any check box that isn't already marked—**Status Bar**, **Horizontal Scroll Bar**, and/or **Vertical Scroll Bar**—and then choose **OK**.

How to Work with Personalized Menus

Microsoft has changed the way menus work in Word 2000 as opposed to previous versions of Word. The new Word offers personalized menus that show only the controls you use the most. Simply put, this means that a menu won't show every available command unless you tell it to; instead, it shows the commands with which you commonly work. You can also customize how menus are displayed. In this task, you learn how to work with the new menus and customize them to suit your needs.

Begin

1 Display a Menu

To open a menu, click on the menu name using the mouse. If you're an avid keyboard user, press the **Alt** key and the underlined letter on the menu name.

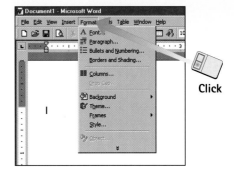

Click

2 Select a Command

To choose a command from the menu, simply click the command or press the command's selection letter (the underlined letter in the command name).

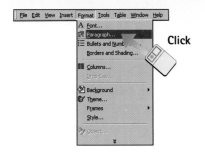

Click

3 View the Whole Menu

To view the entire menu with all of its commands, open the menu and wait a few seconds, or click the double-arrow icon at the bottom of the menu.

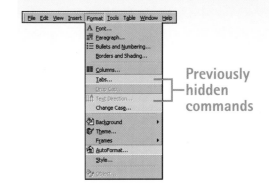

Previously hidden commands

4 View Submenus

A right-pointing arrow next to a menu command means there's a submenu to view. Move your mouse pointer over the arrow to display the submenu. (Some submenus even have submenus from which to select commands.)

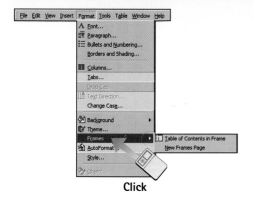

Click

5 Customize Your Menus

To customize your menus, open the **View** menu and select **Toolbars, Customize**. This opens the Customize dialog box.

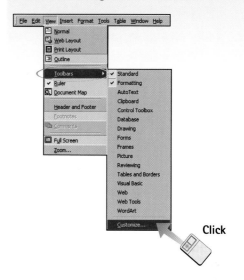

Click

6 Choose an Option

Click the **Options** tab to view menu options. To turn off the personalized menu feature (which means the menus will no longer display just the commands you most recently used), deselect the **Menus show recently used commands first** check box. The remainder of this book will show full menus. Click **Close** to exit the dialog box and apply the changes.

Click

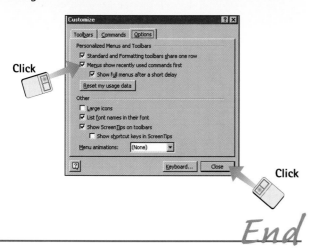

Click

End

How-To Hints

My Personalized Menus Aren't On!

If the personalized menu feature isn't on, open the **Customize** dialog box (another way to open the dialog box is to display the **Tools** menu and choose **Customize**) and click the **Options** tab. Then click the **Show full menus after a short delay** check box. Click **Close** to exit the dialog box.

Use the Shortcut Menu

Almost everything in the Word window has its own shortcut menu, including selected text and misspelled words. To open a shortcut menu that contains often-used commands, click an object with the right mouse button (called a *right-click*), and then use the left mouse button to click the command you want.

How to Work with Toolbars

Toolbars offer you quick shortcuts to commonly used commands with a single click of a button. The toolbars in Word 2000 look and work a little differently than previous versions of Word. For starters, the Standard and Formatting toolbars share the same real estate space onscreen. Secondly, the toolbar buttons you use the most stay visible, and others you don't use as often will no longer appear on the toolbars. This doesn't mean the buttons are gone, just not visible.

As you work with Word, the toolbar buttons displayed will vary, based on how much you use them. If you ever want to know the name of a toolbar button, hover your mouse pointer over the button and a ScreenTip appears with the button's name.

Begin

1 Display Nonvisible Toolbar Buttons

If the button you're looking for isn't onscreen, click the **More Buttons** icon at the far-right end of the toolbar.

Click

2 Select the Button

From the pop-up list that appears, select the toolbar button you want to use. As soon as you do, the command is activated and the button is added to the visible display of buttons on the toolbar.

Click

3 Hide a Toolbar

To hide a toolbar, open the **View** menu and select **Toolbars**. This opens a submenu listing every available toolbar in Word. A check mark next to the toolbar name indicates the toolbar is already displayed. To hide a toolbar, deselect its check mark.

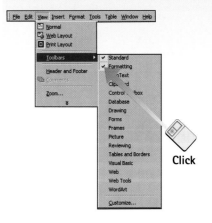

Click

4 The Toolbar Disappears

As soon as you deselect a toolbar from the submenu, it disappears onscreen. In this figure, I've hidden the Formatting toolbar but left the Standard toolbar visible.

5 Display a Toolbar

Another way to turn a toolbar on or off is to use the Toolbar shortcut menu. Right-click over an existing toolbar to display a shortcut menu listing the available toolbars. Click the toolbar you want to display. For example, to redisplay the Formatting toolbar, click **Formatting**. To display a different toolbar, select it from the list.

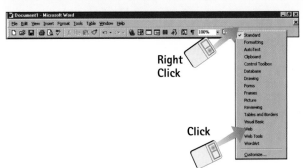

Right Click

Click

6 The Toolbar Appears

As soon as you select a toolbar from the menu, it appears onscreen. In this figure, I've displayed the Web toolbar; it appears below the Standard toolbar.

Web toolbar

End

How-To Hints

Displaying the Default Toolbars

In the remainder of this book, the figures will show both the Standard and Formatting toolbars in their entirety, so your screen may look slightly different than the figures you see in this book.

Lots of Toolbars

There are 16 toolbars available in Word, each one focusing on a particular set of tools. For example, the Drawing toolbar has buttons for using drawing commands. You can also create your own custom toolbar, as explained in Task 5.

Unanchoring Your Toolbars

Some of the toolbars you encounter in Word are floating toolbars, which means they appear in the middle of the screen. Anchored toolbars, like the Standard toolbar, appear lined up along the edges of the program window. All toolbars can become floating toolbars or anchored toolbars. To unanchor an anchored toolbar, hover your mouse pointer over an empty area on the toolbar and drag it out to the middle of the window. To quickly anchor a floating toolbar, double-click its title bar.

How to Customize Your Toolbars

It's easier than ever to customize toolbars to suit your own work needs in Word 2000. For example, by default, the Standard and Formatting toolbars share space, which lets you see more of your document onscreen. But if you prefer to see each toolbar in its entirety, you can revert to the familiar setup of Standard toolbar on top and Formatting toolbar directly below.

You can also specify exactly which buttons you want included on each toolbar in Word. For example, perhaps you never use the Format Painter or Print Preview buttons on the Standard toolbar. You can remove them both. Or maybe you'd rather add a button for Envelopes and Labels. You'll learn how to add and remove buttons in this task, as well as how to change the default toolbar display.

Begin

1 Open the Customize Dialog Box

To customize a toolbar, open the **View** menu and select **Toolbars**, and then **Customize**.

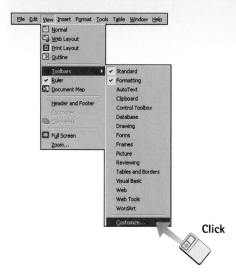

Click

2 Display the Options Tab

From the Customize dialog box, select the **Options** tab to view several toolbar options. To show each of the default toolbars (Standard and Formatting) in full, click the **Standard and Formatting toolbars share one row** check box to deselect the option. Click **Close** to exit the dialog box.

Click

Click

3 Quick Customize

To quickly customize which buttons appear on a particular toolbar, click the **More Buttons** button on the toolbar, and then click **Add or Remove Buttons**.

Click

4 Choose Which Buttons to Display

A list of buttons appears. Those with check marks next to them are currently turned on and are part of the toolbar. Those without check marks are not accessible from the toolbar. To turn a button on or off, select it in the list.

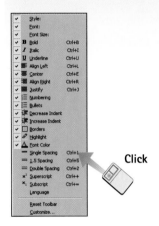

Click

5 Close the List

To exit the toolbar button list, press **Esc** or click anywhere outside the list.

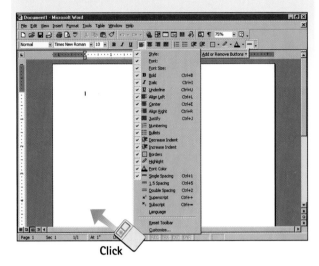

Click

End

How-To Hints

Buttons Too Small?

To switch to larger toolbar button icons, click the **Large icons** check box in the **Options** tab of the **Customize** dialog box.

Can I Get the Default Buttons Back?

If you get too carried away changing buttons, you can always restore the default set. Click the **More Buttons** button for the toolbar, click **Add or Remove Buttons**, and then click **Reset Toolbar**.

Create a Brand-New Toolbar

Open the Customize dialog box, click the **Toolbars** tab, and then click the **New** button. Type in a name and click **OK**. An empty toolbar appears onscreen (you may have to drag the Customize dialog box out of the way to see it). Click the **Commands** tab and look through the **Categories** list box and locate the commands you want to include on your toolbar. Scroll through the **Commands** list box to find the command icon you want to use. Drag it off the list and onto the toolbar where you want it inserted. To remove a button, drag the button off the toolbar. When finished, click **Close**.

How to Work with Dialog Boxes

Many of the commands you activate in Word require additional input from you before Word can carry out the task. That's where dialog boxes come into play. These boxes offer options you can select from to help Word know how to issue the command. Depending on the task you're trying to perform, some dialog boxes contain numerous options, while others offer only a few. Once you've made your selections, click the OK button and Word applies the command.

In this task, you learn how to navigate a typical dialog box and find out how to work with the various options and features found within it. The dialog boxes I'm about to show you will vary so you can see the different kinds of elements available.

Begin

1 Display the Dialog Box

A dialog box may appear when you select certain menu commands or toolbar buttons. For example, menu commands followed by an ellipsis (...) always open a dialog box; if you open the **Format** menu and select **Font**, the Font dialog box opens onscreen.

Click

2 View Tabs

Some dialog boxes have so many options from which to choose that the options are grouped into tabs. To display a tab, click the tab name. This figure shows the Font dialog box, which has three tabs filled with options pertaining to fonts.

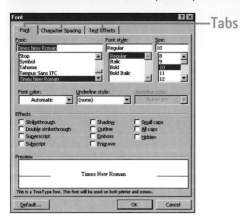
Tabs

3 Use a Text Box

A text box is an obvious place for user input. Click inside the box and enter the appropriate data, whether it's text or numbers. Some text boxes also have spinner arrow buttons you can click to increase or decrease the numeric value in the box.

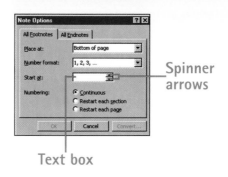
Spinner arrows

Text box

4 Display a Drop-Down List

Many dialog boxes use drop-down lists to display options. To view a list, click the drop-down arrow. To select an item from the list, simply click the item. Other dialog boxes have list boxes, which are permanently displayed lists you can scroll through to select an item.

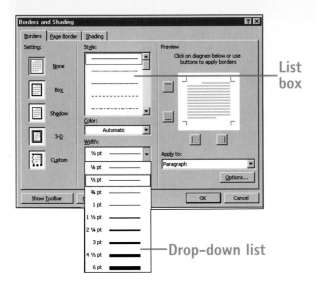

List box

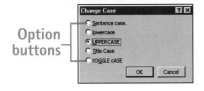

Drop-down list

5 Select a Check Box

To apply a check box option, click the check box to insert a check mark. A check mark inside the check box means the option is selected; no check mark means it's not. You can select as many check box options as you want.

Check boxes

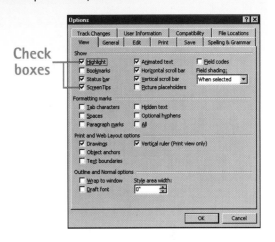

6 Select an Option Button

Like check boxes, round option buttons can also be turned on or off with a click. However, unlike check box options, you can assign only one option button in a group.

Option buttons

7 Use a Command Button

Command buttons look like large buttons in the dialog box. Buttons with ellipsis marks (...) will open additional dialog boxes. To activate a command button, such as Close or OK, click the button.

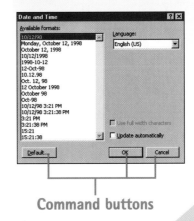

Command buttons

End

Task

2

How to Save, Close, Open, and Create New Files

*T*he world of computers revolves around files, whether they're files you create in a word processing program such as Word or files you create in other types of programs. When you enter data into a Word document and save it, it becomes a file. Files, in turn, are stored in folders. Folders and files are all part of your computer's storage hierarchy.

When you save and open files in Word, the default folder (called *My Documents*) is always at your beck and call in the Save and Open dialog boxes. But you can save your Word files to any other folder you designate. You can also save your files to a floppy disk.

To help you learn how to work with files, this chapter presents seven distinct tasks for using document files you create in Word. You will learn how to start new files, use Word's wizards to create new files, open existing files, save files, assign different file formats, work with multiple files, and find files you think you may have lost.

How to Create a New Document File

When you enter and save your work in Word, it's called a *document* or *file*. By default, Word starts you with a new blank document as soon as you open the program. But you can create additional new files anytime you want. Each new file you create is represented by a button on the Windows taskbar.

Every file you open in Word starts from a *template*, a bare-bones, ready-made document. The blank document that appears when you start Word is actually based on the Normal template—a no-frills template. There are numerous other templates from which you can choose. In this task, you learn two methods for starting new Word files.

Begin

1 Use the New Button

The quickest way to create a new file is to click the **New Blank Document** button on the Standard toolbar.

Click

2 A New File Opens

A new file immediately opens based on the default Normal template, as shown in this figure. Notice the default filename that appears in the title bar.

3 Select File, Then New Command

To open a file based on another template, display the **File** menu and select the **New** command.

Click

4 Select a Tab

From the New dialog box, click the tabs to locate the type of template on which you want to base the new file. To preview the template first, select its icon and then look in the **Preview** area.

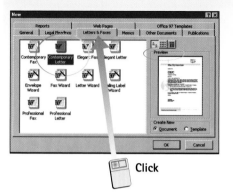

Click

5 Choose a Template

When you find a template to use, double-click to open the new file. You can also select the template, and then click **OK** to exit the New dialog box.

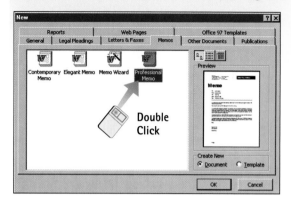

Double Click

6 The File Opens

A new file immediately opens based on the template you selected. Many templates have placeholder text, temporary text you must replace with your own text. To enter your own text, select the placeholder text and start typing.

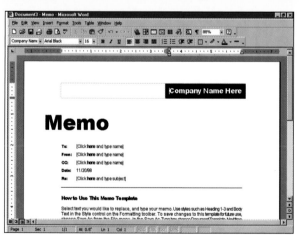

End

How-To Hints

What's a Wizard?

Some of the file types listed in the New dialog box are wizards. Learn more about using a wizard in Task 2, "How to Build a New File with a Wizard."

Use the New Office Document Command

When you install Word, two new commands are added to the top of the **Start** menu. You can use the **New Office Document** command to open new Word files. When you select the command, the New Office Document dialog box appears, which looks and works the same as the New dialog box you learned about in steps 3-6.

How to Build a New File with a Wizard

Word has numerous templates you can choose from, but use Word's template wizards to help you truly tailor-make a document. A template wizard walks you through the steps for creating a document file to suit your specific needs. Depending on the wizard you select, you can customize the document by adding your name, company name, address, and so on. In this task, you'll see how the Memo Wizard helps you create a customized memo document. The steps for using other wizards will vary from those shown, but the process will be similar.

Begin

1 Open the New Dialog Box

Open the **File** menu and select **New** to display the New dialog box.

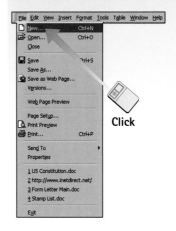

Click

2 Choose a Tab Category

The New dialog box has wizards scattered about in the various tab categories. Click a tab, such as **Memos**, and locate the wizard you want to use. Look for the word Wizard after the template name.

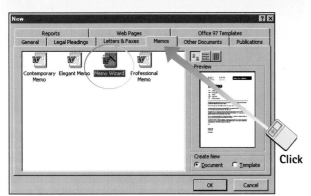

Click

3 Double-Click the Wizard Icon

When you locate a wizard you want to use, double-click its icon. In this example, I chose a Memo wizard.

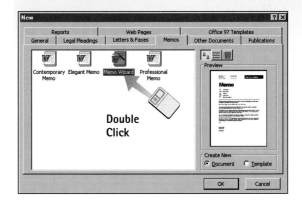

Double Click

4 Start the Wizard

The first wizard dialog box opens. Here you'll see a rundown of the steps you'll follow to create the document. To get started, click the **Next** button.

Click

5 Choose a Style

Select a style for the document, and then click **Next** to continue.

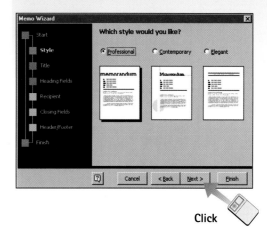

Click

6 Enter a Title

To include a title on the memo, click the **Yes** option and enter a title. Click **Next** to continue.

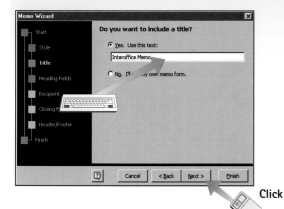

Click

7 Enter Header Text

Use the next dialog box to enter any header items you want included at the top of each memo page. The top two items are selected by default, but to add a subject, click the **Subject** check box and enter the subject text. Click **Next** to continue.

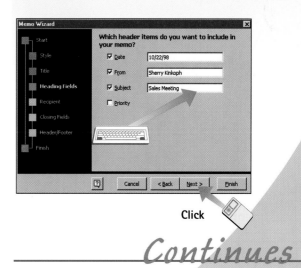

Click

Continues

How to Build a New File with a Wizard Continued

8 Enter the Recipients

In the next dialog box, type in the name of the people receiving the memo. Click inside the **To** text box and enter each name (press **Enter** to start a new line or enter the names on a single line separated by commas). Use the **Cc** text box to enter the names of people you want to "carbon copy." To make the recipient list a separate page from your memo message, click the **Yes** option button; otherwise, leave the default **No** option selected and click **Next** to continue.

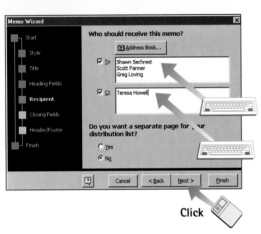

Click

9 Enter Closing Items

Use the next dialog box to add any closing items you want to see in the memo, such as your initials. Select the appropriate options and enter any needed text. When finished, click **Next**.

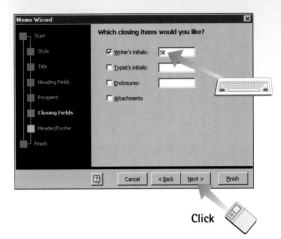

Click

10 Select Header/Footer Items

Select the items you want to include at the top of the page (header) and the items you want at the bottom of the page (footer). To select or deselect a check box, click it. A check mark means the item will appear; no check mark means it won't. Click **Next**.

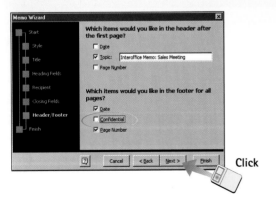

Click

11 Exit the Wizard

In the final dialog box that appears, click **Finish** to exit from the wizard and open the customized document.

Click

12 The Customized Document Opens

Word opens the document onscreen. The document is customized based on the selections you entered by using the wizard. Notice the placeholder text where you can enter your own memo message.

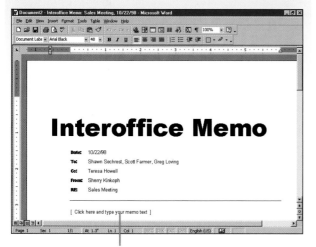

Placeholder text

13 Entering Text

To enter text in the document, click the placeholder text to select it, as shown in this figure, and then enter your own memo message. When finished, you can save and print the file.

Click

End

How-To Hints

Skipping Steps

You can skip the steps the wizard walks you through at any time and complete the document. Just click the **Finish** button at any stage and Word creates the document based on the input you entered up to that point.

Changing Your Input

At any time during the wizard steps, you can stop and return to previous dialog boxes and change your input. Click the **Back** button to navigate to previous boxes.

Types of Wizards

If you take time to peruse the tabs in the New dialog box, you'll notice quite a few wizards you can use to help you create custom documents. Log on to Microsoft's Web site to find even more templates and wizards you can download onto your computer. Open the **Help** menu and select **Office on the Web**. This opens your Web browser and a connect box you can use to log on to your Internet connection and check out the Microsoft Web site for other Word tools, tips, and information.

Saving and Printing Custom Files

You can save and print your custom document just like any other document you create in Word. To learn how to save your work, turn to Task 3, "How to Save Your Work." To learn more about printing your Word files, see Chapter 12, Task 2, "How to Print Files."

How to Save Your Work

After you start working in a Word file, you will want to save it so you can open it again later. It's a good idea to save your work often in case of power failures or other unpredictable computer glitches. When you save a file the first time, you must give the file a name. You can use up to 256 characters, upper- or lowercase letters, in a filename. You can also choose a specific folder or disk to save the file to, and choose to save the file under a specific file format. All of the save options are found in the Save As dialog box.

After you have saved a file, subsequent saves don't require renaming (unless you're saving a duplicate of the file under a different name), and you don't have to reopen the Save As dialog box. Instead, just click the **Save** button on the toolbar to save your changes.

Begin

1 Saving a New File

To save a file for the first time, open the **File** menu and select **Save** or **Save As** to display the Save As dialog box.

Click

2 Designate a Folder

Choose a folder in which to save the file. Open any of the folders displayed in the left pane by clicking the folder icon. You can also use the **Save in** drop-down list to locate the folder you want to save to. To open a list box folder, double-click the folder icon.

Folder   Files   List box

3 Enter a Filename

After you've designated a folder to save to, type a name for the file in the **File Name** text box. Word attempts to define a name for you by using the first bit of text in the document, but you can usually come up with a better name yourself.

4 Click Save

Click the **Save** button and the file is saved.

Click

5 Note the Title Bar Name

Notice that the program's title bar now reflects the name you assigned in the Save As dialog box.

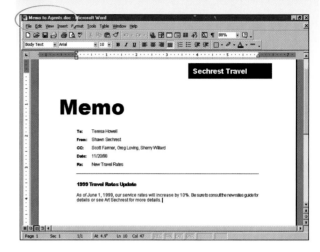

6 Use the Save Button

For subsequent saves of the same file, click the **Save** button on the Standard toolbar.

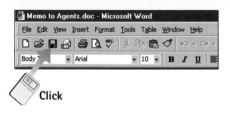

Click

End

How-To Hints

Change the Format

To save a Word file in another format, such as a WordPerfect file to share with someone who uses WordPerfect, open the Save As dialog box (open the **File** menu and choose **Save As**). Click the **Save as type** drop-down arrow and choose a file type from the list. To learn more about saving to other file formats, turn to Task 5, "How to Open and Save Different File Formats."

Saving as a New File

To save an existing file under a new name, use the same steps shown in this task, but enter a different filename. A duplicate of the original file is saved under the new filename and the original file remains intact.

Saving to a New Folder

You can click the **Create New Folder** button in the Save As dialog box to create a new folder to save to; just enter a folder name and click **OK**.

How to Open and Close Files

After you save a file, you will probably want to reopen it and work with it again. You can quickly open existing files you have previously saved by using the Open dialog box. Just locate the folder where you saved the file.

When you're done working with a file but want to keep the program window open, select the **Close** command. This closes only the file, leaving the program window open to work on other files or start new ones. If you haven't saved your work, you will be prompted to do so before closing the file.

Begin

1 Display the Open Dialog Box

Display the **File** menu and select **Open**, or click the **Open** button on the Standard toolbar.

Click

2 Locate the File

Next, you must locate the file you want to open. The list box displays the files stored in the default *My Documents* folder. To open a different folder in the list box, double-click the folder icon to display the folder contents. You may need to use the **Look in** drop-down list to find the folder, or click a folder listed in the left pane of the dialog box.

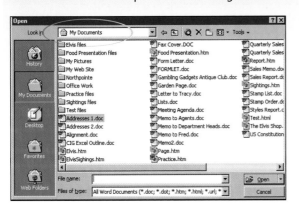

3 Select the File

When you find the file you want to open, double-click the desired filename, or select it and click the **Open** button.

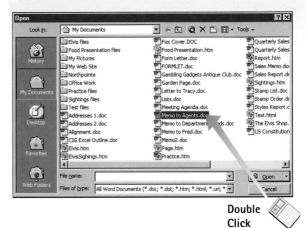

Double Click

4 Open a Recently Used File

To open a file you recently worked on, open the **File** menu and look at the bottom of the menu. Here, you'll find a list of the last four files on which you worked. To select a file from the list, simply click it.

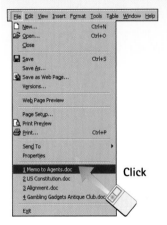

Click

5 Close a File

To close a file, but not the program window, open the **File** menu and choose **Close**.

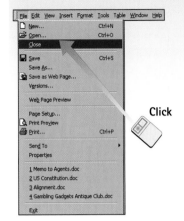

Click

End

How-To Hints

Preview the File

If you're not sure about a file's contents, click the **Views** button on the Open dialog box's toolbar and select the **Preview** command to peek at the file before opening.

Open Options

Notice the Open button in the Open dialog box has a drop-down arrow. Click the **arrow** to display a drop-down list of four Open commands: **Open, Open Read-Only, Open As Copy, Open in Browser**. If you select the **Open Read-Only** command, you can view the file but not make any changes to it. If you select **Open As Copy**, a copy of the file opens, not the original. If you select **Open in Browser**, the file opens in the Internet Explorer browser window.

The Open Office Document Shortcut

Another way to open files is with the Open Office Document command. This is a quick way to open both the file and the Word program window (if it's not already open). Click the **Start** button on the Windows taskbar and choose **Open Office Document** at the top of the menu. The Open Office Document dialog box that appears lists all the Office program files, not just Word files. Locate the Word document you want to open. Double-click the filename or select the file and click **Open**.

How to Open and Save Different File Formats

The files you create in Word are usually saved as document files. Each program you use on your computer requires a different file type or format.

With Word 2000, you can save your documents as different file formats so you can share them with other users who don't have Word 2000. The same holds true for files given to you by others; you can open other file formats into Word 2000. In this task, you learn how to save to different file formats and open other file formats in Word.

Begin

1 Open the Save As Dialog Box

To save your Word file as another file type, first open the file to be saved. Then display the Save As dialog box; open the **File** menu and select **Save As**.

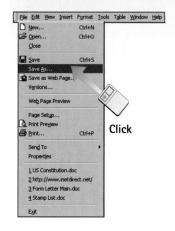

Click

2 Change the Filename or Location

If necessary, give the file another name or designate a specific folder or disk to save the file to (for example, to save the file to a disk, click the **Save in** drop-down arrow and select your floppy disk drive from the list).

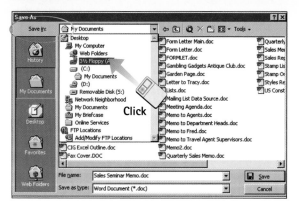

Click

3 Save to Another File Format

To save the file as another file type, click the **Save as type** drop-down arrow and select a file type from the list. Use the scroll arrows to scroll through the list of file types. Click the one you want, and then click the **Save** button to complete the procedure.

Click

4 Open Another File Format

To open a file someone else gave you to read in Word, first open the Open dialog box; display the **File** menu and select **Open** or click the **Open** button on the Standard toolbar.

Click

5 Display the Files of Type List

Click the **Files of type** drop-down arrow and select the file type you want to open, such as **Microsoft Excel Worksheet**.

Click

6 Locate and Open the File

Now locate the folder or drive containing the file you want to open; select the file and click the **Open** button. Word opens the file onscreen.

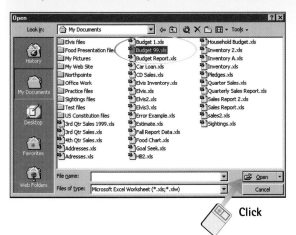

Click

How-To Hints

I Can't Find My Format

Word 2000 can convert files to dozens of other formats, including formats for Macintosh users. If you can't find the file format you're looking for, try checking out the Microsoft Web site. You may find converters you can download and install to work with Word 2000.

End

How to Work with Multiple Files at the Same Time

You can have several files open at the same time while working with Word. The file you're currently working with always appears onscreen; the others are open, but not presently visible. You can easily switch between open files by using the Window menu or the taskbar, or you can choose to view multiple files onscreen at the same time. With multiple files open, you can copy and move data from one file to another.

To try this task, you must first open two or more files. Use the Open dialog box to locate the files, if needed (click the **Open** button on the toolbar or select **File**, **Open**).

Begin

1 Display the Window Menu

One way to switch between open files is to use the Window menu. Click the **Window** menu; the bottom of the menu lists the names of the open files. The currently active file has a check mark next to its name. Click the file you want to view.

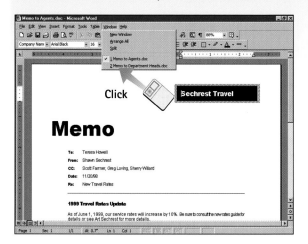

Click

2 Another File Appears Active

The program window now displays the file you selected and it's now the active file.

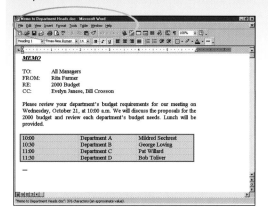

3 Or Use the Taskbar

Another way to switch between open files is to use the taskbar. Simply click the button representing the file you want to view. (Press **Ctrl+Esc** if your taskbar isn't onscreen.)

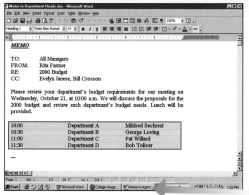

Click

4 View Multiple Files at the Same Time

To see all the open files onscreen at the same time, open the **Window** menu and select **Arrange All**.

Click

5 The Windows Are Arranged

The open files are displayed onscreen at the same time. The active document's title bar is always highlighted.

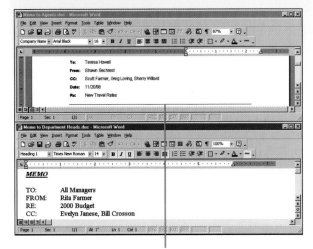

Active document

6 Maximize the Document Window

To return a document window to its full size, click the **Maximize** button on the document's title bar.

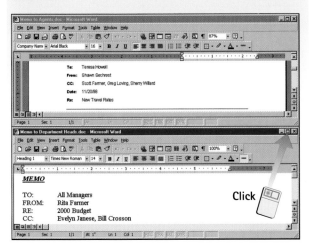

Click

End

How-To Hints

Copy and Move Data

With two or more files open and viewable at the same time, you can drag data from one file to place in another by using the drag-and-drop method. Select the data, click and hold the left mouse button, and drag the data to a new location in the other file. To copy the data, hold down the **Shift** key while dragging.

Moving Data by Using the Taskbar

Another way to move data between files is to use the taskbar. Select the data to move, and then drag it to the taskbar and hover your pointer over the button representing the document you're moving the text to (don't let go of the mouse button yet). After a moment, the document appears and you can continue dragging the text where you want it to go and drop it in place.

How to Find Files

Need to find a specific file you saved? Perhaps you can't remember which folder you saved it in, or maybe you're not sure what filename you assigned but you know what's in the file. Use the Open dialog box to find Word files. This task will show you how to locate files by using the Find features in the Open dialog box.

1 Open the Open Dialog Box

Start by opening the Open dialog box. Click the **Open** button on the Standard toolbar.

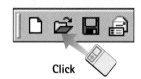

Click

2 Open the Find Dialog Box

Click the **Tools** drop-down arrow on the Open dialog box toolbar and select **Find**.

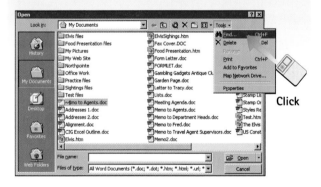

Click

3 Search a Specific Drive or Folder

Use the **Look in** drop-down list to select a drive or folder to search.

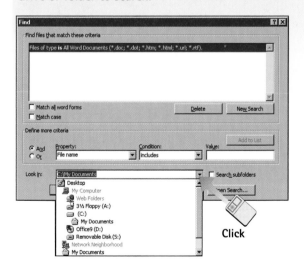

Click

4 Search Subfolders

To search subfolders, too, click the **Search subfolders** check box.

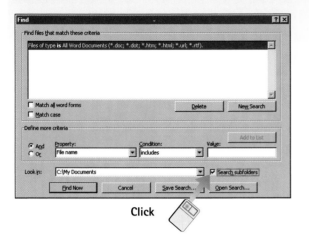

Click

5 Define Search Criteria

Use the **Define more criteria** area to define search criteria. For example, to search for Word filenames containing the word "Sales," choose **File Name** from the **Property** drop-down list, choose **includes** from the **Condition** drop-down list, and then enter the word **sales** in the **Value** text box. Click **Add to List** to add the criteria to the search list.

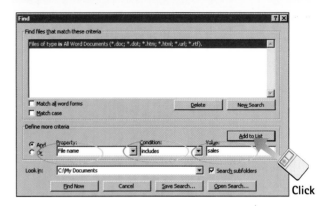

Click

6 Start the Search

Click the **Find Now** button to conduct the search and return to the Open dialog box. After a moment, the results of your search appear in the Open dialog box, as shown in this figure. To open a file, double-click its name in the list box.

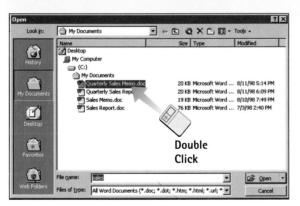

Double Click

End

How-To Hints

Start a New Search

Each time you finish conducting a search and you want to search again, you must open the **Tools** drop-down list and choose **Find**. Then click the **New Search** button to start another search. This clears the previous search criteria.

Task

How to Find Help

here's nothing worse than finding yourself in a jam with no one around to help you. Never fear, Word 2000 has several help options you can pursue to find help with the problem you're experiencing. Word's Help system can show you how to perform a particular task, as well as let you look up topics. It can even point you to help on the Web.

In this chapter, you learn how to employ the Office Assistant, the animated paper clip feature, that appears as soon as you start Word for the first time. Office Assistant is ready to help you whenever you need it, and often appears when you begin a new task or explore a new feature. You also learn how to look up topics and log on to the Internet to find help on the Microsoft Web site. ●

How to Use the Office Assistant

Sooner or later, you're going to need a little help with Word, regardless of your level of computer experience. There's nothing wrong with asking for help from time to time, especially when you're learning a new software program. By default, Microsoft's Office Assistant appears ready to help you as soon as you start Word.

The Office Assistant is an animated help feature you can use to help navigate new tasks or find additional information about a feature. The Office Assistant stays off to the side of the screen, jumping in to offer you help when it thinks you need it. You can use Office Assistant to look up specific instructions or topics you want help with, or you can close the feature if it's distracting to you.

Begin

1 Open Office Assistant

By default, Office Assistant appears when you first use a program or tackle a new feature. If the Office Assistant is onscreen, click the character to open the Office Assistant balloon. If the Office Assistant isn't onscreen, simply press **F1** or open the **Help** menu and select **Show the Office Assistant**.

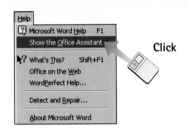

Click

2 Ask a Question

From the Office Assistant balloon, you can type a question or select from options the Assistant lists. To type a question, click inside the text box and enter the question text. Click **Search** or press **Enter**.

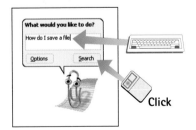

Click

3 Choose a Topic

Office Assistant produces a list of possible topics from which you can choose. Click a topic that most closely matches the information you desire. (If the question you typed didn't produce the results you expected, enter a new question and try again.)

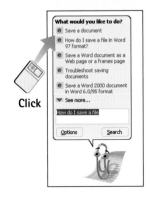

Click

4 Read the Help Window

A Help window appears with more information detailing the topic or shows additional topics you can choose. Underlined text you see are links to related topics. Click a link to view the topic. Learn more about using the Help window in Task 2, "How to Navigate the Help Window."

Help window

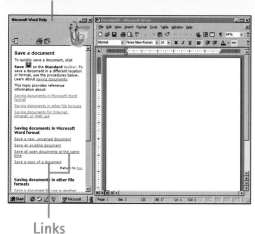

Links

5 Close the Help Window

To close the Help window when you're finished reading, click the window's **Close (X)** button.

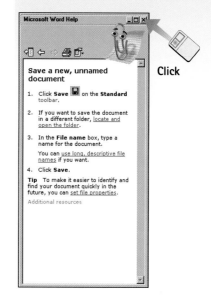

Click

6 Hide the Office Assistant

To hide the Office Assistant so it's no longer in view, open the **Help** menu and select **Hide the Office Assistant** or right-click over the Office Assistant character and select **Hide**. You can also choose to leave the Office Assistant open onscreen in case you need more help. As you work with the document, the Office Assistant will move out of your way as needed.

Click

End

How-To Hints

Customize the Office Assistant

If you don't like the default Clippit character (the animated paper clip), you can change it. There are several other animated characters from which you can choose. Learn how to customize the Office Assistant in Task 3, "How to Customize the Office Assistant."

Or Try the What's This? Feature

To find quick information about an onscreen element, open the **Help** menu and choose **What's This?**. The mouse pointer takes the shape of a question mark. Click the onscreen element you want to know more about, such as a toolbar button or dialog box option, and an information box appears. (Click anywhere onscreen or press **Esc** to close the help information.)

How to Navigate the Help Window

After opening the Help window by using the Office Assistant, you can use the Help window to access a list of help categories, as well as an index for looking up specific terms. For example, if asking the Office Assistant a question didn't reveal the results you were looking for, try a word search or browse through the Help contents. In this task, you learn how to use the various features found in the Help window.

Begin

1 Open the Full Help Window

From the Help window, click the **Show** button to expand the window's size and reveal the available tabs.

Click

2 Ask the Answer Wizard

The **Answer Wizard** tab (click to display) works just like the animated Office Assistant balloon; click inside the text box and type in your question. Click **Search** or press **Enter** when you're ready to view the topic.

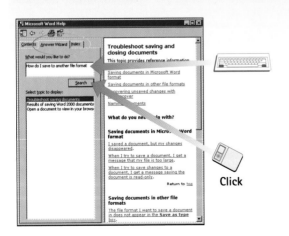

Click

3 Choose Your Topic

Use the **Contents** tab (click to display) like a book's table of contents. Double-click a topic category to open a list of subtopics. From the list of subtopics, click a topic to display more information about the topic.

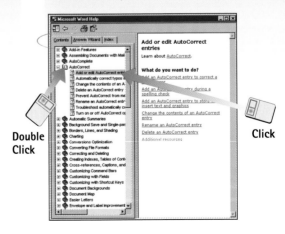

Double Click

Click

4 View the Index Tab

The **Index** tab (click to display) is an alphabetized list of help topics, much like a book's index. You can type the term (or phrase) you want to look up (for example, print), and the middle list box scrolls alphabetically to the term.

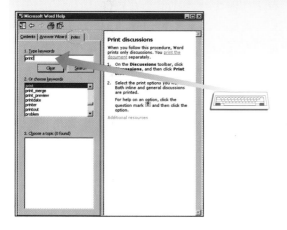

5 Look Up a Term

Double-click an entry in the bottom list in the Index tab to display detailed information about the word or phrase.

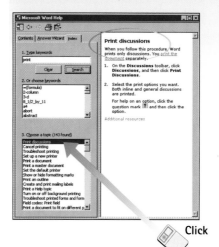

Click

6 Move Between Topics

Click the **Back** and **Forward** buttons to move between topics you've been reading. To close the Help window when you're finished reading, click the window's **Close** (×) button.

Back   **Forward**   Close

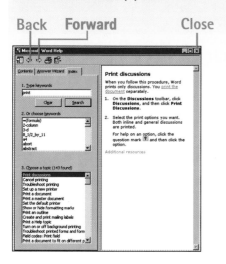

End

How-To Hints

Printing Help Topics

From the Help window, click the **Print** button and click **OK**.

Open the Help Window Directly

You can set the Help window to open without going through the Office Assistant. From the Office Assistant balloon, click the **Options** button. In the **Options** tab, deselect the **Respond to F1 key** check box and click **OK**. The next time you want to access the window, press **F1**.

How to Customize the Office Assistant

By default, the Clippit Assistant character appears when you first use Word. However, there are other characters you can choose from and each has its own personality, so to speak. You can change the character whenever you want using the Office Assistant dialog box.

You can also find other help options in the Office Assistant dialog box that control how the Assistant works. Be sure to check them out as well.

Begin

1 Display the Office Assistant Balloon

Open the Office Assistant balloon by clicking the character. If Office Assistant isn't onscreen, open the **Help** menu and choose **Show the Office Assistant**.

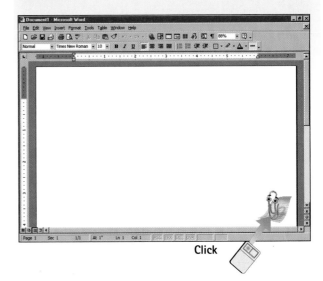

Click

2 Click the Options Button

Click the **Options** button in the Office Assistant balloon. This opens the Office Assistant dialog box.

Click

3 View the Gallery Tab

Click the **Gallery** tab. To view the other available characters, click the **Back** and **Next** buttons. Each character runs through its animated demo and displays a description of the character.

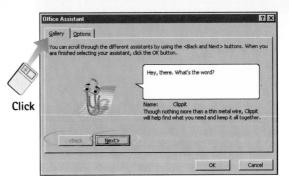

Click

4 Choose a Character

When you find a character you want to use, click **OK** to exit the Office Assistant dialog box.

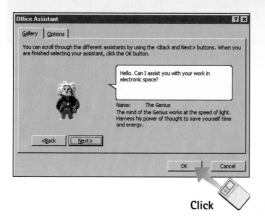

Click

5 View the Options Tab

Use the **Options** tab in the Office Assistant dialog box to change which options are turned on or off. Reopen the dialog box as explained in step 2, and then click the **Options** tab.

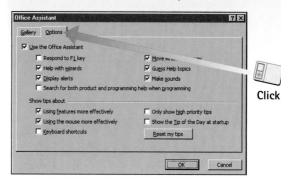

Click

6 Change Office Assistant Options

From this tab, you can change how the Office Assistant works by selecting or deselecting the various check marks. For example, if you prefer that the Office Assistant remain in the same place onscreen, deselect the **Move when in the way** check box. Click **OK** to exit and apply any changes.

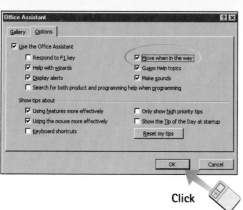

Click

End

How-To Hints

Looking for Tips?

If you're new to Word, consider turning on the **Show the Tip of the Day at startup** check box in the Office Assistant dialog box. When the tip feature is activated, the Office Assistant will display a helpful tip each time you open Word.

How to Find Help on the Web

If Word's online Help system doesn't prove helpful, try the Microsoft Web site. If you have an Internet account and a Web browser program, such as Internet Explorer, you can log on to the Internet and look up additional information about the program. For example, you can look up tips and tricks for using Word, access FAQs (frequently asked questions), or find updates for the program. Take time to explore the Web site and find more information about using the program and becoming a more productive Word user.

Begin

1 Open the Help Menu

Open the **Help** menu and select **Office on the Web**.

Click

2 Log On to Your Account

Your Web browser immediately opens along with the Dial-up Connection dialog box, if you're not already logged on to the Internet. Click the **Connect** button to log on to your account.

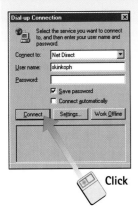

Click

3 View the Web Page

The Office Update page appears in your Web browser window (remember, Word is part of the Microsoft Office suite of programs). Click the **Home** link to open the site's home page.

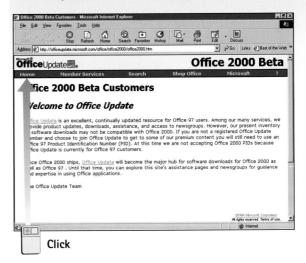

Click

4 Click the Word Link

Click the **Word** link, as shown in this figure.

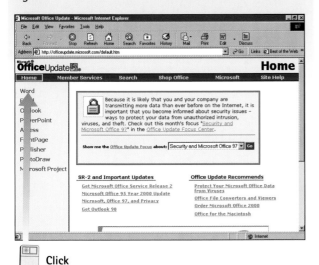

Click

5 Open Assistance

From the Word Updates page, click the **Assistance** link.

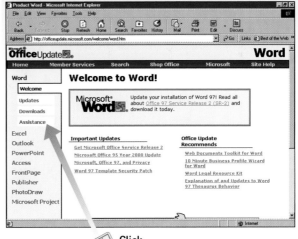

 Click

6 Choose Your Assistance

From the Word Assistance page, you'll find helpful links to Word-related information, including updates, help files, and more. To follow a link, such as the FAQs (Frequently Asked Questions about Word) link, click the link. To close the browser window, click the window's **Close** button in the upper-right corner. Don't forget to log off your Internet account when finished.

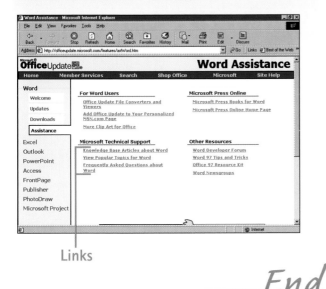

Links

How-To Hints

Navigating Pages

Use the browser program's **Back** and **Forward** buttons to navigate the Office Web site and view pages you've previously looked at.

Switch Between Word and Internet Explorer

To quickly switch between your Word window and Internet Explorer, click the Word document button on the taskbar to view the Word window, or click the Internet Explorer document button to view the browser window. If the taskbar isn't visible, press **Ctrl+Esc** to view it.

End

Task

How to Change Your Document View

*W*ord's flexibility offers numerous ways to view your documents. There are several view modes to use, depending on how you want to work on your document or the type of document you're creating. You can also use Word's zoom controls to give you different perspectives; for example, you can zoom out to see the entire page or zoom in for a closer look. You can even choose to split the screen to view different portions of the same document at the same time. You can also choose to turn off various onscreen elements to free up more space for viewing your work. In this chapter, you learn several tasks for controlling how your document is displayed. ●

How to Display Your Document Differently

Word offers you four main view modes to help you as you work with your documents: Normal, Web Layout, Print Layout, and Outline. For example, if you're typing a letter, Normal and Print Layout views work best. If you're constructing a long document that's based on an outline, use Outline view to help you modify the document's structure. If you're creating Web pages, Web Layout view is the best view to use.

The view mode you select has much to do with the type of document with which you're working. Most users stick with Normal and Print Layout views to work with and view document pages. In this task, you'll sample each of the view modes available.

Begin

1 Select a View Button

The quickest way to switch views is to use the View buttons in the lower-left corner of the Word window. You'll find buttons for Normal, Web Layout, Print Layout, and Outline views. For example, to switch to Normal view mode, click **Normal View**.

View buttons

Click

2 Use the View Menu

You can also switch views using the View menu; open the **View** menu, and then click the view you want to use.

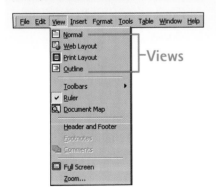

Views

3 Normal View

In Normal view, the document page displays only text, no graphics or other special objects you might add. The work area shows the document page without edges, as shown in this figure.

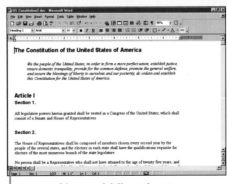

Normal View button

4 Print Layout View

Switch to Print Layout view to see clip art, page margins, and elements such as headers and footers. In Print Layout view, Word displays the document just as it will print. This includes any special objects, such as graphics. The work area in Print Layout view shows the edges of the page, as shown in this figure, and the vertical ruler.

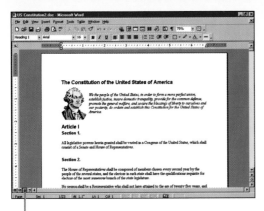

Print Layout View

5 Outline View

Use Outline view to help you build and maintain outline levels in your document. When you switch to this view, the Outline toolbar appears. You can move headings and any body text by dragging and dropping; hide and display heading levels by clicking toolbar buttons. You can also apply heading styles or outline levels.

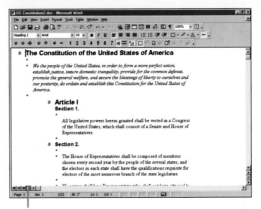

Outline View

6 Web Layout View

Web Layout view takes its cue from Web pages, allowing you to take advantage of the full width of a Web page document. In Web Layout view, Word displays the document as it will appear in a Web browser window. (Learn more about Word's Web features in Chapter 14, "How to Use Word on the Web.")

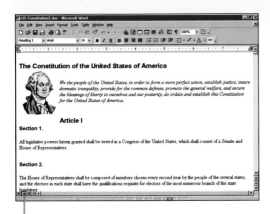

Web Layout View

How-To Hints

Which Button Is Which?

To find out which view button is which, simply hover your mouse pointer over the button to reveal the ScreenTip name.

Building an Outline

To learn more about working with an outline in Outline view, check out Task 6, "How to Work with an Outline in Outline View," later in this chapter.

End

How to Magnify Your View

Another way you can change the way you look at your document is to use Word's Zoom controls. You can zoom in up close and see your text or other elements (such as graphics), in great detail, or you can zoom out to see the document from a bird's-eye view. You can use the Zoom controls in any view mode, in Print Preview mode, and there's even a Zoom dialog box you can open. In this task, you'll explore the various methods for zooming your view.

Begin

1 Use the Zoom Button

The quickest way to zoom your view of the document is to use the **Zoom** control on the Standard toolbar. Click the drop-down arrow to display the list of zoom percentages, and then click a percentage (such as 200%) to zoom your view.

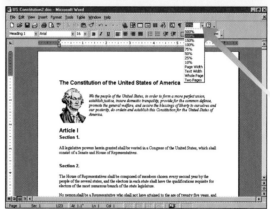

Click

2 Your View Is Zoomed

Word zooms your view of the document to the percentage you selected in step 1. In this example, 200% was selected.

3 Open the Zoom Dialog Box

Another way you can zoom is to open the Zoom dialog box. For example, you might want to specify an exact zoom percentage. Open the **View** menu and select **Zoom**.

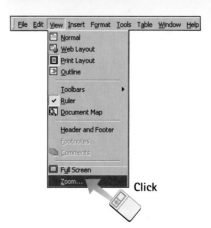
Click

4 Specify a Zoom Percentage

In the Zoom dialog box, you can enter an exact zoom percentage in the **Percent** box (such as 45%). You can also click the spin arrows to change the setting.

5 Preview the Zoom

The **Preview** area gives you an idea of how the zoomed document will look. Click **OK**, exit from the dialog box, and apply the new view.

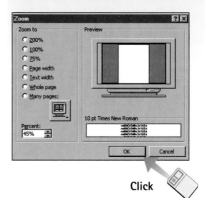

Click

6 Your View Is Zoomed Again

Word zooms your view of the document to the percentage you selected in the Zoom dialog box. In this example, 45%.

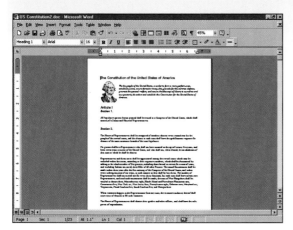

End

How-To Hints

Print Preview Mode

Another view mode you can use to examine your document is Print Preview mode. Learn more about using this feature in Chapter 11, "How to Work with Graphics," Task 5, "How to Preview a File."

What's Full Screen View?

Want to see your document without any program Window elements to distract you? Open the **View** menu and select **Full Screen**. This lets you view your document without the menu bar, toolbars, scroll bars, or other Window elements. To return to regular view again, click the **Close Full Screen** button.

View Multiple Pages

To see multiple pages of a document onscreen, use the **Many pages** option in the Zoom dialog box. Click the option button, click the pages button (the icon looks like a computer monitor), and drag the number of pages you want to view on the drop-down palette that appears. Click **OK** to exit the dialog box and view the pages.

How to Split the Screen

If you've got a particularly long document, you may find yourself needlessly scrolling from top to bottom to view different portions. You can set up Word so that you can view different sections onscreen at the same time. For example, you can split the screen to show the top of your document and the very bottom.

Begin

1 Select Split from the Window Menu

Open the **Window** menu and select **Split**.

Click

2 Place the Split

A horizontal bar appears onscreen. Drag the bar to where you want the split to occur and click in place.

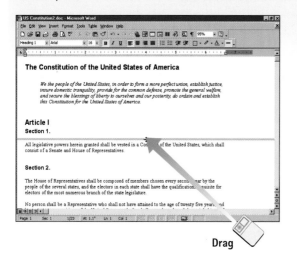

Drag

3 The Screen Is Split

The screen is now split into two parts. Each part has its own scroll bars and rulers.

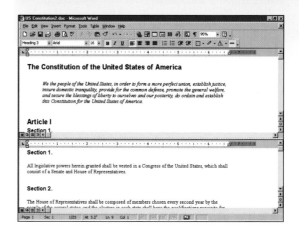

4 Scroll Your View

Click inside the section you want to work with, and then use the scroll arrows to move the document view. In this figure, I'm viewing both the top and bottom portions of a 23-page document.

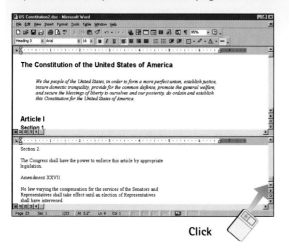

Click

5 Remove the Split

To return your screen to normal, open the **Window** menu and select **Remove Split**.

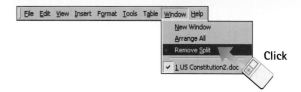

Click

6 Or Drag a Split

Another way to insert a split is to drag the split marker from the vertical scroll bar onto the document page and drop it where you want the split to occur. This figure points out the split marker. To remove the split, simply drag the splitter bar off-screen.

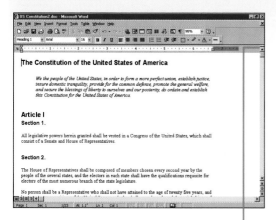

Split marker

End

How-To Hints

Moving and Copying Between Screens

One of the advantages of working with a split screen document is that you can easily move text from one section to the other. You can move or copy text by dragging it from one screen section to another. Learn more about moving and copying text in Chapter 5, "How to Enter and Edit Text," Task 5, "How to Move and Copy Text."

Making Changes

Splitting the document only provides an additional view—not an additional copy—of your document. If you make changes to the document on one side of the split, those changes will appear to the other side of the split as well.

How to Free Up Onscreen Work Space

Although the programmers who created Word 2000 have tried to make the work area as large as possible by combining toolbar space, sometimes it's just not enough. There are times when you want to see more of your document onscreen or want to remove an item that you find distracting. To do so, you can turn off various onscreen elements, as explained in this task. This frees up valuable onscreen real estate. You can always turn the elements back on again when you need them.

Begin

1 Turn Off the Ruler

To hide both the horizontal and vertical rulers (if you're in Print Layout view), open the **View** menu and select **Ruler**.

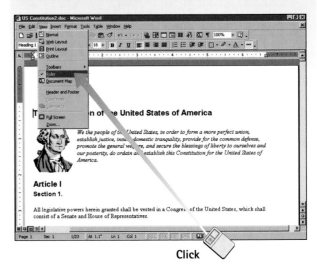

Click

2 Turn Off the Toolbars

To turn off all your toolbars, open the **View** menu and select **Toolbars** to reveal a submenu of available toolbars. Click the toolbar you want to turn off (toolbars with a check mark next to their name means they're displayed onscreen; no check mark means they're already turned off). You may need to repeat this step again to turn off every toolbar.

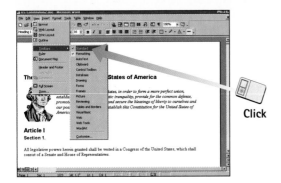

Click

3 Check Out the Space

Just turning off the rulers and toolbars frees up considerable space onscreen, as shown in this figure.

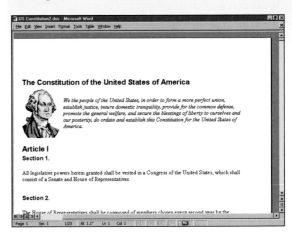

4 Open the Options Dialog Box

To turn off the remaining onscreen elements (with the exception of the Menu bar), open the **Tools** menu and select **Options**. This opens the Options dialog box.

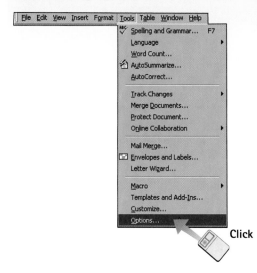

Click

5 Turn Off the Remaining Bars

Click the **View** tab and find the check boxes for the **Status bar**, **Horizontal scroll bar**, and **Vertical scroll bar**. Deselect each item to remove the check mark next to the element's name. Click **OK** to exit the dialog box.

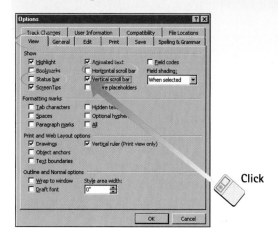

Click

6 Extra Space Revealed

Now your screen will resemble the one in this figure, with plenty of room to view your document without the distraction of the various elements. To navigate the document without the scroll bars, use the keyboard arrow keys.

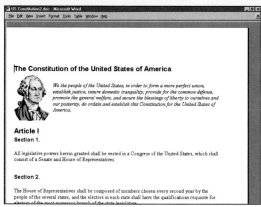

End

How-To Hints

Turn Them Back On

Repeat these steps to turn all or any of the elements back on again, this time selecting the options to place check marks beside their names.

What About the Menu Bar?

Sorry, you can't turn off the Menu bar. You probably wouldn't want to anyway because it has all the commands necessary for working with the document.

Or Try the Shortcut Menu

To quickly turn on toolbars, right-click over the Menu bar or an existing toolbar to display a shortcut menu of available toolbars. Click the one you want to view again.

How to View Paragraph Marks and Other Non-printing Symbols

Although you can't see them by default, Word inserts nonprinting symbols, also called *paragraph* or *formatting marks*, every time you press the **Spacebar**, the **Enter** key, and the **Tab** key.

When you're checking your document for errors, sometimes it's necessary to view nonprinting symbols to see whether you inserted an extra space between words or tabs, or whether you need to check the number of blank lines between paragraphs. You can choose to view Word's nonprinting symbols to see every place you typed something in the document, even if it was a space. As their name implies, these symbols do not print when you print your document file.

Begin

1 The Default View

Here's an example of text entered into a document using the default view, which doesn't show nonprinting symbols.

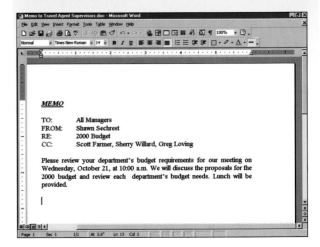

2 Use the Show/Hide Button

Use the **Show/Hide** paragraph button on the Standard toolbar to quickly turn on your view of nonprinting symbols. Click the button to toggle the feature on.

Click

3 View Nonprinting Symbols

The document now shows nonprinting symbols. Notice that a dot represents places where I pressed the **Spacebar**, an arrow represents areas where I pressed the **Tab** key, and a paragraph mark represents every place I pressed the **Enter** key to start a new paragraph.

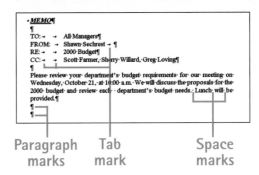

Paragraph marks   Tab mark   Space marks

4 Edit Paragraph Marks

You can make changes to your text while viewing nonprinting symbols, including edits to the nonprinting symbols. For example, to remove an extra space between words, click next to the space, and then use the **Backspace** or **Delete** key to remove the symbol.

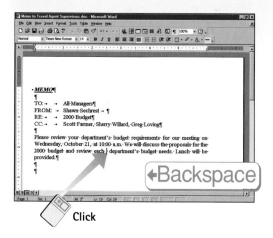

Click

5 Turn Nonprinting Symbols Off

To turn off your view of nonprinting symbols, click the **Show/Hide** button again.

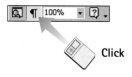

Click

6 Back to the Default View

Word returns you to the default view without revealing paragraph marks and other non-printing characters.

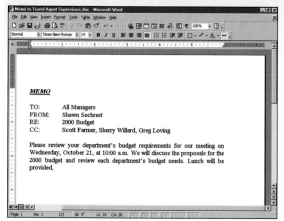

End

How to Work with an Outline in Outline View

When you need to prepare long, complicated documents, an outline can make it easier to organize your material. Use Word's Outline view to help you arrange your outline's headings, subheadings, and body text. The Outlining toolbar has buttons to help you assign heading levels and view different portions of your outline.

In this task, you learn how to switch to Outline view and demote and promote headings. Be sure to explore all the options available on the Outlining toolbar as you assemble your own outlines.

Begin

1 Enter the Outline Text

Begin entering the outline text, including headings, subheadings, and body text for your document. Don't worry about leaving anything out; you can always add more text later.

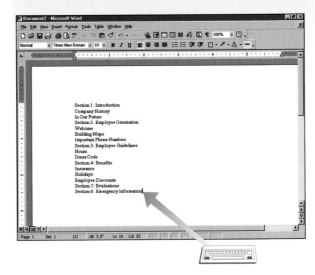

2 Switch to Outline View

Click the **Outline View** button in the bottom-left corner of the Word window to switch to Outline view.

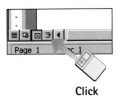

Click

3 Outline Displayed

Word displays your text in Outline view and the Outlining toolbar appears onscreen. No headings are currently assigned.

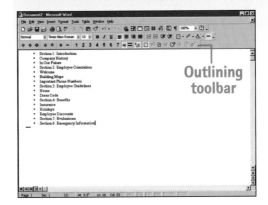

Outlining toolbar

4 Promote a Heading

To promote a heading in the outline, click anywhere in the text you want to turn into a heading, and then click the **Promote** button.

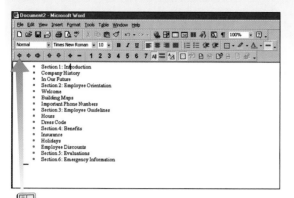

Click

5 New Heading Assigned

Word assigns the new heading level. Continue promoting headings as needed.

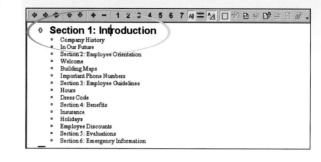

6 Demote a Heading

To demote a heading, click inside the text, and then click the **Demote** button on the Outlining toolbar. This demotes the text by one level. To demote the text to body text, click the **Demote to Body Text** button to the right of the **Demote** button.

Demote   Demote to Body Text

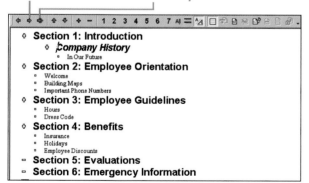

End

How-To Hints

Moving Headings

To move a heading or body text up or down in the outline, click inside the line of text, and then click the **Move Up** or **Move Down** button on the Outlining toolbar as many times as needed to move the text to the desired location in the outline.

Expand or Collapse Your Outline

Use the **Expand** and **Collapse** buttons on the Outlining toolbar to view or hide subheadings and body text. You can also choose to view only certain levels of your outline by using the numbered buttons. Take note that moving a collapsed heading up or down also moves its hidden subheadings or body text.

TASK 7

How to Navigate with Document Map View

Another great tool for working with exceptionally long documents is Word's Document Map view. This view mode lets you see various portions of your document and keep the main parts in view all the time. Document Map view works the same way some Web sites are set up. Two panes appear onscreen; use one to view your overall document structure and use the other to scroll to specific areas.

Begin

1 Select the Document Map Command

Display the **View** menu and select Document Map.

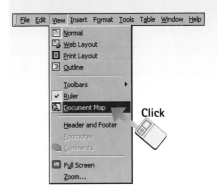

Click

2 Two Panes Appear

Word displays two panes onscreen. The left pane shows the overall document structure and the right pane displays the document work area.

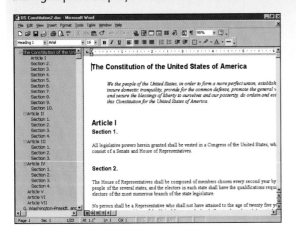

3 Quick Navigation

To quickly go to a section of text in the document, click the section in the left pane. The right pane immediately scrolls to the section.

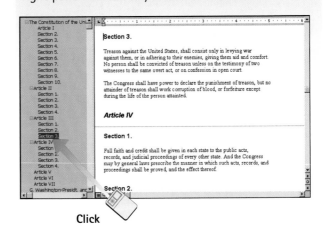

Click

4 Resize the Pane

To resize the map pane, hover your mouse pointer over the border between the left and right panes until it becomes a two-sided Resize pointer.

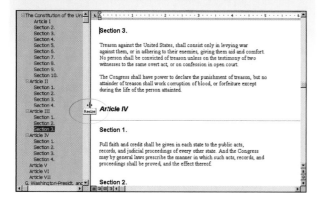

5 Drag to Resize

Drag the two-sided arrow pointer to the right to make the left pane wider, or drag to the left to make the document pane wider.

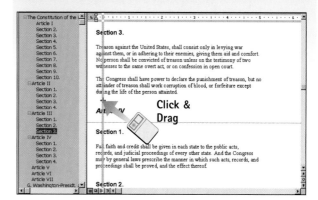

6 The Panes Are Resized

Release the mouse button and the panes are resized.

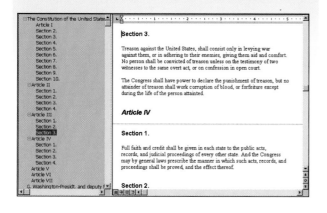

7 Close Document Map View

To exit from Document Map view mode, reopen the **View** menu and select **Document Map**.

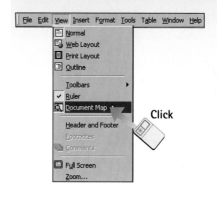

End

Task

How to Enter and Edit Text

*T*here's absolutely no end to the type of documents you can create in Word. This feature-packed program can handle everything from simple letters to large manuscript volumes that incorporate all manner of footnotes, endnotes, and so on. You can whip up memos, reports, grocery lists, or a letter to Mom in no time at all. Of course, it's up to you to enter the text to create your document; however, rest assured that Word can handle any type of text-based file you need to compose.

There are a variety of methods you can employ to enter and edit text in your Word documents. There's even a new technique in Word 2000, called Click-and-Type, to learn about. In this chapter, we'll cover all the basic ways you can enter and edit your text, including how to navigate a document page, how to move and copy text, how to insert the date and time, and much more. ●

How to Enter and Edit Text

Microsoft Word opens with a blank document window ready for you to begin typing text, whether it's in the form of a bestseller novel, a personal letter, or an interoffice memo. You can enter text by using any of Word's view modes. The flashing insertion point indicates where the next character you type will appear. If you're using Normal view, as shown in this task, the end of document marker shows the last line on which you entered text. Simply start typing to enter text. If you make any mistakes, use the **Backspace** key to delete unwanted characters.

Begin

1 Start a New Paragraph

Each time you press **Enter**, you start a new paragraph. Don't worry about pressing **Enter** when you reach the right margin, Word automatically wraps the text to the next line for you. The only time you need to press **Enter** is to end short lines of text, to create blank lines, and to end paragraphs.

> To enter text, just start typing. Don't worry about reaching the end of the line, Word will automatically wrap the text to the next line for you. The only time you need to press Enter is to start a new paragraph.
>
> Press Enter twice to add extra space between paragraphs.

↵Enter

End of document marker   Cursor

2 Indent with the Tab Key

Press the **Tab** key to quickly indent the first line of a paragraph. If you keep pressing **Tab**, you increase the indent one-half inch at a time.

> To enter text, just start typing. Don't worry about reaching the end of the line, Word will automatically wrap the text to the next line for you. The only time you need to press Enter is to start a new paragraph.
>
> Press Enter twice to add extra space between paragraphs.
>
> Press Tab to create an indent like this. The Tab key is handy for quick indents. If you prefer to use specific types of indents, open the Paragraph dialog box instead (right-click in the paragraph and choose Paragraph on the shortcut menu).

 Tab

3 Typing Repeating Characters

To type the same character repeatedly, hold the key down. Word automatically converts some repeated characters into different types of lines, as shown here. If you type three or more asterisks (*) and press **Enter**, for example, Word replaces them with a dotted line. Do the same with the equal sign (=) for a double line, the tilde (~) for a wavy line, the pound (#) symbol for a thick decorative line, or the underscore (_) for a thick single line.

> To enter text, just start typing. Don't worry about reaching the end of the line, Word will automatically wrap the text to the next line for you. The only time you need to press Enter is to start a new paragraph.
>
> Press Enter twice to add extra space between paragraphs.
>
> Press Tab to create an indent like this. The Tab key is handy for quick indents. If you prefer to use specific types of indents, open the Paragraph dialog box instead (right-click in the paragraph and choose Paragraph on the shortcut menu).
>
> Hold down the Shift key and press the asterisk character (*) to fill the line. The asterisks become a dotted line, like below
> ....

4 Typing Uppercase Letters

To produce all uppercase letters without having to hold down the **Shift** key, press the **Caps Lock** key once before you begin typing. Press the **Caps Lock** key again when you're ready to switch caps off. Caps Lock affects only the letter keys, not the number and punctuation keys. So you always have to press **Shift** to type a character on the upper half of a number or punctuation key, such as @ or %.

To enter text, just start typing. Don't worry about reaching the end of the line, Word will automatically wrap the text to the next line for you. The only time you need to press Enter is to start a new paragraph.

Press Enter twice to add extra space between paragraphs.

Press Tab to create an indent like this. The Tab key is handy for quick indents. If you prefer to use specific types of indents, open the Paragraph dialog box instead (right-click in the paragraph and choose Paragraph on the shortcut menu).

Hold down the Shift key and press the asterisk character (*) to fill the line. The asterisks become a dotted line, like below

CLICK THE CAPS LOCK KEY TO TYPE ALL CAPS

5 Fix Mistakes as You Type

Press the **Backspace** key to delete characters to the left of the cursor.

To enter text, just start typing. Don't worry about reaching the end of the line, Word will automatically wrap the text to the next line for you. The only time you need to press Enter is to start a new paragraph.

Press Enter twice to add extra space between paragraphs.

Press Tab to create an indent like this. The Tab key is handy for quick indents. If you prefer to use specific types of indents, open the Paragraph dialog box instead (right-click in the paragraph and choose Paragraph on the shortcut menu).

Hold down the Shift key and press the asterisk character (*) to fill the line. The asterisks become a dotted line, like below

CLICK THE CAPS LOCK KEY TO TYPE ALL CA

← Backspace

6 Edit Existing Text

To fix mistakes in text you've already typed, click inside the word and press the **Delete** key to remove characters to the right of the cursor or press **Backspace** to remove characters to the left of the cursor.

To enter text, just start typing. Don't worry about reaching the end of the line, Word will automatically wrap the text to the next line for you. The only time you need to press Enter is to start a new paragraph.

Press Enter twice to add extra space between paragraphs.

Press Tab to create an indent like this. The Tab key is handy for quick indents. If you prefer to use specific types of indents, open the Paragraph dialog box instead (right-click in the paragraph and choose Paragraph on the shortcut menu).

Hold down the Shift key and press the asterisk character (*) to fill the line. The asterisks become a dotted line, like below

CLICK THE CAPS LOCK KEY TO TYPE ALL

Del

End

How-To Hints

Overtype and Insert Modes

By default, Word starts you in Insert mode, which means anytime you click the cursor in the document and start typing, any existing text moves to the right to make room for new text you type. If you prefer to replace the existing text entirely, use the Overtype mode. Press the **Insert** key to toggle Overtype mode on or off. You can also double-click the letters OVR on the status bar to toggle the feature on or off (the letters OVR appear in black when Overtype mode is on).

Need a New Page?

By default, Word starts a new page when the current page is filled with text. At times, you may want to start a new page without filling the current page (when you want a title page, for example). Press **Ctrl+Enter** to insert a manual page break.

How to Use Click-and-Type

A new feature in Word 2000 is *Click-and-Type*. If you're using Print Layout view, you can move the mouse anywhere on the document page, double-click, and immediately start typing. In previous versions of Word, you could enter text only at the top of the page, never beyond the end-of-document marker. You had to use the Enter key and Tab key to position the cursor in a certain area on a blank page. The new Click-and-Type feature lets you choose to enter text anywhere, for example, you can double-click smack dab in the middle of the document and enter text.

Begin

1 Switch to Print Layout View

If you're not already using the Print Layout view mode, click the **Print Layout View** button at the bottom of the Word window.

Click

2 Move the Pointer

To use Click-and-Type, move the mouse pointer where you want to insert text. As you hover the mouse pointer over the area of the page where you want to enter text, an icon appears indicating the type of alignment that will be applied. For example, if you move the pointer to the center of the page, a center-align icon appears indicating the text you type there will be centered. You can always change the alignment after you enter the text.

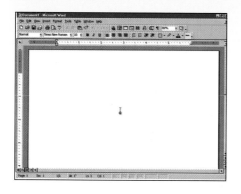

3 Double-Click

Double-click to insert the cursor.

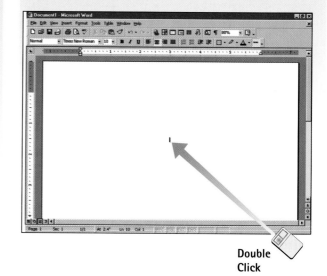

Double Click

4 Start Typing

Begin typing the text you want to enter.

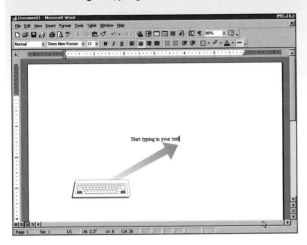

5 Text Is Entered

Word displays the text and automatically wraps it to the next line as needed. In this example, because I double-clicked in the center of the document, center alignment is applied to the text I entered.

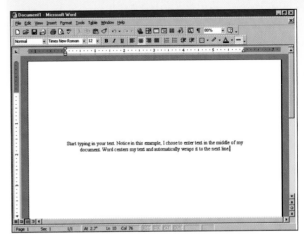

End

How-To Hints

What's Alignment?

Alignment controls how the text lines up between the margins. By default, Word applies left alignment when you first enter text, but when you use Click-and-Type, the alignment used depends on where you click on the page. Learn more about changing alignment in Chapter 8, Task 2, "How to Align Text."

Don't Like Click-and-Type?

If you're not too keen on this new Click-and-Type feature, you can turn it off. Open the **Tools** menu and select **Options**. This opens the Options dialog box. Click the **Edit** tab and deselect the **Enable Click and Type** check box. Click **OK** to exit the dialog box. Remember, Click-and-Type works only in Print Layout view or Web Layout view modes. If you're using another Word view, the feature won't work.

TASK **3**

How to Navigate a Document

As you begin filling a document with text, the view area will move down to show your current cursor location as you type. When your document becomes longer or wider than a full screen of text, use Word's navigation tools to view different parts of the document.

Begin

1 Use the Scrollbars

Depending on the size of your document, use the vertical or horizontal scrollbars to view different portions of the document. Click the scrollbar's **arrow** buttons to scroll in the appropriate direction. For example, to scroll down, click the **down arrow** on the vertical scrollbar.

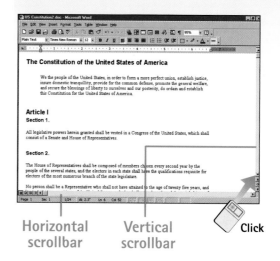

Horizontal scrollbar   Vertical scrollbar   Click

2 Drag the Scroll Box

You can also drag the scroll box to move your view. Drag the vertical scroll box up or down or drag the horizontal scroll box to the left or right to move your view of the document page. A ScreenTip appears while you drag to indicate which page you're on if your document has more than one page.

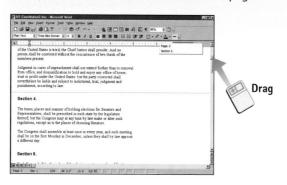

Drag

3 Use the Page Buttons

If your document is longer than a page, click the **Next Page** button to immediately scroll to the next page. Click the **Previous Page** button to scroll back a page.

—Previous Page
—Next Page

68 CHAPTER 5: HOW TO ENTER AND EDIT TEXT

4 Use the Mouse

Click the mouse anywhere in your document to move the insertion point to that spot.

Section 4.

The times, places and manner of holding elections for Senators and Representatives, shall be prescribed in each state by the legislature thereof; but the Congress may at any time by law make or alter such regulations, except as to the places of choosing Senators.

The Congress shall assemble at least once in every year, and such meeting shall be on the first Monday in December, unless they shall by law appoint a different day.

 Click

5 Use the Arrow Keys

Use the arrow keys on the keyboard to move up, down, right, or left in the document. Press the **left arrow** key, for example, to move left one character; hold the **left arrow** key down to quickly move across many characters.

Section 4.

The times, places and manner of holding elections for Senators and Representatives, shall be prescribed in each state by the legislature thereof; but the Congress may at any time by law make or alter such regulations, except as to the places of choosing Senators.

The Congress shall assemble at least once in every year, and such meeting shall be on the first Monday in December, unless they shall by law appoint a different day.

6 Use Keyboard Shortcuts

In addition to the navigational arrow keys, you can use numerous other keyboard shortcuts to navigate documents. Press **Ctrl+→** to move right one word, for example; press **Ctrl+←** to move left one word. Be sure to check out the inside back cover of this book to learn more helpful shortcut keys you can use in Word.

Section 4.

The times, places and manner of holding elections for Senators and Representatives, shall be prescribed in each state by the legislature thereof; but the Congress may at any time by law make or alter such regulations, except as to the places of choosing Senators.

The Congress shall assemble at least once in every year, and such meeting shall be on the first Monday in December, unless they shall by law appoint a different day.

  Control

End

How-To Hints

Go To

If you know the page you want to view onscreen, use the Go To command to get there. Select **Edit**, **Go To**, or click the **Select Browse Object** button on the vertical scrollbar, and then click the **Go To** icon. In the Go To tab, enter the page number, and then click the **Go To** button. (You can also locate specific document elements, such as footnotes or headings.)

Scrolling with the Wheel

If you're using a Microsoft IntelliMouse, you can quickly scroll around your Word documents by rolling the mouse wheel that sits between the left and right mouse buttons up or down with your finger.

Page Up, Page Down

Keyboard users can press the **Page Up** and **Page Down** keys to move a screen at a time through the document.

How to Select Text

After entering text, you can do a variety of things with it, such as applying formatting or moving and copying the text. But before you can do any of these things, you must first learn to select text. *Selecting text* means to highlight the specific text you want to change or to which to apply commands. Selected text, whether it's a single character, a word, a paragraph, or an entire document, always appears highlighted onscreen with a black bar.

Begin

1 Select Text with the Mouse

To select a character, word, or phrase, click at the beginning of the text you want to select, and then hold down the left mouse button and drag to the end of the selection. Release the mouse button and the text is selected.

Memo

To: Carmen Laudneschlager
From: Alicia Gray
Cc: Alan Oglesby

Re: Monthly Sales Report

Carmen:

se turn all monthly sales reports over to Alan
Oglesby in Sales (extension x4329). He'll be compiling all department sales
reports from now on. Thanks!

 Click & Drag   **Release**

2 Select Text with the Keyboard

To select text by using the keyboard, press the arrow keys to move the cursor to the beginning of the word or phrase you want to select. Hold down the **Shift** key and move the appropriate arrow key to select the desired text. To select a word, for example, move the cursor to the beginning of the word, hold down the **Shift** key, and press the right arrow key until the text is selected.

Memo

To: Carmen Laudneschlager
From: Alicia Gray
Cc: Alan Oglesby

Re: Monthly Sales Report

Carmen:

As of next month, please turn all monthly sales reports over to Alan
Oglesby in Sales (extension x4329). He'll be compiling all department sales
reports from now on. Thanks!

 ⬆Shift

3 Mouse Shortcuts

To quickly select a single word, double-click inside the word. To select a paragraph, triple-click inside the paragraph.

Memo

To: Carmen Laudneschlager
From: Alicia Gray
Cc: Alan Oglesby

Re: Quarterly Sales Report

Carmen:

As of next month, please turn all monthly sales reports over to Alan
Oglesby in Sales (extension x4329). He'll be compiling all department sales
reports from now on. Thanks!

 Double Click

4 Click Inside the Left Margin

You can also click inside the left margin to select lines of text. Hover your mouse pointer to the left of the line you want to highlight until the mouse pointer takes the shape of a northeast-pointing arrow; click once to select the line.

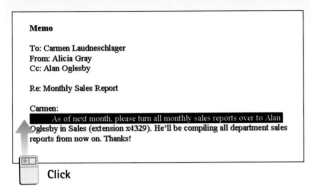

Click

5 Select a Paragraph

Use the left margin to also select a paragraph; double-click next to the paragraph you want to select.

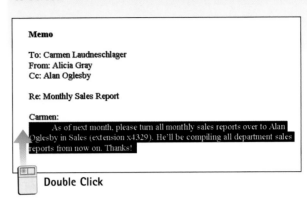

Double Click

6 Select the Entire Document

You can also use the left margin to select the entire document; triple-click anywhere in the left margin to select the entire document.

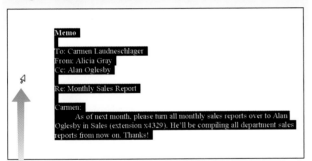

Triple Click

End

How-To Hints

Unselecting Text

To quickly unselect text, click anywhere outside the text or press any arrow key.

Edit Selected Text

You can easily replace selected text with new text. Just start typing, and the selected text is deleted and replaced with any new text you type. To delete selected text without typing new text, press the **Delete** key.

Keyboard Shortcuts

To quickly select one word at a time by using the keyboard keys, start at the beginning or end of the word and press **Ctrl+Shift+→** or **Ctrl+Shift+←**. To select one paragraph at a time, press **Ctrl+Shift+↑** or **Ctrl+Shift+↓**. To select all the text from the insertion point onward, press **Ctrl+Shift+End**. To select all text above the insertion point, press **Ctrl+Shift+Home**.

How to Move and Copy Text

Use Word's Cut, Copy, and Paste functions to move and copy text from one location to another. Word makes it easy to pick up characters, words, sentences, paragraphs and more, and move or copy them to a new location. You can even move and copy them between files.

You can apply a variety of methods to move and copy text. You can use menu commands, shortcut menu commands, toolbar buttons, keyboard shortcuts, and drag-and-drop techniques; everyone finds his or her favorite method. To move text, you cut it from its position and paste it somewhere else; to copy text, you make a copy of the text and paste it elsewhere.

Begin

1 Select the Text

Select the text you want to cut or copy.

2 Click Cut or Copy

To move the text, click the **Cut** button in the Standard toolbar. The text is deleted from your document, but it remains in a special Windows storage area called the *Clipboard*. To copy the text, click the **Copy** button. When you copy text, nothing appears to happen because the text remains in its original location, but a copy of the selected text is sent to the Clipboard.

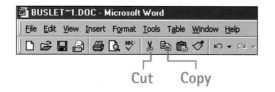

Cut   Copy

3 Relocate the Cursor

Click to place the cursor in the document where you want to paste the cut or copied text. If necessary, you can open another document or switch to a document you already have open to paste text there.

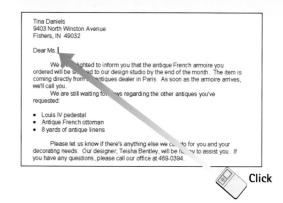

Click

4 Click Paste

Click the **Paste** button in the Standard toolbar to paste the text. The text is pasted into the document beginning at the position of the insertion point.

Paste

5 Drag-and-Drop to Move Text

Another easy method to move or copy text is to drag-and-drop it. To move text, click in the selected text and hold the mouse button down. *Drag* the mouse where you want to paste the text. Release the mouse button to *drop*, or paste, the cut text.

Click & Drag

Release

6 Drag-and-Drop to Copy Text

To copy text by dragging and dropping it, select the text you want to copy. Click in the selected text and hold the mouse button down, hold down the **Ctrl** key, and then *drag* the mouse to the new location. Release the mouse button to *drop*, or paste, the copied text.

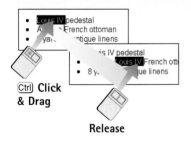

Ctrl Click & Drag

Release

 End

How-To Hints

Keyboard Shortcuts

If you prefer using the keyboard, try these shortcut commands: **Ctrl+X** for Cut, **Ctrl+C** for Copy, and **Ctrl+V** for Paste. These keyboard shortcuts are standard for all Windows-based programs.

Keep Pasting

After you cut or copy text, a copy of it remains in the Clipboard, so you can repeatedly paste more copies of the text without cutting or copying it again.

Pasting to Other Programs

You can also cut or copy text to other programs. Cut or copy the desired text, switch to the other program and open the file in which you want to paste the text; position the insertion point, and then use the Paste command provided in that program.

How to Paste Multiple Items with the Clipboard Toolbar

A new feature added to Word 2000 is the Clipboard toolbar. It allows you to paste multiple items you cut or copy in your documents. For example, you might cut two or three different paragraphs, and then paste them back into your document in a different order. The Clipboard toolbar lets you pick exactly which item to paste and you can choose to cut or copy up to 12 items.

Begin

1 Cut or Copy Text

Use the skills you learned in the previous task to cut or copy text. You can cut or copy up to 12 different items. When you cut or copy more than one item, the Clipboard toolbar automatically appears.

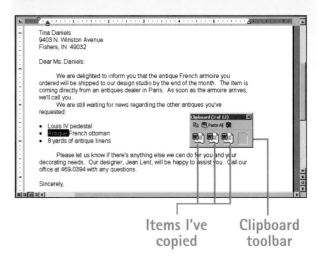

Items I've copied   Clipboard toolbar

2 Place the Insertion Point

Click in place where you want to paste an item you cut or copied.

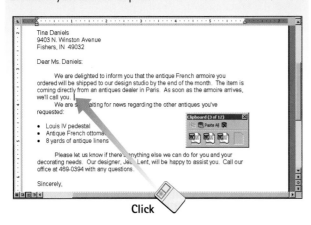

Click

3 Select an Item to Paste

From the Clipboard toolbar, choose the item you want to paste. If you're not too sure which item is which, hover your mouse pointer over an icon and a ScreenTip appears describing the cut or copied text.

Call our office at 469-0394 with any questions.

4 Click to Paste

Click the icon representing the text you want to paste.

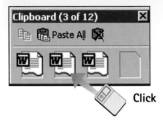

Click

5 The Item Is Pasted

The text is immediately pasted into your document. To paste another Clipboard item, repeat steps 3-5.

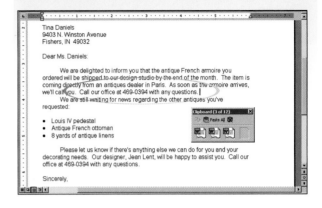

6 Close the Clipboard Toolbar

To close the Clipboard toolbar when you're finished pasting, click the **Close** (×) button.

Click

End

How-To Hints

Using Other Clipboard Buttons

The items you copy remain on the Clipboard even when you close it, just in case you want to paste more copies later. To clear the Clipboard's contents, click the **Clear Clipboard** button to the left of the **Close** button. To paste all the cut or copied items at once, click the **Paste All** button.

Where's My Clipboard Toolbar?

If you can't see your Clipboard toolbar, or you've accidentally closed it before you could use it, you can open it by displaying the **View** menu, selecting **Toolbars**, **Clipboard**.

It's in the Way!

If the Clipboard toolbar is blocking your view of the area you want to paste to, you can drag it out of the way. Drag the toolbar's title bar to move the toolbar to a new location onscreen.

How to Delete Text

In the process of making changes (also called *edits*) to your document, you'll inevitably need to delete unwanted text. There are several different methods you can employ to remove text from your document page. Try each one and see which method works best for you. If you make a mistake and delete text unnecessarily, click the **Undo** button on the Standard toolbar to bring the text back.

Begin

1 Select the Text

To delete text, whether it's a word, a sentence, or several paragraphs, you must first select the text you want to remove.

2 Press the Delete Key

Probably the fastest method to remove the selected text is to simply press the **Delete** key on the keyboard.

3 Click the Cut Button

If you're in the habit of using your mouse to do everything, you can quickly click the **Cut** button on the Standard toolbar.

Click

4 Display the Shortcut Menu

You can also right-click over the selected text to display a shortcut menu.

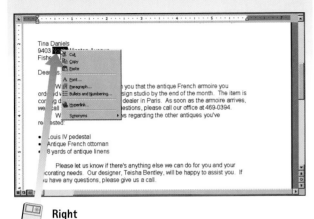

Right Click

5 Select the Cut Command

Select **Cut** from the shortcut menu to delete the text.

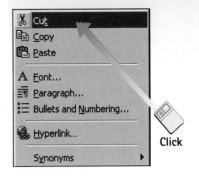

Click

6 Press Backspace

A tried-and-true method of deleting text while typing is to use the Backspace key. Simply press **Backspace** to delete a character to the left of the cursor. Hold down the **Backspace** key to delete more than one character at a time.

End

How-To Hints

Undo and Redo

If you accidentally delete something and decide you need it back, use Word's Undo command to retrieve the text. Learn more about this feature in the next task, "How to Use Undo and Redo."

How to Use Undo and Redo

Two very useful tools for editing documents are Word's Undo and Redo commands. These commands do exactly as their names imply; the Undo command undoes your last action, and the Redo command redoes the action. For example, perhaps you've accidentally deleted a paragraph. Click the **Undo** button and the entire paragraph reappears. If you decide, after reading the paragraph again, that you were better off without it, click the **Redo** button and it's deleted all over again.

In this task, you learn the various ways to use Undo and Redo to help you edit your document. This task focuses on the Undo and Redo buttons on the Standard toolbar, but you can also find these commands on the Edit menu.

Begin

1 Delete Some Text

To show you how the Undo command works, select and delete some text in your document. Use the skills you learned in the previous task. In this example, I'm deleting the year.

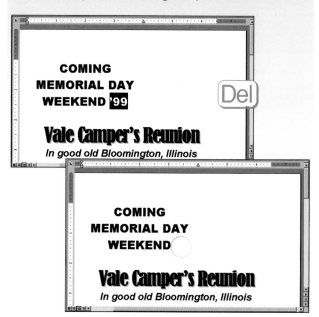

2 Undo Your Last Action

To quickly undo the last action you performed in the document, whether it was deleting text, copying and pasting, applying formatting, or any other action, simply click the **Undo** button on the Standard toolbar.

Click

3 My Text Is Restored

If you deleted text in step 1, as I did, clicking the **Undo** button in step 2 will immediately retrieve the deleted text. In this example, the year I deleted reappears.

4 Using Redo

To see how the Redo command works, let's redo the deletion again. Click the **Redo** button on the Standard toolbar.

Click

5 The Text Is Deleted Again

As soon as you click the **Redo** button, the last thing you did with the Undo command is restored. In this example, the text is deleted again.

COMING
MEMORIAL DAY
WEEKEND

Vale Camper's Reunion

In good old Bloomington, Illinois

6 Undoing Multiple Actions

In addition to undoing the last action you performed, you can also go back and undo the last several actions (the same is true for the Redo command as well). Undo keeps track of every edit you make and lists each action in the Undo list. To display the list, click the down arrow next to the **Undo** button.

Click

7 Choose an Action

Select the action you want to undo from the list. Word undoes not only that action, but every action you've performed since that action. In this example, I'm undoing the last four actions I performed.

Click

End

How to Save Time with AutoText

AutoText is a great tool for saving you time entering text. If you find yourself typing in the same company name, phrase, or address over and over again, make the text an AutoText entry. Assign the entry a brief abbreviation, and the next time you enter the abbreviation, AutoText inserts the entire text entry for you. AutoText entries can be of any length, from a short sentence to an entire letter, and they are easy to save and use.

Begin

1 Select the Text

Type the text you want to include in your AutoText entry and apply any formatting you want (for example, "Human Resources Department").

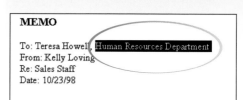

2 Choose the AutoText Command

Open the **Insert** menu and select **AutoText, New**.

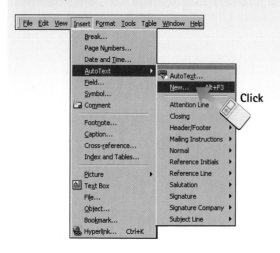

3 Enter a Name

In the Create AutoText dialog box, type a name for the entry in the **Please name your AutoText entry** box, such as *Human Resources*, or use the default suggestion, and choose **OK**. Although you can have AutoText names that are more than one word long, it's best to use a name or abbreviation that's short and memorable.

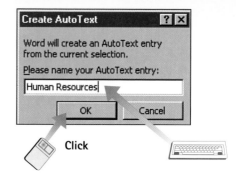

4 Insert AutoText

The next time you're ready to use the entry, click your document where you want the entry inserted and type the first few letters of an AutoText entry's name. As you type, an AutoComplete tip containing the name may appear next to the characters you typed; if you press **Enter**, the AutoText entry is inserted at the location.

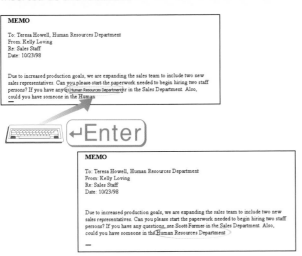

5 Open the AutoText Tab

You can also choose which AutoText entry you want to use by opening the **Insert** menu and selecting **AutoText**, **AutoText**. This opens the AutoCorrect dialog box with the AutoText tab displayed.

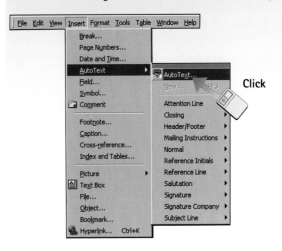

6 Choose an Entry

On the list of AutoText categories, point to the category where your entry is stored and click the name of the entry. Click the **Insert** button and the entry is pasted into your document.

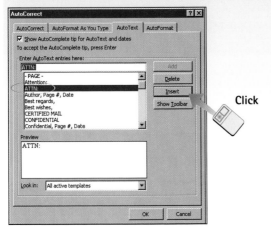

How-To Hints

Deleting Entries

To delete an AutoText entry, open the **Insert** menu and select **AutoText**, **AutoText** to display the AutoText tab of the AutoCorrect dialog box. Click the entry you want to delete from the list; click the **Delete** button, and click **OK**.

Use the AutoText Toolbar

Another way to create and insert AutoText entries is with the AutoText toolbar. Display the toolbar on your screen (select **View**, **Toolbars**, **AutoText**), and then use the **New** button to add new entries as you encounter them. To insert an entry, click the **AutoText** button and choose the entry from the list, and then click **Insert**.

Turn AutoComplete On or Off

To turn automatic AutoText entries on or off, choose **Tools**, **AutoCorrect**. At the top of the AutoText tab, mark or clear the **Show AutoComplete tip for AutoText and dates** check box. Click **OK** to exit.

End

How to Insert Symbols

Need to insert a special character or symbol not found on the keyboard? Tap into Word's collection of characters and symbols to find exactly what you're looking for. You can insert a copyright or trademark symbol, for example, into your text for products you mention. Depending on what fonts you have installed, you may have access to additional symbols, such as mathematical or Greek symbols, architectural symbols, and more.

Begin

1 Open the Symbol Dialog Box

Click the insertion point where you want the symbol inserted, and then open the **Insert** menu and select **Symbol**.

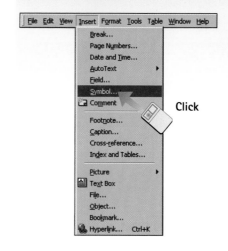

Click

2 Choose a Symbol

From the **Symbols** tab, click a symbol to magnify it. Each symbol you click is magnified so you can see clearly what it looks like (for example, click the "TM" symbol).

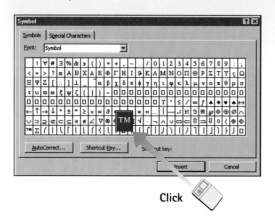

Click

3 Insert the Symbol

After selecting the symbol you want to use, click the **Insert** button and the symbol is placed in your text.

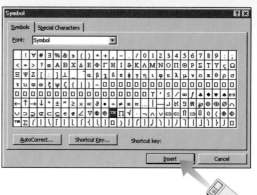

Click

4 Choose a Special Character

If you want a special character inserted, click the **Special Character** tab to view what's available.

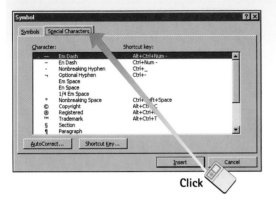

Click

5 Insert the Special Character

Select the special character you want to insert, and then click the **Insert** button. The character is added to your text.

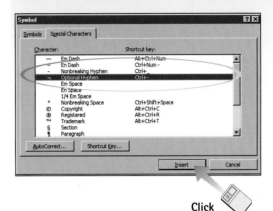

Click

6 Close the Dialog Box

The Symbol dialog box remains open in case you want to add another symbol. Click the **Close** button to exit the dialog box.

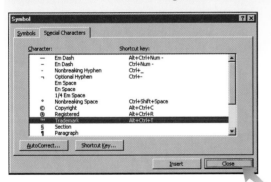

Click

End

How-To Hints

Customize the Symbols

Use the **Font** drop-down list in the Symbol dialog box to change the font used. Use WingDings, for example, to insert character icons such as clocks and telephones. Be sure to check out the symbols available for the fonts you have installed on your computer.

11

How to Change Case and Add Drop Caps

In some documents you create, you may want the first letter of the first word in a paragraph to stand out—perhaps larger than the rest or in a different font. Use Word's Drop Cap command to format the letter.

In other documents, you may decide you need to use all capital letters, or turn an all-caps title into upper- and lowercase letters. Use Word's Change Case command to change the text case exactly as you want it.

In this task, you learn how to use both of these features.

Begin

_1_ Select the Text

Select the letter you want to change to a drop-cap character.

The Vacation Begins

Day 1: September 6, 1997

A long time coming, the day of our vacation finally arrives. It's been nearly 10 years since our first visit to San Francisco, and lots of things have happened in both our lives...but time always seems to stand still when we embark on adventures such as these, and this trip will prove to be no exception.

_2_ Open the Drop Cap Dialog Box

Open the **Format** menu and select **Drop Cap** to display the Drop Cap dialog box.

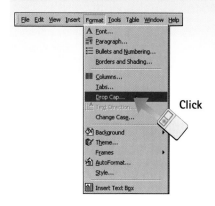

Click

_3_ Choose a Drop Cap

Choose a position for the drop cap: **Dropped** or **In Margin**. Then assign any formatting, such as a new font or change the positioning.

Click

4 Apply the Settings

Click **OK** to exit the dialog box and apply the new settings. Word immediately switches to Print Layout view, if you're not already using the view, so you can see the drop-cap character in your paragraph. Notice the character is surrounded by a border with selection handles. Word now treats the drop cap as an object. Learn more about working with objects in Chapter 11, "How to Work with Graphics."

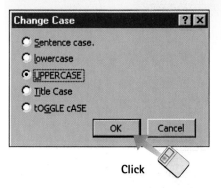

5 Change Text Case

Select the text whose case you want to change, and then open the **Format** menu and choose **Change Case** to display the Change Case dialog box.

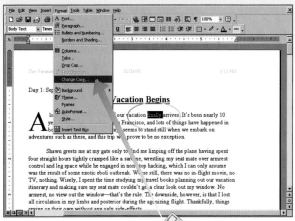

Click

6 Select a Case Option

Choose a case option from those available. To make lowercase letters all caps, for example, click the **UPPERCASE** option. To make capital letters all lowercase, choose **lowercase**. Click **OK** to exit and apply the new case.

Click

End

How-To Hints

Format the Drop Cap

To change the position, text wrap, and other formatting options for your drop-cap character, double-click the drop cap's border to open the Frame dialog box. From this box, you can tinker with the positioning of the drop cap. To learn more about applying options to objects, check out Chapter 11.

Which Is Which?

The way the options are written in the Change Case dialog box shows how the text case will appear. For example, the **Sentence case.** option capitalizes the S in sentence and ends the phrase with a period. The **lowercase** option is written in all lowercase letters.

How to Insert the Date and Time

When you're typing a letter or another type of document that requires the current date, don't bother typing the date yourself—let Word do all the work for you. You can insert the current date in a number of different formats to suit your document's style. You can also turn on the Update automatically option and Word updates the date to the current date every time you open the document.

Begin

1 Place the Insertion Point

Click in your document where you want to insert the date or time.

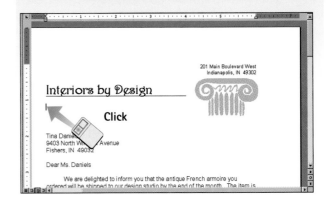

2 Open the Insert Menu

Open the **Insert** menu and select **Date and Time**. This opens the Date and Time dialog box.

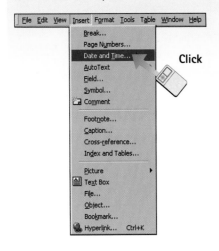

3 Choose a Date and Time Format

Scroll through the Available formats list box to find the format you want to use. Click the format to select it.

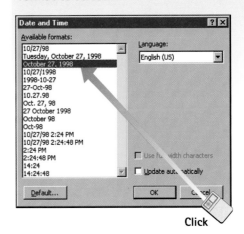

4 Update Automatically

If you want the date or time automatically updated every time you open the document, click the **Update automatically** check box.

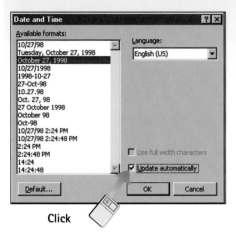

Click

5 Exit the Dialog Box

To exit the dialog box, click **OK**.

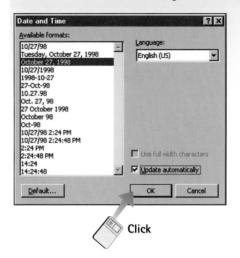

Click

6 The Date or Time Is Inserted

The date or time, depending on which format you selected, now appears in the document.

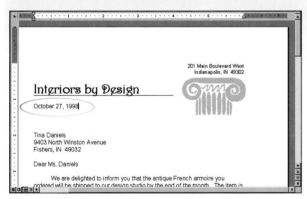

End

How-To Hints

Other Languages

Different countries have different ways of expressing the date or time in correspondence. Depending on what language version of Word you're using, you can use the **Language** drop-down list in the Date and Time dialog box to change the list of available formats.

Task

4 Find and Replace Text

To find the text and replace it with new text, use the Replace command. Open the **Edit** menu and select **Replace**. This opens the Find and Replace dialog box with the Replace tab up front.

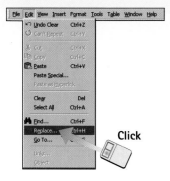

Click

5 Enter the Text

Type the word or words you're looking for in the **Find what** text box (such as **trip**). Type the replacement text in the **Replace with** text box (such as **journey**). (If you want to specify any search criteria, click the **More** button and select from the available options.)

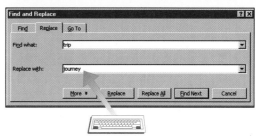

6 Search and Replace

Click the **Find Next** button to locate the first occurrence. Word highlights the text in the document. Click the **Replace** button to replace the text with the new text. Click **Replace All** to replace every occurrence in the document. Click **Find Next** to ignore the first occurrence and move on to the next.

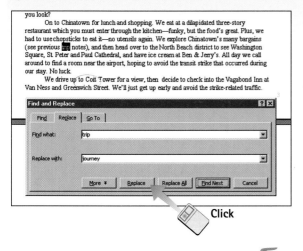

Click

How-To Hints

Search Complete

When Word completes a search, it displays a prompt box telling you the search is complete. Click **OK**. If the search didn't reveal any occurrences of the text, a prompt box alerts you; click **OK** and try another search.

Search and Delete

Use the Find and Replace tools to delete text from your document. Open the Find and Replace dialog box, type a space and the word you're looking for in the **Find what** text box, but leave the **Replace with** box empty. Word will search and delete the text from your document without replacing it with new text.

End

How to Check Your Spelling and Grammar

The Spelling and Grammar Checker enables you to check the spelling and grammar of a document as you type, or check the entire document's spelling all at once. Because most of us tend to forget about running the Spelling Checker when we finish typing, the Automatic Spelling Checker can save errors by pointing them out as we type and making them difficult to ignore.

If Automatic Spelling Checker isn't on, choose **Tools**, **Options**, and click the **Spelling and Grammar** tab. Click the **Check spelling as you type** check box to turn it on (click the **Check grammar as you type** check box if you want to turn on Automatic Grammar Checking).

Begin

1 Find the Red Wavy Line

When you type, any word that Word can't find in its dictionary gets a red wavy line under it to tell you it may be misspelled (in this figure, for example, Word points out "visists" as a misspelling).

> Day 2: September 7, 1997
> **A Day in the Park**
> No visit to San Francisco would be complete without spending a Sunday in Golden Gate Park. Starting with a tour of the Palace of Fine Arts (which I unknowingly missed in my first two SF visists), we wind our way through the Presidio and Lands End to finally arrive in the middle of Golden Gate Park. Here we begin yet another glorious, memorable San Francisco Sunday afternoon, with air so crisp and sky so blue, the vision is permanently seared in our minds.

2 Display the Shortcut Menu

Right-click the word to open a shortcut menu displaying possible alternative spellings at the top and a few additional commands. To choose an alternative spelling from the shortcut menu, click it. If your spelling is correct (for example, someone's last name), click **Add**; the word is added to Word's dictionary and won't be picked up by the Spelling Checker ever again.

Right Click

3 Ignore the Spelling

If you don't want to add the word to the dictionary, but want to leave the word spelled as is in the current document, click **Ignore All**. To add the correct spelling to your AutoCorrect list so that future misspellings will be corrected automatically as you type, click **AutoCorrect** (see Task 4, "How to Correct Text with AutoCorrect," to learn about AutoCorrect). To open the Spelling dialog box, click **Spelling**.

Click

4 Find the Green Wavy Line

If the wavy underline is green, Word detects a possible grammatical error. Follow steps 2 and 3 of this task to fix the error or rectify the problem yourself. (If you're not clear about what the problem is, right-click over the error and select Grammar to open a dialog box explaining the error.)

> Quickly, we make our way to a shuttle and eventually to our generic rental car, which Shawn has already secured in advance. It's no station wagon, but it's transportation nonetheless (hats off to dedicated Hertz employees everywhere). By 2:00 pm, our vacation is in full swing.
>
> We head directly downtown to look for a hotel, stopping at the Travelodge at the corner of Lombard and Van Ness. In a matter of moments, we've checked in, changed clothes and set out on foot to see the sights. Climbing Russian Hill, with repeated stops to gaze in amazement at the seriously steep incline and rest our out-of-shape midwestern legs, we reach the crookedest street in the world and take a quick cable car ride down to the bay (for free!). We then proceed to spend a glorious afternoon at Ghirardelli Square sampling delicacies at a chocolate tasting festival. Heaven must surely be like a Ghirardelli chocolate truffle.

5 Check Your Entire Document

To run the Spelling and Grammar Checker for the whole document at one time, click the **Spelling and Grammar** button on the Standard toolbar, or open the **Tools** menu and select **Spelling and Grammar**.

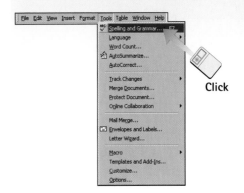

Click

6 Fix or Ignore Errors

Word checks every word in your document against its dictionary and list of grammatical rules and presents the Spelling and Grammar dialog box when it encounters a word that is not in its dictionary or does not conform to a grammatical rule. Click **Change** to fix the problem with Word's suggestion, or click **Ignore** to skip the error.

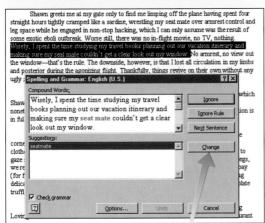

Click

End

How-To Hints

Turn It Off

To turn the Automatic Spelling checker off, choose **Tools, Options**; on the **Spelling and Grammar** tab, clear the **Check spelling as you type** check box. To turn the Automatic Grammar Checker off, clear the **Check grammar as you type** check box. Click **OK** to exit.

Check Selected Text

To check the spelling and grammar of only a portion of the document, select that portion before starting the check. When Word finishes checking the selection, it asks whether you want to check the rest of the document. Click **No** to end the check.

Check the Writing Style

To modify what Word looks for in a grammar check, choose **Tools, Options**, and click the **Spelling and Grammar** tab. In the **Writing style** drop-down list, select a style that best describes your document. You can choose which items Word checks by clicking the **Settings** button. Mark or clear check boxes for items such as wordiness or passive sentences. Choose **OK**.

How to Use the Thesaurus

In addition to spelling and grammar checking, Word can also help you with your writing endeavors with the Thesaurus tool. The Thesaurus lets you look up synonyms (words that mean the same or nearly the same), and check other meanings for words you type into your document. Use this tool to help you when you find yourself overusing a word and to make a better impact on the reader.

Begin

1 Select a Word

Select the word in your document that you want to look up by using the Thesaurus tool.

Day 2: September 7, 1997
A Day in the Park
No visit to San Francisco would be complete without spending a Sunday in Golden Gate Park. Starting with a tour of the Palace of Fine Arts (which I unknowingly missed in my first two SF visits), we wind our way through the Presidio and Lands End to finally arrive in the middle of Golden Gate Park. Here we begin yet another glorious, memorable San Francisco Sunday afternoon, with air so crisp and sky so blue, the vision is permanently seared in our minds.

2 Open the Thesaurus

Open the **Tools** menu and select **Language**, **Thesaurus**. This opens the Thesaurus dialog box.

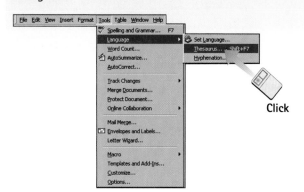

Click

3 View Synonyms

The Thesaurus dialog box displays the word you want to look up in the **Looked Up** text box. A list of synonyms appears in the list box on the right.

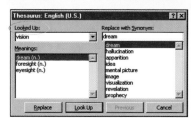

4 Look Up a Word

To look up a word's meanings, select it from the Synonym list box. For example, in this figure, I've selected "image." Click the **Look Up** button.

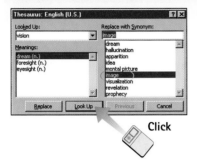

Click

5 View a Meaning

The Thesaurus displays the word you selected along with its meanings and another synonym list. Continue looking up words and meanings until you find the word you want to use. To return to the previous word viewed, click the **Previous** button.

Click

6 Replace the Word

Highlight the word you want to use, and then click the **Replace** button. This replaces the previous word you selected in the document with the new word you looked up.

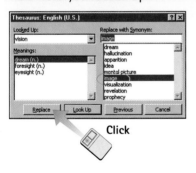

Click

End

How-To Hints

Forget It

To exit the Thesaurus without choosing a word, simply click the **Cancel** button.

Viewing Synonyms

You can also right-click over a selected word in the document to reveal a shortcut menu. Select **Synonyms** from the menu to display a list of possible synonyms (only if Word has any listed in its dictionary). You can click any word on the list and it immediately replaces the word you originally selected.

How to Correct Text with AutoCorrect

Word's AutoCorrect feature can save you time by automatically correcting misspelled words as you type—no need to run a spelling checker. AutoCorrect comes with a list of common misspellings, but the list isn't comprehensive; you can add your own common misspellings to the list to personalize it to your work habits.

What makes AutoCorrect even more useful is that you can use it to do your typing for you. If you often type a particular word or long phrase, you can create an AutoCorrect entry that types the word for you when you type a short abbreviation or acronym. For example, I got tired of typing the word "AutoCorrect," so I made it an Auto-Correct entry; now I type "ac" and a space, and Word types out the whole word for me, capitals and all. Or, if you have a long phrase, such as "Lake City High School Alumni Association," you can make it an AutoCorrect entry that responds to a short abbreviation such as "lca."

Begin

1 Try It Out

Test AutoCorrect to see how it performs—type **teh**, and then press the Spacebar or type a punctuation mark such as a comma or a period. Because "teh" is a common misspelling, AutoCorrect corrects it to "the" before you realize you mistyped it.

Memo

To: Carmen Laudneschlager
From: Alicia Gray
Cc: Alan Oglesby

Re: Monthly Sales Report

Carmen:
    As of next month, please turn all monthly sales reports over to Alan Oglesby in Sales (extension x4329). He'll be compiling all department sales reports from now on. We hope teh

Memo

To: Carmen Laudneschlager
From: Alicia Gray
Cc: Alan Oglesby

Re: Monthly Sales Report

Carmen:
    As of next month, please turn all monthly sales reports over to Alan Oglesby in Sales (extension x4329). He'll be compiling all department sales reports from now on. We hope the

2 Undo AutoCorrect

If you type something you don't want corrected (for example, "Mr. Edmund Teh"), press **Ctrl+Z** to undo the correction before you type any other characters. The AutoCorrection is undone, and you can continue typing.

Mr. Edmund The

Mr. Edmund Teh

3 Remove a Word from AutoCorrect

To remove a word from the AutoCorrect list, open the **Tools** menu and select **AutoCorrect**.

Click

4 Delete the Word

Click the **AutoCorrect** tab. In the **Replace** box, type the first few letters of the word you want to delete from AutoCorrect; the list of words and replacements scrolls to the point in the list where you can find your word. Click your word in the list, and then click **Delete**. Click **OK** to exit the dialog box.

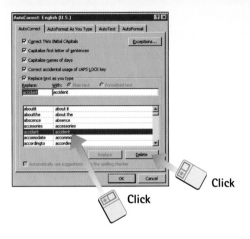

Click

Click

5 Add a Misspelling

To add a word you frequently misspell to the AutoCorrect list, open a document and type the correct spelling. (You can also add a long phrase for which you want to create a shortcut; type in the phrase, including any special capitalization.) Select the word, and then choose **Tools, AutoCorrect**.

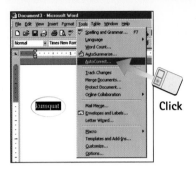

Click

6 Click Add

Click the **AutoCorrect** tab. Your word or phrase appears in the **With** box. In the **Replace** box, type the incorrect word (for example, "kumqat") or acronym you want to replace (this text is what you will mistype in your document). If you want to add only a single word, choose **OK** to close the dialog box; if you want to add more words to the AutoCorrect list, click **Add** to add each word, and choose **OK** when you're finished.

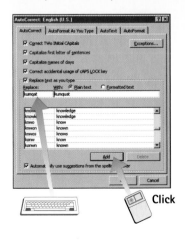

Click

How-To Hints

Turn It Off

Turn AutoCorrect off or on by clearing or marking the **Replace text as you type** check box on the AutoCorrect tab in the AutoCorrect dialog box.

Other Options

As you can see in the AutoCorrect tab, Word automatically corrects other items. Set or turn off other convenient automated options, such as capitalization of weekday names and the first word in sentences, by marking or clearing those check boxes.

AutoCorrect Long Phrases

To add a long word or phrase to the AutoCorrect list, enter the complete phrase in the **With** box. Enter an abbreviation or acronym you want to substitute for the phrase in the **Replace** box. Next time you need to insert the phrase, type the abbreviation or acronym you assigned and AutoCorrect handles the rest.

End

How to Count Words and Characters

If you're creating a document that requires a set number of characters, use Word's Word Count command to help you keep track of how much text you enter. For example, perhaps you're writing an article for a newsletter and know in advance that you have room for only a thousand words, including spaces. You can use the Word Count feature to check your progress and find out exactly how many words or characters you've entered. Word Count even tells you how many paragraphs and lines you entered.

Begin

1 Select Text

To count the words or characters in a portion of the document, select the text to be counted.

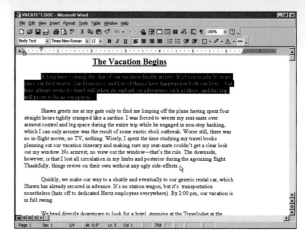

2 Or Click in the Document

To perform a word count on the entire document, click to place the cursor in the document.

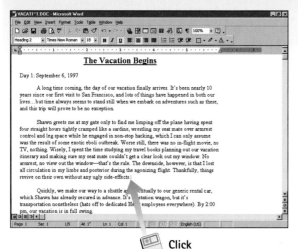

Click

3 Select the Word Count Command

Next, open the **Tools** menu and select the **Word Count** command.

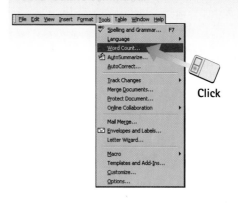

Click

4 View Your Word Count

The Word Count dialog box gives details about the number of pages, words, characters without spaces, characters with spaces, paragraphs, and lines.

5 Close the Dialog Box

To exit the dialog box, click the **Cancel** button.

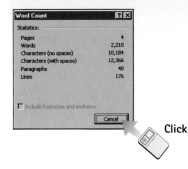

Click

End

How-To Hints

Keeping Track of Pages

Notice Word also keeps track of how many pages the document contains by displaying the current page and the total pages on the Status bar at the bottom of the program window.

How to Track Document Changes Between Users

If you're using Word in an office or network situation, you can utilize the program's tracking features to help you and your colleagues collaborate on documents. For example, let's say you create a rough draft of a report and pass it off to your department head to add his or her input, and he or she, in turn, passes it on to someone else. Each person who views the document file adds his or her comments to your work. If Word's tracking features are turned on, you can see exactly what each person adds to the document. Each person's edits (also called *revision marks*) appear in a different color.

After the document is returned to you, you can view each person's comments and revision marks and choose to incorporate them into the final document or not. See the next task to learn how to review changes.

Begin

1 Open the Highlight Changes Dialog

Start by opening the document you want to share with your colleagues, and then open the **Tools** menu and select **Track Changes**, **Highlight Changes**. This displays the Highlight Changes dialog box.

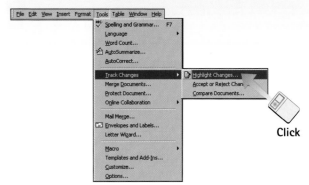

Click

2 Turn Tracking On

To turn the tracking feature on, click the **Track changes while editing** check box.

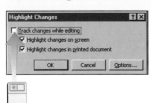

Click

3 Open the Track Changes Dialog

To control which revision marks are used to show changes between users, click the **Options** button. This opens the Track Changes dialog box.

Click

4 Change Revision Marks

Word offers you four ways to control the revision marks that will appear in the document; you can control how newly inserted text appears, how deleted text appears, changes in formatting, or changes to lines. For most users, the default settings are sufficient. If you do need to change the revision marks, however, you can click the **Mark** drop-down arrow in each category and change the revision mark used. Click **OK** when finished.

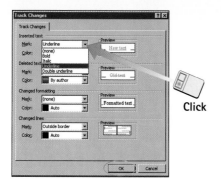

Click

5 Exit the Dialog Box

Click **OK** again to exit the Highlight Changes dialog box. Now you're ready to hand off the document to another user.

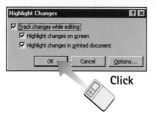

Click

6 Changes Marked in Color

Any changes made to the document by you or another user will appear marked in a different color (along with the revision marks determined by choices made in step 4).

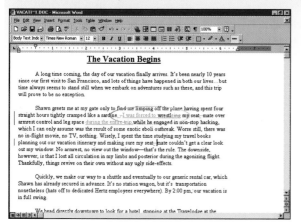

End

How-To Hints

Author Color

If you're passing the document to other users, be sure to leave the **Color** options set to **By author** and **Auto** in the Track Changes dialog box. This lets Word keep track by applying a new color for every different person who works on the document. Unfortunately, you can't change which color is used each time, Word determines the color choice and keeps track of it for you.

Preview It

If you make changes to the revision marks used, the **Preview** box next to the revision mark category lets you see how the revision mark will appear in the document.

Comparing Documents

If you failed to turn on the track changes feature, you can still compare changes made to the document against the original file. Use Word's Compare Documents command to open and view each file and locate differences between the two documents. To use this feature, open the **Tools** menu and select **Track Changes, Compare Documents**.

How to Review and Accept Document Changes

After you've passed around your document (see the previous task about tracking changes), you're ready to view what other users have changed in the document. Open the document and check over all the edits that have been made. When you're ready to create the final document, follow the steps in this task to help you accept or reject the changes your colleagues have made to your text.

Begin

1 Review the Edits

Start by reviewing all the edits that have been made to the document. Notice a different color designates each user's input.

> **The Vacation Begins**
>
> A long time coming, the day of our vacation finally arrives. It's been nearly 10 years since our first visit to San Francisco, and lots of things have happened in both our lives...but time always seems to stand still when we embark on adventures such as these, and this trip will prove to be no exception.
>
> Shawn greets me at my gate only to find me limping off the plane having spent four straight hours tightly cramped like a sardine. I was forced to wrestling my seat–mate over armrest control and leg space during the entire trip while he engaged in non-stop hacking, which I can only assume was the result of some exotic eboli outbreak. Worse still, there was no in-flight movie, no TV, nothing. I spent four hours on that flight, and all I got was a lousy sandwich. Wisely, I spent the time studying my travel books planning out our vacation itinerary and making sure my seat–mate couldn't get a clear look out my window. No armrest, no view out the window—that's the rule. Besides, if you're going to cough at me for four hours, you don't deserve a view. The downside, however, is that I lost all circulation in my limbs and posterior during the agonizing flight. Thankfully, things revive on their own without any ugly side-effects.
>
> Quickly, we make our way to a shuttle and eventually to our generic rental car, which Shawn has already secured in advance. It's no station wagon, but it's transportation nonetheless (hats off to dedicated Hertz employees everywhere). By 2:00 pm, our vacation is in full swing.

Changes

2 Open the Dialog Box

Next, open the **Tools** menu, select **Track Changes**, and then select **Accept or Reject Changes**. This displays the Accept or Reject Changes dialog box onscreen.

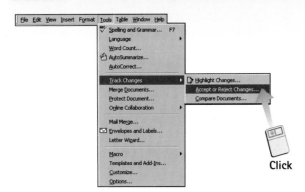

Click

3 Find the First Change

Click the **Find** button to find the first change that occurs in the document. Word highlights the change, as shown in this figure.

> Shawn greets me at my gate only to find me limping off the plane having spent four straight hours tightly cramped like a sardine. I was forced to wrestling my seat–mate over armrest control and leg space during the entire trip while he engaged in non-stop hacking, which I can only assume was the result of some exotic eboli outbreak. Worse still, there was no in-flight movie, no TV, nothing. I spent four hours on that flight, and all I got was a lousy sandwich. Wisely, I spent the time studying my travel books planning out our vacation
>
> itinerary and makin...
>
> armrest, no view ou...
>
> four hours, you don...
>
> my limbs and poste...
>
> without any ugly si...
>
> **Accept or Reject Changes** [? X]
>
> Changes
> Sherry Kinkoph
> Inserted
> 12/5/98 1:01 PM
>
> View
> ○ Changes with highlighting
> ○ Changes without highlighting
> ○ Original
>
> Find / Find
>
> Accept | Reject | Accept All | Reject All | Undo | Ck
>
> Quickly, we make our way to a shuttle and eventually to our generic rental car, which Shawn has already secured in advance. It's no station wagon, but it's transportation nonetheless (hats off to dedicated Hertz employees everywhere). By 2:00 pm, our vacation is in full swing.

Click

4 Accept or Reject the Change

To accept the change, click the **Accept** button. To reject the change and keep the original text intact, click the **Reject** button.

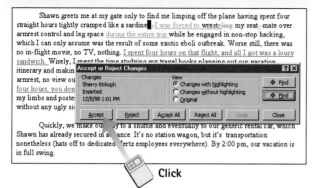

Click

5 On to the Next Change

Word moves on to the next change and highlights it in the document. You can choose to accept or reject the change again. Continue doing this to check over each change made to the document.

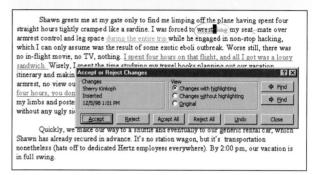

6 Close the Dialog Box

When finished checking all the edits, Word prompts you it's reached the end; click **OK**. Then click **Close** to exit the Accept or Reject Changes dialog box.

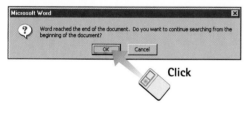

Click

End

How-To Hints

Accept or Reject All

If you don't want to check every edit individually, or perhaps you've already read over everyone's input, you can choose to accept or reject all the changes in one fell swoop. To accept all edits, click the **Accept All** button. To reject them, click **Reject All**. Word prompts you with a box asking whether you want to accept or reject all; click **Yes**.

Oops!

If you accidentally accept or a reject a change that you change your mind about, click the **Undo** button in the Accept or Reject Changes dialog box to immediately undo the situation.

Task

7

How to Change the Way Your Text Looks

*T*he real beauty of a word processing program such as Word 2000 lies in its myriad of formatting options. The term *formatting* refers to all the techniques that enhance the appearance of your document, including character, paragraph, and page formatting. Character formatting refers to all the features that can affect individual text characters, such as fonts, sizes, bold, or italic. With character formatting, you can choose to make a single word stand out in your document or change the appearance of every character throughout the entire document. You can even change the color of text, which can be put to great use if you have a color printer or if you're creating Web pages.

In this chapter, you'll learn how to use Word's character formatting options to change the way your text looks. The easiest way to see how formatting changes the text is to apply the commands to existing text you've already typed in. However, you can also apply these commands before entering any text. In the chapters to follow, you see how to build on these formatting techniques to change the way your paragraphs and pages look. ●

How to Apply Bold, Italic, and Color Formatting

By far the easiest formatting to apply is bold, italic, and underline. You can turn these three options on or off by using the toolbar buttons. You can also find these three commands in the *Font dialog box*, a comprehensive dialog box for applying formatting options in one fell swoop.

You can also add color to your text by using the Font Color and Highlight tools. Apply color to a single character, a word, or your entire text by using the Font Color button on the Formatting toolbar. Use the Highlight button to highlight the background behind your text.

Begin

1 Use the Formatting Buttons

Select the text you want to format, or choose the formatting commands before typing in the text. To boldface, italicize, or underline text, click on the Formatting toolbar.

2 Formatting Is Applied

Depending on which buttons you select, the formatting is immediately applied to your selected text. In this example, all three formatting types are applied.

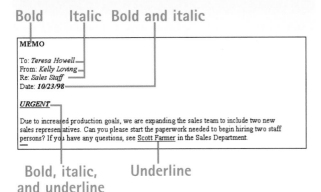

3 Or Open the Font Dialog Box

If you want to see what the formatting will look like before you apply it, open the **Format** menu and choose **Font**.

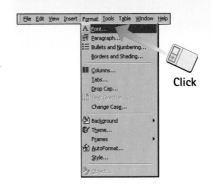

4 Select Bold, Italic, or Both

In the **Font style** list, choose **Bold**, **Italic**, or **Bold Italic** to boldface and/or italicize your text. To underline text, click the down arrow on the **Underline** list box to display the list of choices, and then click the desired underline style.

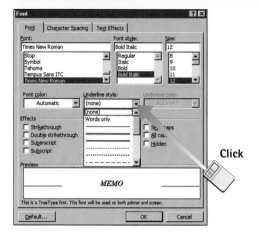

Click

5 Preview Your Selections

In the **Preview** area at the bottom of the dialog box, you can preview how your choices will affect the text.

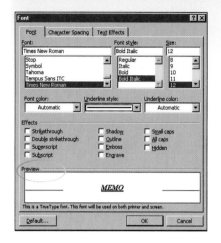

6 Exit the Dialog Box

When you've made your selections, choose **OK** to close the dialog box and apply the changes to the selected text.

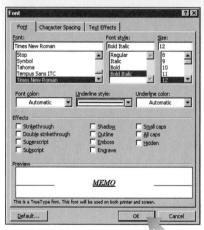

Click

7 Use the Font Color Button

To quickly change the color of text, select the text and click the arrow next to the **Font Color** button on the Formatting toolbar. This displays a palette of colors from which you can choose.

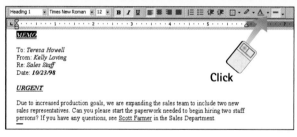

Click

Continues

8 Select a Color

Click the color you want to use.

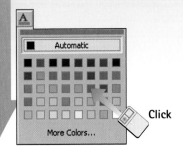

Click

9 The Color Is Applied

The color is immediately applied to the selected text. I deselected the text so you could see the results. In this example, I chose a shade of blue. Notice that the **Font Color** button now displays the last color you selected. It does this so you can reuse the color again elsewhere in your document with just a single click of a button.

10 Use the Highlight Tool

Want to highlight your text instead? To use the default yellow color, click the **Highlight** button on the Formatting toolbar. The mouse pointer takes the shape of a highlighter pen icon.

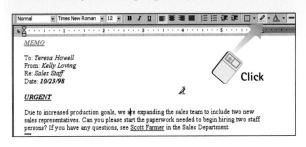

Click

11 Drag to Highlight

Drag over the text you want to highlight; hold down the left mouse button and drag the mouse to select the text.

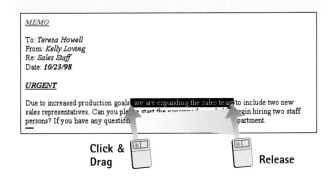

Click & Drag

Release

12 The Highlight Is Applied

When you're finished selecting the text to highlight, release the mouse button. The highlight color is applied to the text.

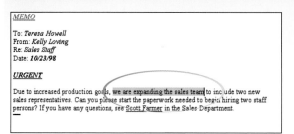

13 Change the Highlight Color

To change the color of the highlight, click the arrow next to the **Highlight** button to display a palette of colors. Click a color to use as your highlight. Now you can drag across the text and the new color is used.

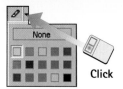

Click

14 Turn the Highlight Tool Off

To turn off the highlighting feature, click the **Highlight** button again.

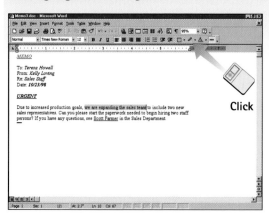

Click

End

How-To Hints

Toggle On or Off

In addition to formatting selected text, most of the Formatting toolbar buttons, such as Italic or Highlight, toggle on or off. Click a button to turn the formatting on (the button looks pushed in), click again to turn it off.

Keyboard Shortcuts

To format text from the keyboard, select the text, and then use these keyboard shortcuts: **Ctrl+B** for boldface, **Ctrl+I** for italic, **Ctrl+U** for underline, or **Ctrl+Shift+D** for double underline.

Adding Color by Using the Font Dialog Box

You can also add color from the Font dialog box. Click the **Font Color** drop-down arrow to display the list of choices, and then click the color you want to use. To add color to an underline, click the **Underline Color** drop-down arrow and select a color.

TASK 2

How to Change the Font and Size

Changing fonts and sizes is an easy way to alter the appearance of words to change the appearance of the document. A font is a set of characters distinguished by their style, and font size is the size of the characters measured in points (72 points in an inch). By default, Word assigns Times New Roman, 12 point, every time you open a new document. But you can easily apply another font or size anytime you want. You can change the font or size for one word, a paragraph, or the entire document.

Don't go overboard and use so many fonts and sizes that the document becomes excessively busy and difficult to read. Two or three fonts per document is sufficient.

Begin

1 Select the Text

Select the text whose font you want to change.

2 Choose a Font

On the Formatting toolbar, click the down arrow on the **Font** box to display a list of your installed fonts. Scroll through the list to find the font you want, and then click it to apply it to the selected text. (Word places the fonts you've used recently above a double line at the top of the list; below the double line is an alphabetical list of all the fonts.)

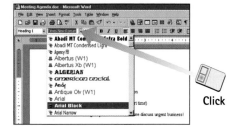

Click

3 Choose a Size

After you have chosen a font, you can make it larger or smaller by changing the font size. On the Formatting toolbar, click the down arrow on the **Font Size** box to display the list of font sizes. Scroll, if necessary, to find the size you want, and then click it to apply it to the selected text. (You can also click in the **Font Size** box and type a point size that's not on the list.)

Click

4 Open the Font Dialog Box

The quickest way to experiment with fonts, sizes, and other characteristics all at the same time is to use the Font dialog box. Select the text you want to format, and then open the **Format** menu and choose **Font**.

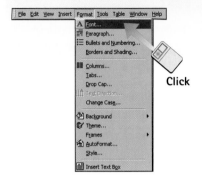

Click

5 Preview Font and Size

Use the Font tab to change the font and size, and then check the results in the **Preview** area.

6 Exit the Dialog Box

After you select a font or any other formatting options on the Font tab, click **OK** to exit the Font dialog box and apply the new settings.

Click

End

How-To Hints

Don't Like It?

If, after applying a new font or size, you decide you don't like it, click the **Undo** button on the Standard toolbar; the text will revert to the previous font or size.

Different Fonts

The number and type of available fonts depend on what has been installed on your computer, but most computers have a wide selection of TrueType fonts. They're displayed in font lists with a TT symbol next to their names. The advantage of TrueType fonts is that they look the same onscreen as they do when printed out.

What's Assigned?

The buttons and list boxes on the Formatting toolbar—for font, font size, style, and so on—always reflect the formatting at the current location of the insertion point. This comes in handy when you aren't sure which font is applied to a particular block of text. Click the text, and then look at the Formatting toolbar to see what characteristics are in effect.

How to Copy Text Formatting

If you have applied several character formats—such as a font, a font size, and a format (bold, italic, underline)—to a block of text in your document, and then later decide you would like to apply the same formatting to another block of text, you don't have to apply those formats one by one to the new location. Instead, you can use the Format Painter button to take all the formats from the original block of text and "paint" them across the new text.

Begin

1 Select the Text

Select the text that has the formatting you want to copy (characters, words, whole paragraphs, headings, and so on).

The Constitution of the United States of America

We the people of the United States, in order to form a more perfect union, establish justice, insure domestic tranquility, provide for the common defense, promote the general welfare, and secure the blessings of liberty to ourselves and our posterity, do ordain and establish this Constitution for the United States of America.

Article I
Section 1.

All legislative powers herein granted shall be vested in a Congress of the United States, which shall consist of a Senate and House of Representatives.

Section 2.

The House of Representatives shall be composed of members chosen every second year by the people of the several states, and the electors in each state shall have the qualifications requisite for electors of the most numerous branch of the state legislature.

2 Choose Format Painter

Click the **Format Painter** button in the Standard toolbar.

Click

3 Mouse Pointer Changes

Your mouse pointer changes to a paintbrush pointer.

The Constitution of the United States of America

We the people of the United States, in order to form a more perfect union, establish justice, insure domestic tranquility, provide for the common defense, promote the general welfare, and secure the blessings of liberty to ourselves and our posterity, do ordain and establish this Constitution for the United States of America.

Article I
Section 1.

All legislative powers herein granted shall be vested in a Congress of the United States, which shall consist of a Senate and House of Representatives.

Section 2.

The House of Representatives shall be composed of members chosen every second year by the people of the several states, and the electors in each state shall have the qualifications requisite for electors of the most numerous branch of the state legislature.

4 Drag to Copy Formatting

Click and drag the paintbrush pointer across the text where you want to paint the format.

> **Article I**
> Section 1.
>
> All legislative powers herein granted shall be vested in a Congress of the United States, which shall consist of a Senate and House of Representatives.
>
> Section 2.
>
> The House of Representatives shall be composed of members chosen every second year by the people of the several states, and the electors in each state shall have the qualifications requisite for electors of the most numerous branch of the state legislature.

Click

5 Formatting Is Applied

Release the mouse. The formatting is painted to the block of text (click anywhere to deselect the text).

> **Article I**
> **Section 1.**
>
> All legislative powers herein granted shall be vested in a Congress of the United States, which shall consist of a Senate and House of Representatives.
>
> Section 2.
>
> The House of Representatives shall be composed of members chosen every second year by the people of the several states, and the electors in each state shall have the qualifications requisite for electors of the most numerous branch of the state legislature.

End

How-To Hints

Keep Painting

To paint the same formatting to several blocks of text more quickly, double-click the **Format Painter** button. Format Painter remains turned on so you can paint the formatting repeatedly. For example, you could paint across all the headings in the document shown here. When you're finished painting the formatting, click the **Format Painter** button again to turn it off.

Another Route

Another way to copy formatting is to apply formatting to a selection with the Font dialog box (by using the Font dialog box, you can apply several formatting characteristics at once); select a block of text where you want to copy the formatting, and choose **Edit, Repeat Font Formatting**. You can also press **F4** or press **Ctrl+Y** to repeat an action.

Use AutoFormat

Don't like the pressures of coming up with formatting yourself? Use Word's AutoFormat feature to automatically format your documents. Open the **Format** menu and select **AutoFormat**. In the AutoFormat dialog box, select the type of document you're creating and click **OK**. Learn more about working with the AutoFormat feature in Chapter 8, "How to Change Paragraph Formatting," Task 10, "How to Use AutoFormat."

Task

How to Change Paragraph Formatting

*P*aragraph formatting commands can be used to improve the appearance of paragraphs on the document page. For example, you can change the horizontal positioning of your text by altering the alignment or changing the margins—perhaps you want to indent a paragraph so it stands out from the rest. You can change the vertical positioning of paragraphs by altering the line spacing. For example, a draft document with double-spaced lines is easier to mark up with changes than a single-spaced document.

Unlike character formatting that affects only the appearance of text characters, paragraph formatting affects as many blocks of text as you designate, whether it's a single paragraph or the entire document. In addition to controlling how the paragraph is situated on the page, you can also format the paragraph as a numbered or bulleted list, apply one of Word's many styles, or set tab columns throughout the document. In this chapter, you'll learn how to utilize Word's many paragraph formatting commands. ●

How to Set Line Spacing

Line spacing is the amount of space between lines within a paragraph. By default, Word starts each new document with single spacing, which sets just enough space between lines so that characters don't overlap. You might want to switch to double-spacing for document drafts because it gives you extra room to write in edits by hand.

You can also control the amount of space between paragraphs. For example, documents with an extra half-line of space between paragraphs are easier to read, and you don't need to type an extra blank line between paragraphs.

Begin

1 Select the Paragraph

To change the line spacing of only one paragraph, click in the paragraph. To change the line spacing of several paragraphs, select them first. To change the line spacing for the entire document, press **Ctrl+A** to select the entire document.

2 Open the Paragraph Dialog Box

Open the **Format** menu and select **Paragraph** to display the Paragraph dialog box.

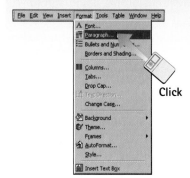

Click

3 Choose a Line Spacing

At the top of the Paragraph dialog box, click the **Indents and Spacing** tab if it's not already in front. Then click the down arrow on the **Line spacing** list box and select a line spacing: **Single**, **1.5 lines**, or **Double**.

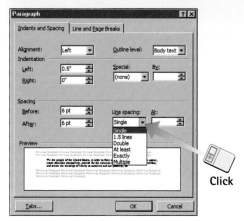

Click

4 Change Spacing Between Paragraphs

To change spacing between paragraphs, designate a new setting in the **Before** and **After** boxes. The **Before** box sets spacing at the top of the paragraph; the **After** box sets spacing at the bottom of the paragraph. Use the spin arrows to set paragraph spacing in points, or type in a setting.

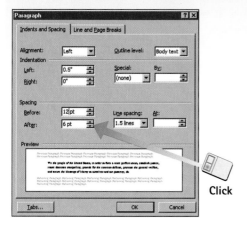

Click

5 Exit the Dialog Box

Choose **OK** to close the Paragraph dialog box.

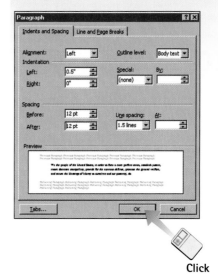

Click

6 Line Spacing Is Applied

Any changes you made in the Paragraph dialog box are applied to the selected text.

End

How-To Hints

Preview First

When changing the settings in the Paragraph dialog box, check out the effects in the Preview area to see how similar effects will appear in your own text.

Set an Exact Spacing Measurement

If your document requires an exact spacing measurement, use the **At least** or **Exactly** options on the **Line spacing** drop-down list. When either of these options is selected, you can enter a measurement in the **At** text box to define the amount of spacing you want between lines.

How to
Align Text

Use Word's alignment commands to change the way your text is positioned horizontally on the document page. By default, Word automatically aligns your text with the left margin as you type (unless you use the Click-and-Type method to enter text anywhere on the document page). You can choose to align text to the right margin, center text between the left and right margins, or justify text so it aligns at both the left and right margins.

For example, if you're creating a title page for a report, you might want to center the title text. If you're creating a newsletter or columns of text, justify the text to create even alignments on both sides.

Begin

1 Select the Text

Select the text or paragraphs you want to align.

> Centered Text
> aligns in the center of the document
>
> Right-aligned text
> lines up at the right margin
>
> Left-aligned text
> lines up at the left margin
>
> Justified text lines up at both the left and right margins. Newspaper columns, magazine articles, and books use justified alignment. In Word, you can't justify a single word or sentence; justification works best with paragraphs. Use justified text when creating your own newsletters and brochures.

Click & Drag

2 Click the Alignment Buttons

The alignment buttons on the Formatting toolbar will quickly align the text for you. Click **Align Left** to left-align text. Click **Center** to center text, click **Align Right** to right-align text. Click **Justify** to justify text between the left and right margins.

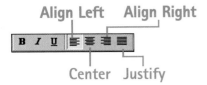

Align Left   Align Right

B *I* U

Center   Justify

3 Word Aligns Your Text

Depending on which alignment button you chose, Word aligns your text accordingly. This figure shows several alignment examples in effect.

> Centered Text
> aligns in the center of the document
>
>   Right-aligned text
>   lines up at the right margin
>
> Left-aligned text
> lines up at the left margin
>
> Justified text lines up at both the left and right margins. Newspaper columns, magazine articles, and books use justified alignment. In Word, you can't justify a single word or sentence; justification works best with paragraphs. Use justified text when creating your own newsletters and brochures.

4 Or Open the Paragraph Dialog Box

Another way to apply alignment is with the Paragraph dialog box—one-stop shopping for paragraph formatting commands. With the text selected, open the **Format** menu and choose **Paragraph**.

Click

5 Choose an Alignment

In the Indents and Spacing tab, click the **Alignment** drop-down arrow to display a list of alignment options. Click the one you want to use.

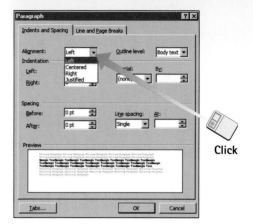

Click

6 Exit the Dialog Box

Notice that the **Preview** area gives you a glimpse of what the alignment will do to your text. Click **OK** to exit the dialog box and apply the settings to your document.

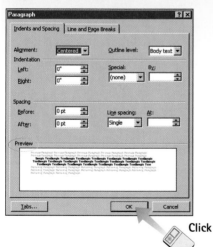

Click

End

How-To Hints

Keyboard Shortcuts

To center text by using only the keyboard, press **Ctrl+E**. Press **Ctrl+L** for left alignment, **Ctrl+R** for right alignment, and **Ctrl+J** for justified alignment.

Vertical Alignment

In addition to horizontal alignment, you can also change your document's vertical alignment. Learn how in Chapter 9, "How to Change Page Formatting," Task 4, "How to Apply Vertical Alignment."

How to Indent Text

Indents are simply margins that affect individual paragraphs or lines. Indents can help make paragraphs easier to distinguish. The quickest way to indent a line of text is with the Tab key; however, other ways will indent text more precisely. You can set exact measurements for left and right indents, choose to indent only the first line of text, or create a hanging indent that leaves the first line intact but indents the rest of the paragraph.

Begin

1 Click the Indent Buttons

For a quick indent, click in front of the paragraph or sentence you want to indent, and then use the Indent buttons on the Formatting toolbar. To increase the indent, click the **Increase Indent** button. To decrease the indent, click **Decrease Indent**.

Decrease Indent

Increase Indent

2 Or Open the Paragraph Dialog Box

For specific kinds of indents or to set an exact indent, click in front of the paragraph or text you want to indent. Then open the **Format** menu and select **Paragraph** to open the Paragraph dialog box.

Click

3 Specify a Measurement

From the Indents and Spacing tab, use the **Left** or **Right** indent boxes to set a specific measurement for the indent. You can type a measurement directly into the boxes or use the spin arrows to increase the settings.

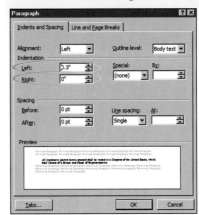

4 Set a Special Indent

To set a first-line or a hanging indent, click the **Special** drop-down list and make a selection.

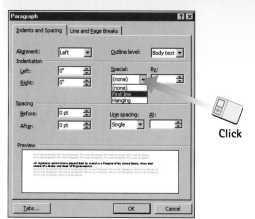

Click

5 Exit the Dialog Box

After setting the indent, check the **Preview** area to see how it will look. Click **OK** to exit from the dialog box.

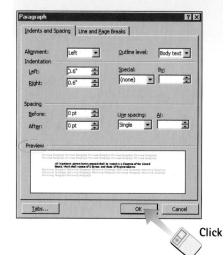

Click

6 Indents Applied

Word applies your indent specifications to the paragraph. This figure shows an example of a first-line indent and a hanging indent.

First-Line Indent

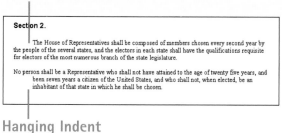

Hanging Indent

End

How-To Hints

Another Quick Indent

For a quick indent while you're typing a new paragraph, press the Tab key. This indents your text line by 1/2", which is perfect for starting most paragraphs.

Indents on the Ruler

You can also set indents on the ruler, including first-line and hanging indents. To set an indent, drag the appropriate indent marker on the ruler bar. The indent markers are funny-looking triangle shapes on the ends of the ruler. If you hover your mouse pointer over an indent marker, a ScreenTip appears identifying the marker.

Other Ideas

Use both a left and right indent to indent quotes or special text you want to set off in a document.

How to Work with Bulleted and Numbered Lists

Use Word's Bulleted and Numbered List features to set off lists of information in your documents. For example, a bulleted list can make a list of related information easy to spot on a page, and a numbered list organizes items that must be listed in a certain order.

You can start a bulleted or numbered list before typing in text, or you can turn existing text into an organized list.

Begin

1 Select Text

To turn existing text into a list, first select the text.

2 Click the Formatting Buttons

To add bullets, click the **Bullets** button on the Formatting toolbar. To turn the text into a numbered list, click the **Numbering** button.

Numbering

Bullets

3 Bullets or Numbers Are Applied

If you selected bullets, the text is immediately indented with bullet points in front of each line. If you selected numbering, the list is numbered sequentially, as shown in the following figure.

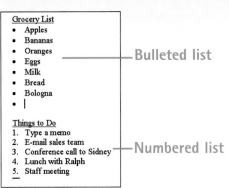

Bulleted list

Numbered list

4 Add to the List

To add items to the list, click at the end of the line before the place where you want to add another item and press **Enter**. Word inserts a new bullet or numbered step for you; just type in the new text. After you type the last item in the list, press **Enter** twice to turn the numbered or bulleted list off, or click the **Numbering** or **Bullets** button on the toolbar to turn the feature off.

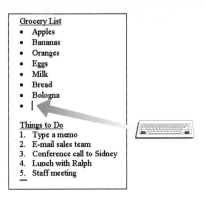

5 Change the Style

If you prefer to use a different bullet or numbering style in your list, open the **Bullets and Numbering** dialog box. Select the list text, open the **Format** menu, and choose **Bullets and Numbering**.

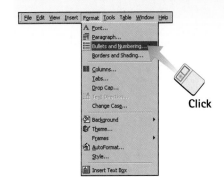

Click

6 Select a Bullet or Number Style

To change the bullet style, click the **Bulleted** tab and choose another style. To change the number style, click the **Numbered** tab and select another style. Click **OK** to exit the dialog box and apply the new style.

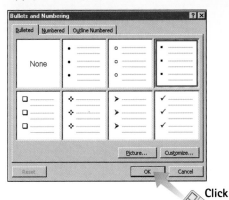

Click

End

How-To Hints

Create the List As You Type

You can also create a bulleted or numbered list as you type. For a numbered list, type **1.** followed by a space, type the text for the first item, and press **Enter**. To create a bulleted list, type an asterisk (*) followed by a space, type the text for the first item, and press **Enter**. Continue entering list items as needed. Press **Enter** twice after the last item to turn off the list feature.

Customizing Bullets or Numbers

Use the **Customize** button in the Bullets and Numbering dialog box to set another font for the bullets or numbers you use or customize the way in which they are positioned in the document. Learn more about customizing in Task 5, "How to Customize Bulleted and Numbered Lists."

How to Customize Bulleted and Numbered Lists

Word automatically assigns a default bullet style or a default number style when creating bulleted and numbered lists. You can customize the appearance of the bullets or numbers used in such lists as well as change the position of the bullets or numbers as they appear in the lists. For example, you may want the text closer to the bullets or numbers or prefer larger bullets or picture bullets instead. If you're using Word to create a Web page, for instance, you may want to use a colorful bullet image that really shows up on the page.

In this task, you learn how to customize the positioning of a bulleted or numbered list and assign picture bullets.

Begin

1 Select List Text

To customize an existing bulleted or numbered list, first select the list. You can also follow these steps to set custom bullets or numbers before typing in the list.

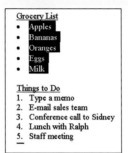

2 Open the Dialog Box

Open the **Format** menu and choose **Bullets and Numbering**. This opens the Bullets and Numbering dialog box.

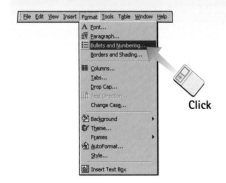

Click

3 Open the Customize Dialog Box

To customize the placement of the bullets or numbers in the list text or change the bullet style, click the **Customize** button (be sure to select a bullet style first). This opens the Customize Bulleted List or Customize Numbered List dialog box.

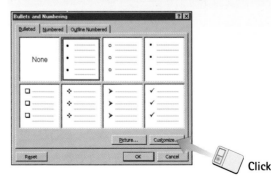

Click

4 Change the Indents

Use the position controls to change how the bulleted or numbered list is indented. Enter a new measurement in the **Indent at** text box or use the spin arrows to set a new setting. Check the **Preview** area to see how the indents look. Click **OK** to exit and apply the new indents.

Click

5 Assign a Picture Bullet

You can assign Web page bullets to a bulleted list. Click the **Picture** button in the Bullets and Numbering dialog box to open the Picture Bullet dialog box.

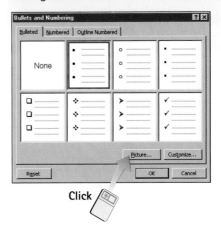

Click

6 Choose a Picture Bullet

Scroll through the list of picture bullets in the **Pictures** tab and select the one you want to use.

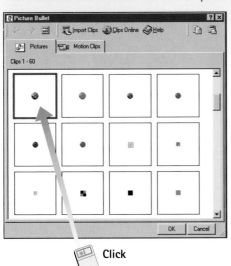

Click

7 Exit and Apply

A balloon list pops up; click the **Insert Clip** icon and click **OK**. The bullet pictures replace any default bullets in the list.

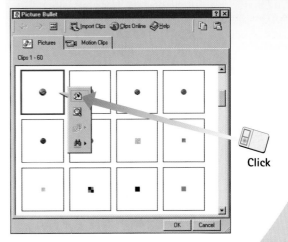

Click

End

How to Set Tabs Using the Ruler

Tabs are used to indent and create vertically aligned columns of text. By default, Word has tab stops set at every half-inch interval in your document. Whenever you press the Tab key, the cursor moves to the next tab column. The tab text is always aligned at the left, which means it lines up at the left edge of the tab column.

You can create your own tab stops and change how the tab text is aligned at a tab stop. For example, you can align tab text to the right edge of the tab column, center the text in the column, or use the decimal point tab to line up decimal points in the tab column. You can even apply a bar tab which sets a vertical bar between tab columns. In this task, you learn how to create quick tabs by using the ruler.

Begin

1 Choose a Tab Alignment

To set a tab stop on the ruler, first select the type of tab alignment. By default, the Left Tab alignment is selected. To select another, you must cycle through the selections. Each click on the alignment button displays a different tab alignment symbol (hover your mouse pointer over the button to display the tab alignment name).

Tab alignment button

⌊—Left tab

⌊—Center tab

⌊—Right tab

⌊—Decimal tab

⌊—Bar tab

2 Click in Place

On the ruler, click where you want the tab inserted; the tab symbol is added to the ruler.

Click

3 Apply a Tab

To use the new tab stop, place the cursor at the beginning of the line and press **Tab**, or place your cursor in front of the text you want to reposition and then press **Tab**. In the next figure, I'm creating a two-column tab list of grocery items.

Tab

4 Enter Text

Enter the text for the tab column. In my grocery list, I press **Enter** to start a new line, and then enter text and press the **Tab** key to move to the next column. The tab I set on the ruler is in effect until I change it to another setting.

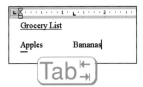

5 Remove a Tab

To remove a tab you've set on the ruler, simply drag it off the ruler. Click the tab symbol, drag it off the ruler, and release the mouse button. You can remove a tab for a single line of text or an entire list (select all the text first).

Click & Drag

6 Tab Stop Is Deleted

The tab symbol no longer appears on the ruler.

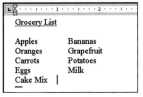

End

How-To Hints

How Many Tabs Can I Set?

You can set as many tab columns as will fit in your document page, and you can use different tab stops for different paragraphs or lists. To apply a tab stop to an existing paragraph, first click inside the paragraph, and then set the tab stop. If you previously pressed the Tab key to use the default tab setting, the tab stop adjusts to the new setting you apply.

How to Set Custom Tabs

In the previous task, you learned how to set tabs by using the horizontal ruler. Another way to create custom tabs to use throughout your document is to set tabs with the Tabs dialog box. Word keeps track of the tabs you set in this dialog box. When you set tabs in the Tabs dialog box, you can always reapply the setting to a new document or to another area in your existing document.

Begin

1 Open the Tabs Dialog Box

Another way to set tabs is to use the Tabs dialog box; click where you want to insert a tab stop, open the **Format** menu, and choose **Tabs**.

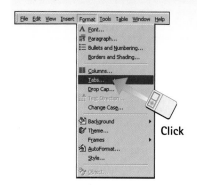

Click

2 Enter a Tab Stop

In the **Tab stop position** text box, enter a new tab stop measurement. Tab stops are measured in inch-increments, so if you enter 1.5, the tab column will appear 1 and ½ inches from the left margin.

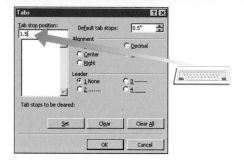

3 Set an Alignment

Use the **Alignment** options to change the tab stop alignment. The alignment affects how text lines up within a tab column. The default setting is Left, but you can change it to another alignment. Click the alignment you want to use.

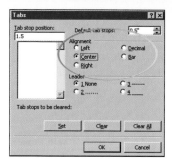

4 Add the Setting to the List Box

After setting a tab stop, you can add it to Word's list box by clicking the **Set** button.

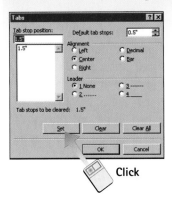

Click

5 Exit the Dialog Box

Click **OK** to exit the dialog box. The new tab stop is ready to go.

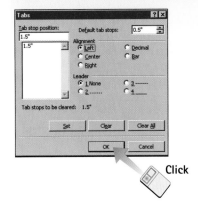

Click

6 Clear Tab Settings

To remove a tab setting you've added to the list box, reopen the Tabs dialog box and select the tab from the list box, and then click the **Clear** button. To remove all the tab stops you've set, click the **Clear All** button.

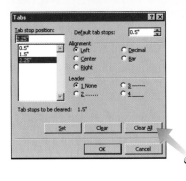

Click

 End

How-To Hints

Changing the Default Tab

By default, Word's tabs are set up at half-inch intervals across the document page. If you prefer a different default tab, set a new default tab measurement in the Tabs dialog box. Click inside the **Default tab stops** text box and enter a new setting or use the spin arrows to change the existing setting. Click **OK** and the new default tab stop is applied.

How to Apply Preformatted Styles

A *style* is a collection of formatting specifications that has been assigned a name and saved. You might have a report, for example, that uses specific formatting for every heading. Rather than reapply the formatting for every heading, assign the formatting to a style. You can then quickly apply the style whenever you need it. Word comes with a few predefined styles, but you can easily create your own and use them over and over.

Begin

1 Format the Text

Format the text as desired. You can apply any of Word's formatting commands, including character, paragraph, and page formatting. Then select the text or click anywhere in the formatted text.

Article I

Section 1.

All legislative powers herein granted shall be vested in a Congress of the United States, which shall consist of a Senate and House of Representatives.

Section 2.

The House of Representatives shall be composed of members chosen every second year by the people of the several states, and the electors in each state shall have the qualifications requisite for electors of the most numerous branch of the state legislature.

2 Locate the Style List Box

Click inside the **Style** list box on the Formatting toolbar.

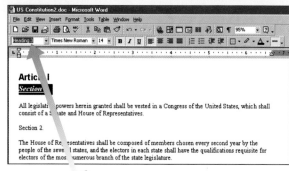

 Click

3 Enter a Name

Type a name for the new style. Be careful not to use any of the existing style names. Press **Enter** when finished. The style is added to the list and ready to assign. For example, I assigned a new style called **Paragraph Title**.

4 Assign a Style

To assign a style to text, select the text first.

Article I
Section 1.

All legislative powers herein granted shall be vested in a Congress of the United States, which shall consist of a Senate and House of Representatives.

Section 2.

The House of Representatives shall be composed of members chosen every second year by the people of the several states, and the electors in each state shall have the qualifications requisite for electors of the most numerous branch of the state legislature.

5 Open the Style List

Click the **Style** drop-down arrow and select the style you want to apply.

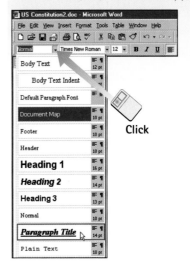

Click

6 Formatting Is Applied

The style is immediately applied to the selected text. Continue applying the style to other text in your document as needed.

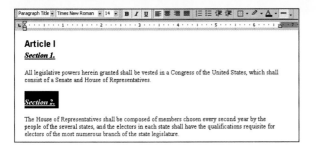

End

How-To Hints

Remove a Style

To remove a style, open the **Format** menu and choose **Style**. From the Style dialog box, locate the style you want to delete in the **Styles** list box and select the style. Click the **Delete** button to permanently remove the style from the list, and then click **Apply** to exit the dialog box. Learn how to customize a style in Task 9, "How to Change a Style."

Understanding Style Formatting

To check out what formatting commands are used by a style, open the Style dialog box and select the style (open the **Format** menu and choose **Style**). The **Description** box tells what formatting is assigned to the style and the **Character preview** area shows an example of the style.

How to Change a Style

Word's styles, whether they're preformatted styles or styles you assign yourself, make it easy to format similar text throughout a document. In some cases, you may decide you need to make a few adjustments to your style after you've already applied it several times in your document. You can easily make modifications to the style, including changing font or alignment or even assigning a new name for the style. Any changes you make to the style are applied wherever the style is used throughout the text.

Begin

1 Open the Style Dialog Box

To make changes to an existing style, open the **Format** menu and choose **Style**. This opens the Style dialog box.

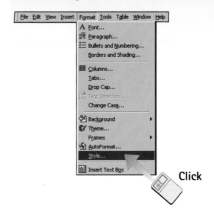

Click

2 Choose a Style to Modify

From the Styles list box, select the style you want to make changes to, and then click the **Modify** button. This opens the Modify Style dialog box.

Click

3 Change the Formatting

To make changes to the style's formatting, click the **Format** button to display a list of formatting options. Select the type of formatting you want to change; for example, select **Font** to open the Font dialog box.

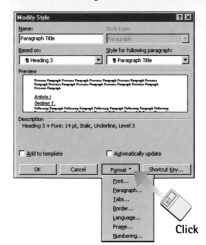

Click

4 Modify the Settings

From the dialog box that appears, make any necessary changes to the formatting. For example, if you're changing the font or size in the Font dialog box, select the options you want and then click **OK** to return to the Modify Style dialog box.

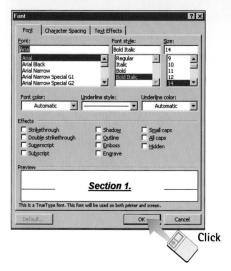

Click

5 Assign a Shortcut Key

One way to speed up the way you assign styles to your text is to assign a shortcut key to the style. Then, instead of using the Style drop-down list to assign a style, just press the keyboard shortcut key. Click the **Shortcut Key** button to open the Customize Keyboard dialog box.

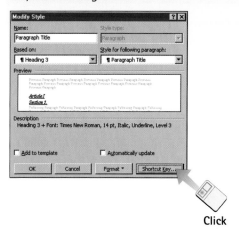

Click

6 Enter a Key Combination

Click inside the **Press new shortcut key** text box and type in the shortcut key you want to use. Word will tell you whether the key combination is currently in use or not. When you find a shortcut key to use, click the **Assign** button. Click **Close** to return to the Modify Style dialog box.

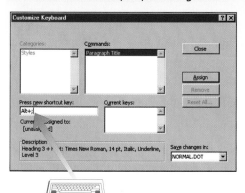

7 Exit the Dialog Boxes

From the Modify Style dialog box, click **OK**. From the Style dialog box, click **Apply** and the modifications are put into effect to any text with the altered style assigned.

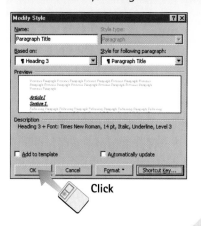

Click

End

How to Use AutoFormat

If you're not too confident about applying formatting controls to your documents, you can let Word's AutoFormat feature do all the work for you. AutoFormat checks your document and applies formatting for you. You can even look through a gallery of styles and choose formatting that suits the message you're trying to communicate, whether it's a letter, an email message, or a regular document.

Begin

1 Start AutoFormat

Open the document you want to apply autoformatting to, and then open the **Format** menu and choose **AutoFormat**. This opens the AutoFormat dialog box.

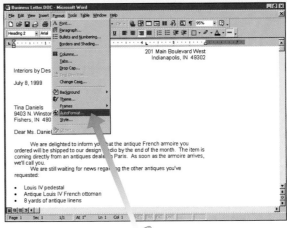

Click

2 Review Each Change

Click the **AutoFormat and review each change** option if you want to go over each format AutoFormat suggests for your document.

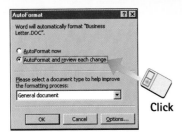
Click

3 Select a Document Type

Click the drop-down arrow and select the type of document you're trying to create. For example, if you're applying the AutoFormat feature to a letter, select **Letter** from the list.

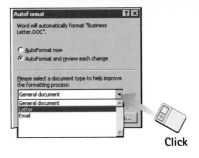
Click

4 Click OK

Click **OK** to exit the first AutoFormat dialog box and proceed with the formatting.

Click

5 Open the Style Gallery

To select from a variety of formatting styles to apply, click the **Style Gallery** button. This opens the Style Gallery dialog box.

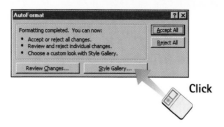

Click

6 Choose a Template Style

From the **Template** list box, select a document style to apply. The **Preview** area lets you see what the template style looks like. Click **OK** to exit and apply the formatting to your document.

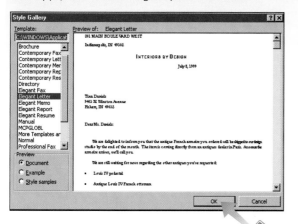

Click

7 Check Over the Changes

Review your document with the new formatting applied; click **Accept All** to keep the formatting. If you don't like the formatting, follow steps 5 and 6 again and choose another style.

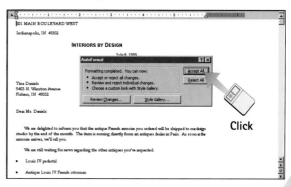

Click

End

Project

To fully explore all the formatting and document-building skills you've acquired so far, take a moment and try your hand at creating a basic letter document. In this exercise, you'll learn how to build and format a business letter. You can easily apply these same steps to create a personal letter.

1 Start a New File

Start by using a template to base your letter on; open the **File** menu and choose **New** to open the New dialog box.

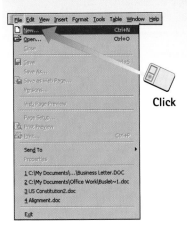

Click

2 Choose a Template

Click the **Letters & Faxes** tab and choose the letter template you want to use. To follow along with this example, double-click the **Professional Letter** icon.

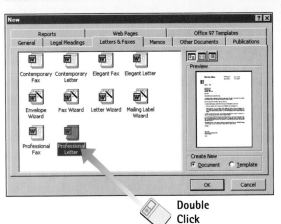

Double Click

3 A New File Opens

A document opens based on the Professional Letter template. Notice the document has placeholder text you can replace with your own.

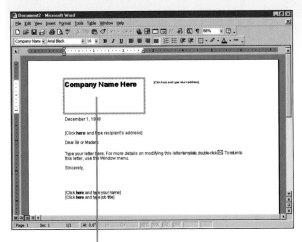

Placeholder text

4 Enter Your Text

Begin filling in the text needed for your letter. Click inside the **Company Name Here** box and type in your own company name.

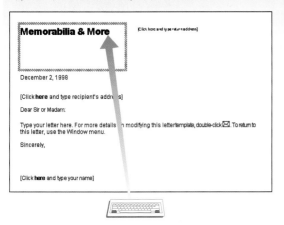

5 Zoom Your View

Click inside the return address placeholder box and type in your own address. If you're having trouble seeing what you're typing, click the **Zoom** drop-down list and zoom your view to **100%**.

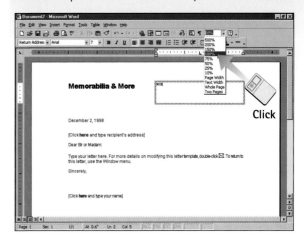

6 Finish the Letter

Continue entering text for your letter. To replace the body text, select the text and start typing. You can type the letter shown in this figure, or enter your own letter text.

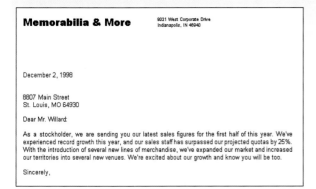

7 Start a Spell Check

To check your letter over for errors, click the **Spelling and Grammar** button on the Standard toolbar. This starts Word's spell check tool.

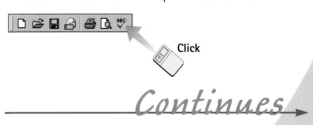

Continues

8 Fix Any Mistakes

Depending on what the spell check finds, fix any spelling or grammar errors. If the spell check finds a proper name, click the **Ignore** button. When the spell check is complete, click **OK**.

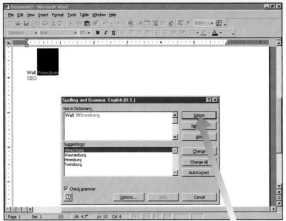

Click

9 Change a Font

Select the company name and change the font. Click the **Font** drop-down arrow on the Formatting toolbar and select another font from the list.

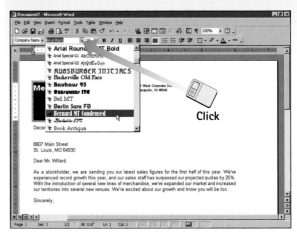

Click

10 The Font Is Applied

As soon as you make your selection, the new font is assigned to the selected text.

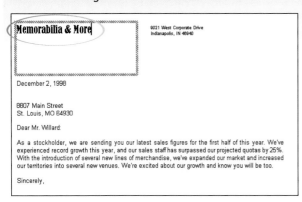

11 Change the Font Size

To change the font size of the company name, select the text, click the **Font Size** drop-down arrow on the Formatting toolbar, and choose a new size.

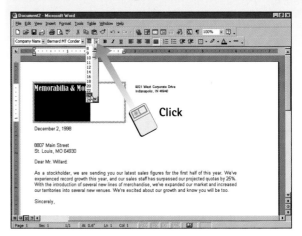

Click

12 New Size Applied

As soon as you click a new size on the list, it's applied to the selected text. In this figure, I assigned 24-point as the font size.

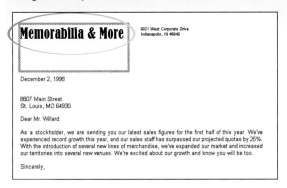

13 Change the Body Text Size

The font size applied to the body text of your letter is rather small. To enlarge it, first select all the text in the letter you want to enlarge. Don't forget to include the recipient's address and the closing salutation.

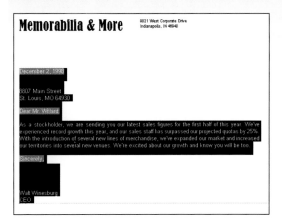

14 Increase the Size

Click the **Font Size** drop-down arrow and enlarge the body text to 12-point.

15 View the New Size

Word applies the new size. The letter text is much easier to read now at 12-point.

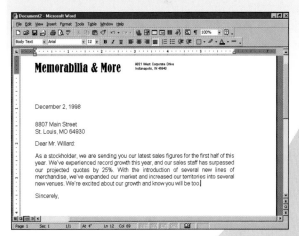

Continues

16 Set an Indent

To make a paragraph stand out, set an indent for the first line of text. Click in front of the line you want to indent.

Dear Mr. Willard:

As a stockholder, we are sending you our latest sales figures for the first half of this year. We've experienced record growth this year, and our sales staff has surpassed our projected quotas by 25%. With the introduction of several new lines of merchandise, we've expanded our market and increased our territories into several new venues. We're excited about our growth and know you will be too.

Click

17 Drag the First Line Indent Marker

Move your mouse pointer up to the horizontal ruler and hover it over the First Line Indent marker. Then click and drag the marker to the location on the ruler where you want the indent to appear.

18 Release the Mouse Button

When the indent marker appears where you want it, release the mouse button.

19 The Line Is Indented

The first line of the paragraph is indented as you specified.

Dear Mr. Willard:

As a stockholder, we are sending you our latest sales figures for the first half of this year. We've experienced record growth this year, and our sales staff has surpassed our projected quotas by 25%. With the introduction of several new lines of merchandise, we've expanded our market and increased our territories into several new venues. We're excited about our growth and know you will be too.

20 Save the Letter

To save your letter, click the **Save** button on the Standard toolbar. This opens the Save As dialog box.

Click

21 Give the File a Name

Select a folder where you want to save the letter to, or use the default My Documents folder. Then enter a name for the file in the **File name** text box.

22 Click Save

When you're ready to save the file, click the **Save** button.

Click

23 The Filename Is Saved

The title bar now reflects the filename you assigned. To close the file, click the **Close** button (**X**) in the upper-right corner of the program window. Congratulations on building a basic letter.

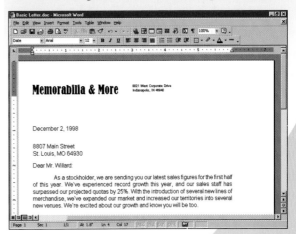

End

Task

9

How to Change Page Formatting

Chapter 7, "How to Change the Way Your Text Looks," and Chapter 8, "How to Change Paragraph Formatting," focused on character and paragraph formatting. In this chapter, you learn about the third type of formatting you can apply to your documents—page formatting. Page formatting includes tools you can use to change the appearance of the entire document page. For example, you can adjust the page margins to fit more or less text on a page, or you can turn your paragraphs into columns of text—much like a newspaper. Page formatting also includes headers and footers (text that appears at the top or bottom of every page), page numbers, and page breaks. In this chapter, you learn all about the various ways you can change the appearance of your pages. ●

How to Set Margins

Margins define the edge of your document's typing area. The default margins in Word are 1 inch on the top and bottom of the page and 1.25 inches on the left and right. These margins are fine for most documents but, like all features in Word, they can be changed to your benefit.

For example, you may find you have just a line or two more than will fit on a page, but if you adjust the margins slightly, everything fits.

Begin

1 Open the Page Setup Dialog Box

Open the **File** menu and select **Page Setup**.

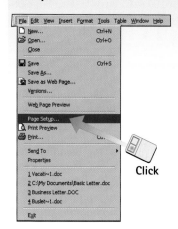

Click

2 View the Margins Tab

In the Page Setup dialog box, click the **Margins** tab if it's not already displayed.

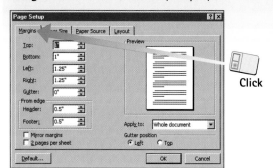

Click

3 Change the Margins

Type new margin settings in the **Top**, **Bottom**, **Left**, and **Right** boxes; the settings are measured in inches. You can also use the spin arrows to set new measurements: Click the up arrow to increase the measurement, and click the down arrow to decrease the measurement.

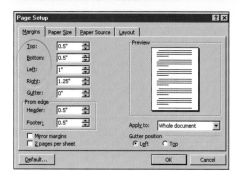

4 Apply the New Settings

Click **OK** to exit the dialog box and apply the new margins to your document.

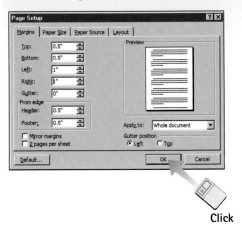

Click

5 View the New Margin Settings

On the Standard toolbar, click the **Print Preview** button to switch the document to Print Preview. In Print Preview, you see a whole-page view of your document, and it's easier to check margin settings.

Click

6 Change Margins Manually

Instead of setting inch measurements by using the Page Setup dialog box, you can change margins manually in any view (except Outline view). The margins are displayed as gray bars at each end of the horizontal and vertical rulers. You can drag a margin marker to reset the margin.

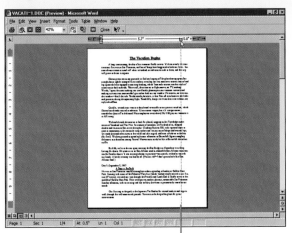

Right margin marker

End

How to Insert Page Breaks

By default, Word keeps track of how much text can fit on a document page and makes page breaks automatically for you. However, you will encounter times where you need to insert a page break yourself. For example, you might create a page for your report that includes only title text. One way to force the start of a second page is to keep pressing the Enter key as many times as it takes to start a new page. However, this method isn't very productive. An easier way to start a second page is to insert a manual page break.

Begin

1 Insert a Manual Page Break

To insert a manual page break yourself, just click in the document where you want the break to occur, and then press **Ctrl+Enter** on the keyboard.

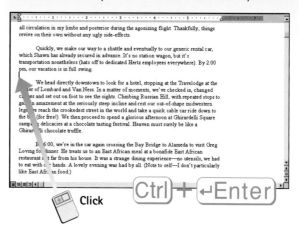

Click

2 View the Break

This inserts a dotted line in the document that represents a page break, seen in Normal view in the next figure.

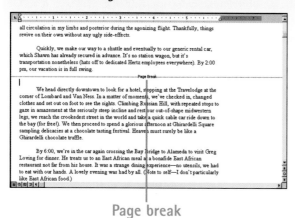

Page break

3 Open the Page Break Dialog Box

For a greater variety of page breaks, column breaks, and section breaks, open the Page Break dialog box, display the **Insert** menu, and choose **Break.**

Click

4 Select an Option

To set a page break, click the **Page break** option.

Click

5 Exit the Dialog Box

Click **OK** to exit from the dialog box and apply the break. Note that the break is applied where the cursor appears on the page.

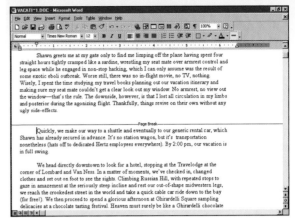

End

How-To Hints

What's a Section Break?

Use sections in your document to vary the layout of text. For example, in a report document you might have an introductory section that summarizes the report, and then a section with text columns that presents the report data. Both sections may reside on the same document page and a section break allows you to divide the page and format each section as you please. Use the four options at the bottom of the Break dialog box to create a specific type of section break: A **Next Page** break starts a new section on the next page, a **Continuous** break starts a section break on the same page, and an **Odd Page** or **Even Page** break inserts a section break on the next odd or even-numbered page.

More About Columns

You can also use the Break dialog box to set breaks for columns of text. Learn more about setting columns on your page in Task 5, "How to Create Newspaper Columns."

Undo a Break

To undo a break, click the page break and press the **Delete** key. To remove a break immediately after applying it, click the **Undo** button on the Standard toolbar.

How to Insert Page Numbers

If you're creating a document with two or more pages, it's a good idea to add page numbers. They can help you keep your pages organized. Word inserts page numbers and adjusts them according to changes you make to the document. For example, if you delete several paragraphs, Word adjusts the page breaks automatically and inserts the page numbers where they're supposed to go. When you're ready to print, the page numbers print, too.

Begin

1 Open the Page Numbers Dialog Box

To add page numbers to your document, open the **Insert** menu and select **Page Numbers**. This opens the Page Numbers dialog box.

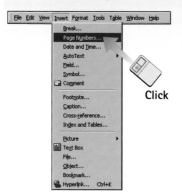

Click

2 Choose a Position

Click the **Position** drop-down arrow to change whether your page numbers appear at the top of the page or the bottom.

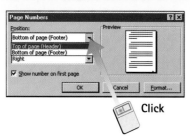

Click

3 Choose the Alignment

Click the **Alignment** drop-down arrow to change how the numbers are aligned on the page.

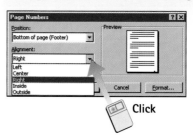

Click

4 Exit the Dialog Box

Click **OK** to exit the dialog box.

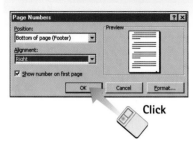

Click

5 View the Numbers

You won't be able to view page numbers in Normal View. Switch to Page Layout View to see page numbers. Click the **Page Layout View** button in the bottom-left corner of the Word window.

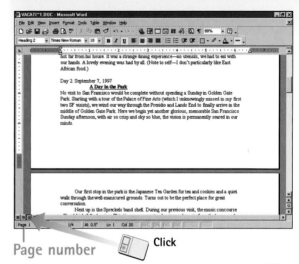

Page number

Click

End

How-To Hints

First Page Numbers

If you prefer the first page in your document not to print with a page number, be sure to deselect the **Show number on first page** check box in the Page Numbers dialog box.

Formatting Page Numbers

To change the number format of your page numbers, click the **Format** button in the Page Numbers dialog box to open the Page Number Format dialog box. Use this box to specify a number style, control page numbering, and chapter numbering. For example, you can choose to use Roman numerals as page numbers, and specify exactly on which pages to start page numbers. To exit the dialog box, click **OK**, and then click **OK** again to close the Page Numbers dialog box.

How to Apply Vertical Alignment

In Chapter 8, you learned to use horizontal alignment commands to control how paragraphs are positioned across the document page. You can use Word's vertical alignment controls to align text from top to bottom on a page. For example, you might want a report title centered smack-dab in the middle of the page, or you may prefer several paragraphs spread out equally from top to bottom.

Begin

1 Open the Page Setup Dialog Box

Open the **File** menu and select **Page Setup**. This displays the Page Setup dialog box.

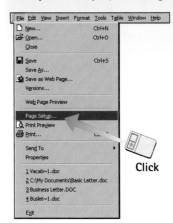

Click

2 Display the Layout Options

Click the **Layout** tab to display the layout options.

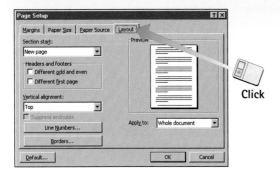

Click

3 Choose an Alignment

Click the **Vertical alignment** drop-down list to choose a new alignment: **Top** (default), **Center**, or **Justified**.

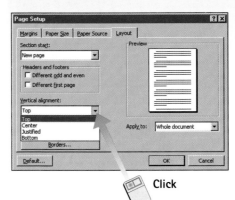

Click

4 Exit the Dialog Box

Click **OK** to exit and apply the alignment to the document.

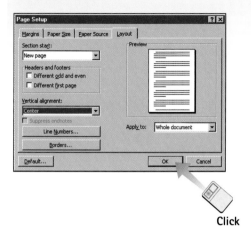

Click

5 Switch to Print Preview

To quickly see the effects of the new alignment, click the **Print Preview** button on the Standard toolbar.

Click

6 View the Alignment

Check out the alignment in Print Preview mode. When finished, click the **Close** button to return to the document page.

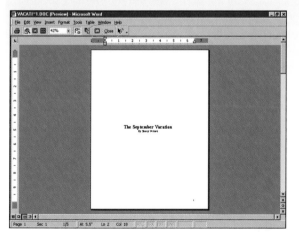

How-To Hints

Undo It!

If you don't like the vertical alignment you just applied, click the **Undo** button on the Standard toolbar to undo the alignment.

End

How to Create Newspaper Columns

If you're creating a newsletter or brochure with Word, consider formatting the text into columns, much like a newspaper or magazine. Word's columns are *newspaper-style columns*, which means the text flows to the bottom of a column on a page and then continues at the top of the next column on the same page. You can then add column breaks to control how columns are displayed on the page, whether they're confined to a particular section or fill the page.

Begin

1 Select the Text

Select the text you want to format into columns, and then open the **Format** menu and choose **Columns**. (You can also set columns before typing any text.)

Click

2 Select a Column Type

Under the **Presets** area, click the type of column style you want to use, such as **Two** or **Three**. Use the **Width** and **Spacing** options to set an exact measurement for the columns and the space between them (or go with the default settings). The **Preview** area lets you see what the columns will look like.

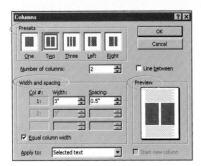

3 Select from the Apply to List

To apply the column format to a specific area, click the **Apply to** drop-down arrow and choose the extent to which the columns apply in the document. Alternatively, choose **Whole document** if you want the entire document to use columns.

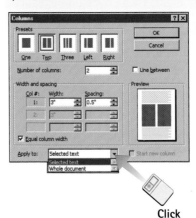

Click

4 Exit the Dialog Box

Click **OK** to exit the dialog box and apply the column format to your text.

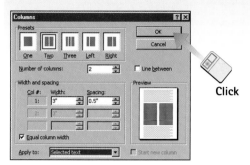

Click

5 Or Create Quick Columns

Another way to set columns is with the Columns button on the Standard toolbar. Select the text to which you want to apply columns, click the **Columns** button on the Standard toolbar, and drag the number of columns you want to use.

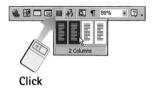

Click

6 Column Format Is Applied

Release the mouse button and the columns are assigned. Word will display the columns in Print Layout View, the best view for seeing columns in Word.

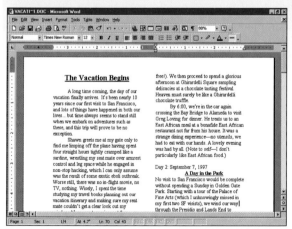

End

How-To Hints

Can't See Them?

The best view for columns is Print Layout View. You can see columns only in Print Layout View or in the Print Preview window. Click the **Print Layout View** button to switch views as needed.

Turning Columns Off

To turn your column text back into normal text (which is really just one column, anyway), select the text, click the **Columns** button on the Standard toolbar, and drag to select a single column.

Inserting a Divider Line

One of the options in the Columns dialog box lets you add a divider line between columns, which defines the columns and gives a nice visual appeal. Click the **Line between** check box to add such a line to your columns.

How to Insert Page Headers and Footers

A *header* appears at the top of every page, and a *footer* appears at the bottom of every page. You might want to use headers and footers to display the document title, your name, the name of your organization, and so on.

You can also insert *fields* in headers and footers—a field is a holding place for information that Word updates automatically, such as the current date or time.

Begin

1 Open the Header and Footer

To add a header and/or a footer to a document, open the **View** menu and select **Header and Footer**.

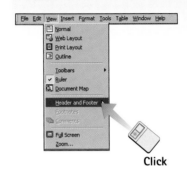

Click

2 Enter Header Text

Word switches to Print Layout View, places the insertion point in the header area, and displays the Header and Footer toolbar. You type and format text in a header or footer just like normal text. By default, Word places the cursor in the header section. Type in any header text. (You may have to zoom your view with the **Zoom** percentage button on the Standard toolbar.)

Header and Footer toolbar   Header

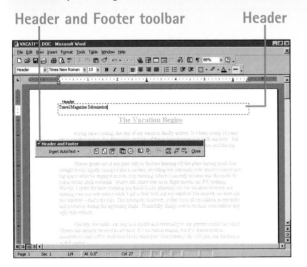

3 Enter Footer Text

To create a footer, click the **Switch Between Header and Footer** button on the Header and Footer toolbar to place the insertion point in the footer area. You can switch between the header and footer by clicking this button.

Switch between
Header and Footer

4 Insert Fields

You can insert fields or select built-in header and footer entries from the **AutoText** button on the Header and Footer toolbar. For example, click the **Date** button to insert a field for the current date. Click the **Page Number** button to insert the current page number. To space out several fields on a single line, click the **Tab** key between entries, as shown in this figure.

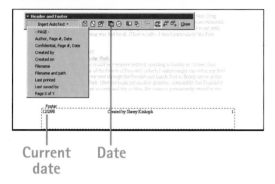

Current
date   Date

5 Close Header and Footer

Click the **Close** button in the Header and Footer toolbar to return to the body of the document.

Click

6 Viewing Headers and Footers

Headers and footers aren't visible in Normal View, but you can see them in both Print Layout View and in Print Preview.

Footer   Header

End

How-To Hints

How Do I Switch?

After you've created a header or footer, you can switch to the header or footer area from within Print Layout View by double-clicking the pale-gray header or footer text. Switch back to the body text by double-clicking the pale-gray body text.

Odd or Even Pages?

If you want different headers or footers on odd and even pages of your document (which is common for documents that are bound), open the **File** menu, choose **Page Setup**, and click the **Layout** tab; mark the **Different Odd and Even** check box, and choose **OK**. You can use the **Show Next** and **Show Previous** buttons in the Header and Footer toolbar to switch between the headers and footers for odd and even pages.

How to Insert Footnotes and Endnotes

Some documents you create in Word may require footnotes or endnotes for identifying the source of your text or referencing other materials. You can easily add such notes to your document pages by using the Footnote and Endnote dialog box. Footnotes appear at the bottom of each page and endnotes appear at the end of the document.

Begin

1 Place the Insertion Point

To add a footnote or endnote, click the insertion point in the document where you want to add a reference number.

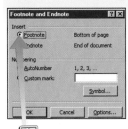

Day 3: September 8, 1997

Valley of the Grapes

After a lovely breakfast (a good sign), we head out to the Silverado Trail for a leisurely drive up the Napa valley. Vineyards roll from one hill to the next, tucked here and there up and down the mountains and along the valley floor. It's as gorgeous as I had hoped, Mediterranean in appearance—what I imagine Italy might look like.

Our destination is the Mumm Napa Valley winery, which offers free tours and an Ansel Adams gallery of photographs. We learn how to make sparkling wine (which is champagne, but you can't call it that unless it's from Champagne, France—how about that for picking up a few things?). We've come at a perfect time, the grapes are being harvested, and hang ripe on the vines in juicy-looking clusters.

As we continue up the valley, Shawn makes an exciting discovery, a sign pointing to the Napa Valley Grapevine Wreath Company, a tiny shop at the edge of a vineyard that sells grapevine wreaths and other decorative grapevine fixings. Having carefully not spent my money thus far, I inexplicably blow a huge wad on grapevine wreaths and make

Click

2 Open the Dialog Box

Open the **Insert** menu and select **Footnote**. This opens the Footnote and Endnote dialog box.

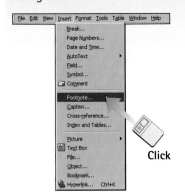

Click

3 Choose an Option

Under the **Insert** area of the dialog box, select either **Footnote** or **Endnote**.

Click

4 Click OK

Click **OK** to exit the dialog box and return to the document page.

Click

5 A Reference Number Is Added

Word adds a superscript reference number to the text and an area opens at the bottom of the page (for footnotes) or the end of the document (for endnotes) to enter the reference text. (If you're using Normal view, the note area appears as a pane at the bottom of the window.)

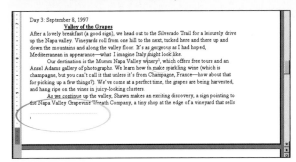

6 Add the Footnote or Endnote

Click inside the area and type in the reference. To view the footnote or endnote, switch to Print Layout View and scroll to the bottom of the page or document where the reference was entered. If you're using Normal view, click **Close** first to exit the note pane.

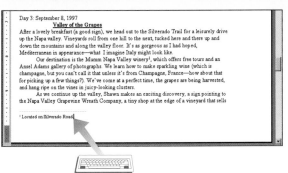

End

How-To Hints

AutoNumbering

By default, Word automatically numbers the references for you. Each new note you add is assigned the next consecutive number. If you prefer another mark, such as a letter or symbol, click the **Custom mark** option in the Footnote and Endnote dialog box and enter the mark. To use a symbol, click the **Symbol** button and select a symbol from the Symbol dialog box.

Changing the Placement

To change the location of footnotes and endnotes and the format used for the numbers, click the **Options** button in the Footnote and Endnote dialog box to open another dialog box for setting such controls.

How to Insert a User Comment

User comments can help you identify various people who work on a document. For example, your office situation may require you to pass along reports for feedback from various department heads. Rather than guess which person contributed which text to the document, insert user comments to add notes to the document.

Begin

1 Start a Comment

Click in the document where you want to insert a comment, open the **Insert** menu, and select **Comment**.

Click

2 Enter a Comment

A separate pane opens at the bottom of the document with space for entering your own comment. Enter the comment text just like you do any other text in Word.

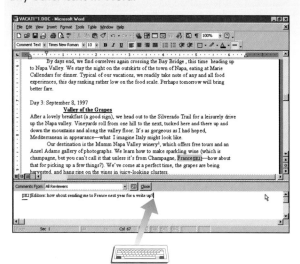

3 Click Close

When finished composing your comment, click the **Close** button on the comment pane.

Click

4 View the Comment

The word to the left of where you clicked to insert the comment is highlighted in yellow. To view the comment, hover your mouse pointer over the highlighted word. The comment box appears, revealing the comment as well as the name of the person who wrote it.

Day 3: September 8, 1997

Valley of the Grapes

After a lovely breakfast (a good sign), we head out to the Silverado Trail for a leisurely drive up the Napa valley. Vineyards roll from one hill to the next, tucked here and there up and down the mountains and along the valley floor. It's as gorgeous as I had hoped, Mediterranean in appearance—what I imagine Italy might look lik

Our destination is the Mumm Napa Valley winery[1], which

Ansel Adams gallery of photographs. We learn how to make spark

champagne, but you can't call it that unless it's from Champagne, France—how about that

for picking up a few things?). We've come at a perfect time, the grapes are being harvested, and hang ripe on the vines in juicy-looking clusters.

Sherry Kinkoph: Editors: how about sending me to France next year for a write up?

5 Edit a Comment

To edit a comment, right-click over the highlighted word and select **Edit Comment** from the shortcut menu. This reopens the comment pane and you can make changes to the comment text.

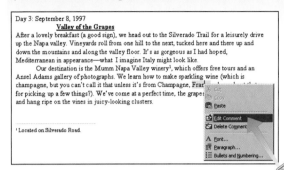

Day 3: September 8, 1997

Valley of the Grapes

After a lovely breakfast (a good sign), we head out to the Silverado Trail for a leisurely drive up the Napa valley. Vineyards roll from one hill to the next, tucked here and there up and down the mountains and along the valley floor. It's as gorgeous as I had hoped, Mediterranean in appearance—what I imagine Italy might look like.

Our destination is the Mumm Napa Valley winery[1], which offers free tours and an Ansel Adams gallery of photographs. We learn how to make sparkling wine (which is champagne, but you can't call it that unless it's from Champagne, Fran

for picking up a few things?). We've come at a perfect time, the grape

and hang ripe on the vines in juicy-looking clusters.

[1] Located on Silverado Road.

Cut
Copy
Paste
Edit Comment
Delete Comment
Font...
Paragraph...
Bullets and Numbering...

Click

6 Remove a Comment

To delete a comment, right-click over the highlighted area and select **Delete Comment** from the shortcut menu.

Day 3: September 8, 1997

Valley of the Grapes

After a lovely breakfast (a good sign), we head out to the Silverado Trail for a leisurely drive up the Napa valley. Vineyards roll from one hill to the next, tucked here and there up and down the mountains and along the valley floor. It's as gorgeous as I had hoped, Mediterranean in appearance—what I imagine Italy might look like.

Our destination is the Mumm Napa Valley winery[1], which offers free tours and an Ansel Adams gallery of photographs. We learn how to make sparkling wine (which is champagne, but you can't call it that unless it's from Champagne, Franc—how about that for picking up a few things?). We've come at a perfect time, the grapes a and hang ripe on the vines in juicy-looking clusters.

[1] Located on Silverado Road.

Cut
Copy
Paste
Edit Comment
Delete Comment
Font...
Paragraph...
Bullets and Numbering...

Click

End

Task

CHAPTER 10

How to Work with Tables

*W*hen it comes to organizing your text, nothing beats a nicely defined table. Word tables allow you to enter text into neat and tidy rows and columns. Tables are great for presenting data such as lists, categorized or related information, inventories, and more. You can create two types of tables in Word. You can create a straightforward, standardized table where all the columns and rows are equally spaced, or you can draw your own table and define exactly how the columns and rows are placed within the table. Once you've created a table, you click inside a table cell (the intersecting column and row) and enter data. You can choose to add borders and shading to the table to dress it up.

In this chapter, you find tasks for creating both types of tables described, and you learn how to enhance your tables with borders and shading. ●

How to Create a Standard Table

A *table* is a grid of rows and columns; each box in a table is called a *cell*. You can use tables to create anything from simple charts to invoices and employee lists. Tables are useful for any kind of information that needs to be organized in a row-and-column format. If you want to create a quick table, look no further than Word's Insert Table command. Word's tables are flexible; you can specify exactly how many rows or columns, control the size and formatting of each cell, and include anything from text to graphics.

Begin

1 Decide Where to Place the Table

To create a table the quick way, first click in the document where you want to place the table.

MEMO

TO: All Managers
FROM: Nancy Wyant
RE: 2000 Budget
CC: Shanda Williams, Jean Jahnssen

Please review your department's budget requirements for our meeting on Wednesday, October 21, at 10:00 a.m. We will discuss the proposals for the 2000 budget and review each department's budget needs. Lunch will be provided.

Click

2 Use the Toolbar Button

Click the **Insert Table** button on the Standard toolbar.

Click

3 Drag Number of Columns and Rows

A grid appears where you can tell Word how many columns and rows you want in the initial table; drag to select squares that represent cells in the table (for example, drag to select 3 columns by 4 rows).

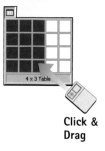

4 x 3 Table

Click & Drag

4 Release the Mouse Button

Release the mouse button, and a table with the number of rows and columns you selected appears on the document page.

MEMO

TO:	All Managers
FROM:	Nancy Wyant
RE:	2000 Budget
CC:	Shanda Williams, Jean Jahnssen

Please review your department's budget requirements for our meeting on Wednesday, October 21, at 10:00 a.m. We will discuss the proposals for the 2000 budget and review each department's budget needs. Lunch will be provided.

5 Enter Table Text

Click in a cell and begin typing. The text in each cell behaves like a paragraph; if you press **Enter**, a new paragraph is started in the same cell. You can format the text in each cell the same way you format text in a normal paragraph.

Dept. A			

6 Move to the Next Cell

Press **Tab** to move cell by cell to the right, and continue entering text to fill your table. You can also click inside any cell and enter text. The following example shows an entire table filled with text.

Dept. A	10:00	Dave Willard
Dept. B	10:30	Melissa Cannon
Dept. C	11:00	Greg Kinkoph
Dept. D	11:30	Donna Williamson

End

How-To Hints

Resize a Table

The table stretches across the width of the page; to make a column narrower, point to a vertical border and drag it to a new position. You can resize rows the same way; drag the row border up or down. To resize the entire table, drag the lower-right corner of the table.

Navigation Tricks

The Tab key is the easiest way to navigate from cell to cell while you're entering text. Press **Shift+Tab** to move cell by cell to the left. (To insert a tab character in a cell, press **Ctrl+Tab**.)

How to Add Rows and Columns

After you've created a table and started entering text into the table, you may find yourself needing an additional row or column. You can easily add to your existing table without changing any text, rows, or columns you already have. You can even delete columns and rows you find you don't need.

Begin

1 Click in Place

To insert a new row within a table, click in the row above or below where you want the new row inserted.

Sales Dept.	10:00	Dave Willard
Human Resources Dept.	10:30	Melissa Cannon
Accounting Dept.	11:00	Greg Kinkoph
Marketing Dept.	11:30	Donna Williamson

Click

2 Select the Command

Open the **Table** menu and select **Insert** to display a submenu, and then click **Rows Above** or **Rows Below**, depending on whether you want a new row above the current row or a new row below.

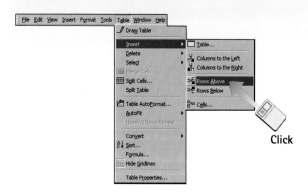

Click

3 The Row Is Added

The row is immediately added. In this example, I added a new row above.

Sales Dept.	10:00	Dave Willard
Human Resources Dept.	10:30	Melissa Cannon
Accounting Dept.	11:00	Greg Kinkoph
Marketing Dept.	11:30	Donna Williamson

4 Click in Place

To insert a column, first click in the column to the left or right of where you want a new column inserted.

Sales Dept.	10:00		Dave Willard
Human Resources Dept.	10:30		Melissa Cannon
Accounting Dept.	11:00		Greg Kinkoph
Marketing Dept.	11:30		Donna Williamson

 Click

5 Insert the Column

Open the **Table** menu, choose **Insert**, and then click **Columns to the Left** or **Columns to the Right** depending on which side of the active column you want to add a new column.

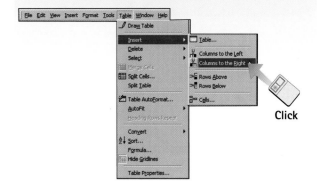 Click

6 The New Column Appears

The new column appears in the table. In this example, I added a new column to the right.

Sales Dept.	10:00		Dave Willard
Human Resources Dept.	10:30		Melissa Cannon
Accounting Dept.	11:00		Greg Kinkoph
Marketing Dept.	11:30		Donna Williamson

7 Delete a Row or Column

To delete a row or column, click in the row or column you want to remove, and then open the **Table** menu and choose **Delete**, **Rows** to delete a row, or **Delete**, **Columns** to delete a column. The row or column is immediately deleted from the table, including any text that may have been in the row or column.

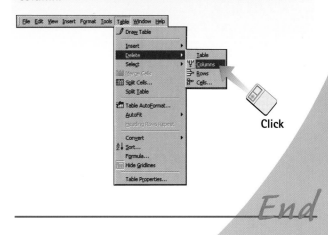 Click

End

How to Add Borders and Shading to Tables

You don't have to know anything about graphics to add attractive borders and shading to tables. They can really make your table stand out and look very professional. One way to issue commands for your table is to use the Tables and Borders toolbar. Another way is to use the Table menu. This task shows you how to work with the options available in the Borders and Shading dialog box as accessed through the Table menu.

Begin

1 Select the Table

To add a border or shading to the entire table, click anywhere inside the table, open the **Table** menu, and choose **Select**, **Table**. This highlights the entire table. (If you want, you can choose to add a border to just one table element: a cell, a row, or a single column; just select the table element first.)

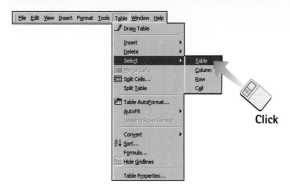

Click

2 Open the Borders and Shading

Open the **Format** menu and select **Borders and Shading** to display the Borders and Shading dialog box.

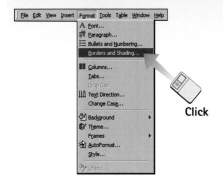

Click

3 Apply a Border

Click the **Borders** tab if it isn't already in front. If you see an option under **Setting** that closely matches the type of border you want to add, click it. In this example, I've selected **All**.

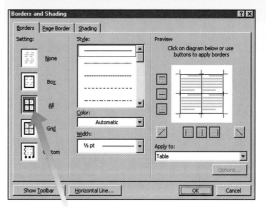

Click

4 Select a Line Style

To change the style of the lines in your border, scroll through the **Style** list and click the desired style. You can also use the **Color** and **Width** drop-down lists to change the color and width of the line style.

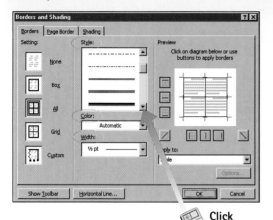

 Click

5 Add Shading

To add shading, click the **Shading** tab, and then click the color you want to use from the **Fill** palette. The Preview area shows what the shading looks like. To add a pattern, click the **Style** drop-down arrow and select a pattern.

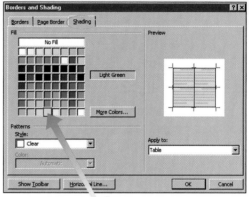

Click

6 Apply the New Settings

Click **OK** to exit the dialog box and apply the new settings to your table.

Sales Dept.	10:00	Dave Willard
Human Resources Dept.	10:30	Melissa Cannon
Accounting Dept.	11:00	Greg Kinkoph
Marketing Dept.	11:30	Donna Williamson

End

How-To Hints

Custom Borders

If you want to design your own border with only the line styles and colors you want to use, choose the **Custom** setting in the Borders and Shading dialog box (on the Borders tab). Select the desired style, color, and width options for one of the lines, and then click the line in the sample box under **Preview**. Repeat this process to create the remaining three lines.

A Word About Patterns

Unless your table text is really bold, most patterns are too busy and will compete with the readability of your text. Be sure to test your choices by printing them out before giving the document to others.

How to Draw a Custom Table

The previous tasks showed you how to insert a standard table by using Word's Insert Table feature. However, sometimes you need a table that doesn't conform to the standard table. You'll be happy to know you can draw your own table and decide for yourself how wide each column should be or how deep each row should appear. The Tables and Borders toolbar has tools to help you customize the appearance of the lines you draw, as well as tools for changing the direction of the text, alignment, and other formatting options.

In this task, you learn how to draw a table and specify the line style, weight, and color. In the following task, you learn how to edit the drawn table.

Begin

_1_ Click the Tables and Borders

To draw an asymmetrical table and control the size and placement of each row and column, click the **Tables and Borders** button on the Standard toolbar.

Click

_2_ The Toolbar Appears

The Tables and Borders toolbar appears, and the mouse pointer becomes a pencil.

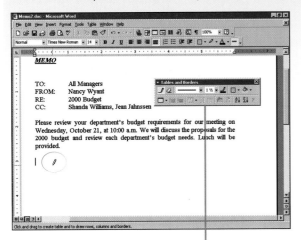

Tables and Borders toolbar

_3_ Choose Table Options

Before you begin drawing the table, use the **Line Style**, **Line Weight**, and **Border Color** buttons on the Tables and Borders toolbar to choose the type and color of line you want for the outside border of your table. Click the appropriate drop-down arrows to display a list of choices.

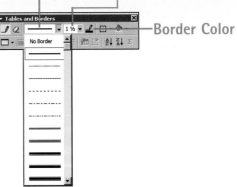

Line Style Line Weight

Border Color

4 Draw the Table Border

Make sure the **Draw Table** button is selected, and then drag the mouse to draw a rectangle for the outside border of the table, as shown in this figure. Click in the document where you want the upper-left corner of the table, and then hold the mouse button down and drag to where you want the lower-right corner of the table. Release the mouse button when finished.

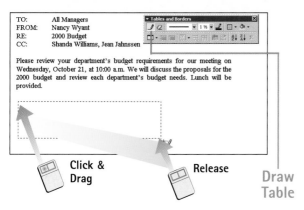

Click & Drag

Release

Draw Table

5 Draw the Row and Column Lines

Now draw the internal lines to delineate rows and columns. As you drag, a dashed line shows you where the line will be inserted. Release the mouse as the line extends across the entire width or height of the table. You can draw a table as complex as you want with this method.

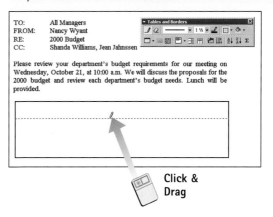

Click & Drag

6 Even Up Your Lines

To evenly space your rows or columns, click the **Distribute Rows Evenly** or **Distribute Columns Evenly** buttons on the toolbar. You can now begin entering text into the table cells just like you do with a standard table.

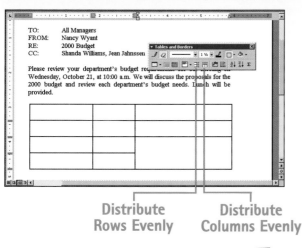

Distribute Rows Evenly

Distribute Columns Evenly

End

How-To Hints

Toggle On or Off

The **Draw Table** button on the Tables and Borders toolbar toggles on or off. If you leave it on, the mouse pointer remains a drawing pen icon. To turn it off, select the button again, or choose another toolbar button.

Change Text Direction

You can change the direction of your text inside a cell in a drawn table, making it read sideways. To do this, click inside the cell, and then click the **Change Text Direction** button on the toolbar. Keep clicking until the text is the direction you want it to read.

Add New Columns and Rows

You can easily add new rows and columns to your custom table just like you add them to standard tables. Select the row or column next to where you want a new row or column inserted, right-click to display a shortcut menu, and select the appropriate **Insert** command.

How to Edit Your Drawn Table

Once you've created a custom table, there are several tools you can use to edit the table. Use the Eraser tool on the Tables and Borders toolbar to erase lines you've drawn. You can erase lines before you enter your table text, or after (any data contained within the cells will be merged). You can always go back and draw new lines by using the technique demonstrated in the previous task. You can also merge cells or split cells using the Tables and Borders toolbar commands. For example, you may find that several rows need to be combined. In this task, you learn how to use the Eraser tool and the Merge and Split commands, just a few editing techniques you can use on your drawn table.

Begin

1 Select the Eraser Tool

Click the **Eraser** button on the Tables and Borders toolbar. This button toggles on or off as needed.

Click

2 Click to Erase

Hover the eraser icon over the line segment you want to erase, and then click. The line is immediately removed. Any existing data contained within the cells is merged.

Accounting	10:00	Dave Willard	
Human Resources	10:30	Melissa Cannon	
Sales Dept.	11:00	Greg Kinkoph	
Marketing Dept.	11:30		

Click

Accounting	10:00	Dave Willard	
Human Resources	10:30	Melissa Cannon	
Sales Dept.	11:00	Greg Kinkoph	
Marketing Dept.	11:30		

3 Drag to Erase

Another method of erasing lines is to drag the eraser over the line. For example, to erase more than one section of the line, drag along the entire line. To turn off the Eraser, click the **Eraser** button on the Tables and Borders toolbar.

Accounting	10:00	Dave Willard	
Human Resources	10:30	Melissa Cannon	
Sales Dept.	11:00	Greg Kinkoph	
Marketing Dept.	11:30		

Click & Drag

Accounting	10:00	Dave Willard	
Human Resources	10:30	Melissa Cannon	
Sales Dept.	11:00	Greg Kinkoph	
Marketing Dept.	11:30		

4 Select an Entire Row or Column

To merge an entire column or row, you must first select the column or row. To select a column, hover your mouse pointer over the top column border until it takes the shape of a downward-pointing arrow, and then click to highlight each cell in the column. To select a row, click in the left margin next to the row.

Accounting	10:00	Dave Willard	
Human Resources	10:30	Melissa Cannon	
Sales Dept. Marketing Dept.	11:00 11:30	Greg Kinkoph	

Click

5 Merge Cells

To merge the cells, click the **Merge Cells** button on the toolbar. The individual cells become one single column or row. In this example, I merged the cells in a column.

Click

Accounting	10:00	Dave Willard	
Human Resources	10:30	Melissa Cannon	
Sales Dept. Marketing Dept.	11:00 11:30	Greg Kinkoph	

6 Split Cells

To split a single column or row into multiple cells, select the column or row, and then click the **Split Cells** button on the toolbar. This opens the Split Cells dialog box.

Click

7 Define the Split

Enter the number of columns or rows you want to split into; you can type in the number or click the spin arrows to designate a number. Click **OK** and the cells split as directed.

Click

End

Task

11

How to Work with Graphics

You can dress up a Word document with a piece of clip art from the Microsoft Clip Gallery or insert an image file from another program file. You can draw your own shapes to include on reports or title pages. Any item you add to the document page, whether it's clip art or a shape, is considered an object. Objects can be moved and resized as needed to fit on the document page.

In this chapter, you'll learn how to utilize the graphics tools to enhance your documents. You'll also learn how to draw basic shapes, insert pictures and clip art, create a WordArt image, and manipulate and format graphics objects. Don't be intimidated by the thought of creating and adding visual objects to your files. The graphics tools make it easy to illustrate any Word item you create. ●

How to Insert Clip Art

One way to add visual impact to your document is to insert clip art. Clip art images are ready-made drawings covering a wide range of topics and categories. You can insert clip art into any document you create. Microsoft Word comes with a gallery of clip art images you can use, including color and black-and-white images and photographs. In addition to the clip art available in the gallery, you can also find clip art on the Web.

Begin

1 Open the Clip Gallery Dialog Box

Click the mouse pointer where you want the clip art inserted on the document page, open the **Insert** menu, and choose **Picture**, and then select **Clip Art**. This opens the Insert ClipArt dialog box.

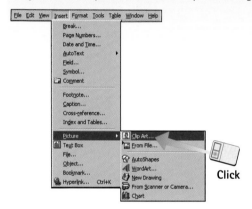

Click

2 View Categories

From the **Pictures** tab, peruse the categories of clip art. Use the scroll box arrows to help you see all the available categories. To choose a category, click it.

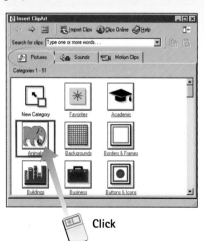

Click

3 View Pictures

Scroll through the available pictures. Some categories may include a Keep Looking link you can click to reveal more pictures. If you can't find the picture you want, click the **Back** button to return to the Category list and try another category (click the **Forward** button to view a previous set of pictures after clicking **Back**).

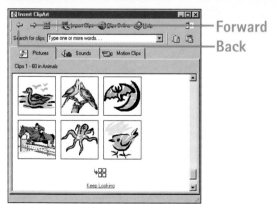

Forward
Back

4 Select a Picture

When you find a clip art piece you want to use, click it to reveal a balloon menu, as shown in this figure. Click the **Insert Clip** button on the menu. To preview the picture before adding it to your file, click the **Preview clip** button.

—Insert clip
—Preview clip

To exit the dialog box, click the **Close** button.

Click

6 The Picture Appears

The clip art appears in your file along with the Picture toolbar. You can now resize or move the image as needed (see Task 5, "How to Move and Resize an Object"). To learn how to wrap text around the clip art, see Task 6, "How to Wrap Text Around Graphics."

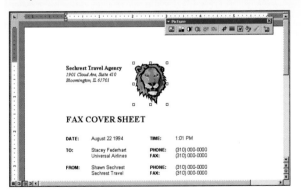

End

How-To Hints

Find Clip Art on the Web

You can import clip art images from Microsoft's Web site. Click the **Clips Online** button in the Clip Gallery dialog box and click **OK**. This opens your Web browser to the Microsoft site where you can choose more clip art. (You must first connect to your Internet account.)

Look Up Clip Art

To search for a specific type of clip art in the clip art gallery, click inside the **Search for Clips** text box in the Insert ClipArt dialog box and enter key words to search for, such as **money** or **elephant**. Press **Enter** and the list box displays any matches.

How to Insert a Picture File

If you have a picture file from another program, you can insert it into your Word file. You can also insert objects such as scanned images, Excel worksheets, and other types of visual objects. Every image you insert into a document is treated like an object, which means it can be resized, moved, cut, or copied. In this task, you learn how to insert an object from another program. Once you've inserted the object, flip to Task 5, "How to Move and Resize an Object," to learn how to resize and move the object around on the document page.

Begin

1 Open the Object Dialog Box

Display the **Insert** menu and select **Object**. This opens the Insert Object dialog box.

Click

2 Click Create from File

Click the **Create from File** tab.

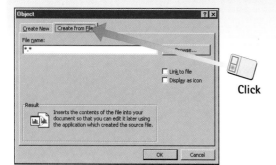

Click

3 Open the Browse Dialog Box

To find the object file you want to insert, click the **Browse** button to open the Browse dialog box.

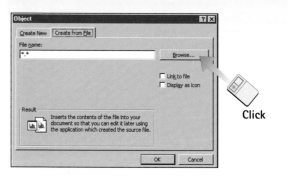

Click

4 Locate the Object File

Locate the picture file or other visual object file you want to use. When you find the file, select it and click **Insert** to return to the Insert Object dialog box.

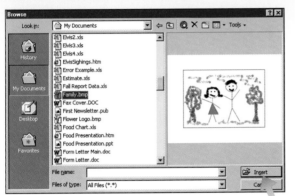

Click

5 Click OK

When you're ready to insert the object file, click **OK**.

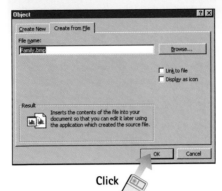

Click

6 The Object Is Inserted

The object appears in your file. You can now resize or move it as needed.

End

How-To Hints

Preview First

To see the picture file before inserting it, use the preview option in the Browse dialog box. Click the **Views** drop-down arrow on the Browse toolbar, and then select **Preview**. Now click the file you want to see and the preview area lets you view the file.

Insert Trick

If you find that you need to add the same picture file repeatedly to Word documents, add the picture file to Word's AutoCorrect collection. First, insert the picture file into a document and select the graphic. Open the **Tools** menu and choose **AutoCorrect**. In the AutoCorrect dialog box, type a text entry for the picture in the **Replace** box. If it's a company logo, for example, you might type **mylogo**. Click **Add** to add the entry to the list and click **OK**. Next time you type **mylogo**, the picture will replace the text.

How to Create Text Shapes with WordArt

One of the more popular features of the Microsoft graphics tools that come with Word is the WordArt application. WordArt enables you to turn text into graphic objects that bend, twist, rotate, and assume a variety of special effects. You can turn ordinary words into works of art.

WordArt is especially helpful when you need to create a company logo, a banner for a newsletter or flyer, or draw attention to important words, such as *sale* or *urgent*. After you design a WordArt object, you can move and resize it as needed (learn how in Task 5).

Begin

1 Open the WordArt Gallery

Open the **Insert** menu and select **Picture**, **WordArt**. This opens the WordArt Gallery dialog box.

Click

2 Choose an Effect

Select a WordArt style that best suits your needs. The samples show the shape and effect of the style. Click **OK** to continue.

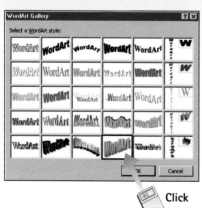

Click

3 Enter Your Own Text

In the Edit WordArt Text dialog box, enter the text you want to use as your WordArt object.

178 CHAPTER 11: HOW TO WORK WITH GRAPHICS

4 Format the Text

Use the **Font** drop-down box to select another font style, if necessary. You can also change the formatting attributes for size, bold, or italic.

5 Click OK

When you have finished with your selections, click **OK** to close the WordArt application.

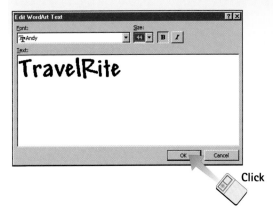

Click

6 WordArt Is Created

The WordArt object appears in your document along with the WordArt toolbar. Use the toolbar buttons to fine-tune your WordArt object. You may have to move or resize the WordArt object. To learn more about moving and resizing objects, see Task 5.

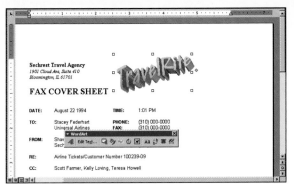

End

How-To Hints

Edit WordArt

Any time you need to edit your WordArt object, double-click it to reopen the text box where you can edit the text. You can use the tools on the WordArt toolbar to format the object.

Try Them All!

To change your WordArt's shape or style, select the WordArt object and click the **WordArt Gallery** button on the WordArt toolbar. This opens the WordArt Gallery dialog box again, and you can choose a new style to apply. By changing the text effects, fonts, sizes, and formatting attributes, you can create different WordArt shapes and designs. To reverse any of the changes you make, click **Undo**.

I Changed My Mind!

If you open the WordArt Gallery and change your mind about using the feature, click **Cancel**. If you have already started creating an image and then change your mind, click outside the picture. To remove a WordArt image you have already created, select it and press the **Delete** key.

How to Draw Basic Shapes

One of the easiest ways to add visual appeal to a document is to add a shape, such as a rectangle or oval. A shape can draw attention to parts of your text or other data, create a nice background effect, or function as a design element. You can also add lines, arcs, and freeform shapes by using the drawing tools. Once you add a shape to your document, you can move and resize it as needed.

You'll find Word's drawing tools available on the Drawing toolbar. To open the toolbar, right-click over any toolbar and select **Drawing**.

Begin

1 Select a Tool

Click the shape tool you want to draw: choose from **Rectangle** or **Oval**. To draw a rectangle, for example, click the **Rectangle** tool on the Drawing toolbar. Your mouse pointer takes the shape of a crosshair.

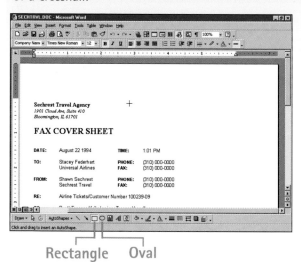

Rectangle   Oval

2 Drag the Shape

Move the mouse pointer to the location in the document where you want the shape to appear. Click and drag the mouse to draw the shape. When the shape reaches the desired shape and size, release the mouse button. You can now resize, move, or format the shape object.

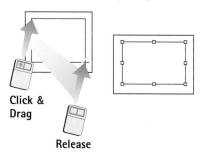

Click & Drag

Release

3 Draw a Line

Drawing lines or arrows is a lot like drawing shapes. Click the tool you want to draw: Choose from **Line** or **Arrow**. To draw a line, for example, click the **Line** tool on the Drawing toolbar. Your mouse pointer takes the shape of a crosshair.

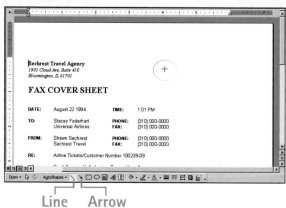

Line   Arrow

4 Drag the Line

Move the mouse pointer to the location on the document, worksheet, or slide where you want the line to appear. Click and drag the mouse to draw the line. When the line is the size you want, release the mouse button.

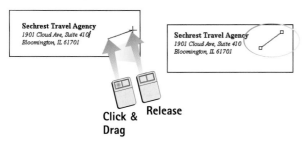

Click & Drag   Release

5 Draw a Freeform Shape

Use the Freeform tool to draw a polygon or freeform shape. To open the Freeform tool, click the **AutoShapes** button on the Drawing toolbar, select the **Lines** category, and choose the **Freeform** tool.

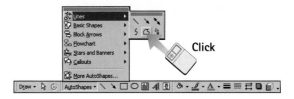

Click

6 Drag or Anchor

To draw a polygon shape, click where you want the shape to start and keep clicking each *anchor point* in place until the shape is finished. To draw a freeform shape, drag the mouse instead of clicking (the mouse pointer takes the shape of a pencil icon) and click in place when finished. The next figure shows the two types of techniques applied.

Polygon shape

Freeform shape

End

How-To Hints

Use AutoShapes

If you're not too keen on drawing your own shapes, use the available predrawn shapes. Click the **AutoShapes** tool on the Drawing toolbar to display a list of categories. Click the category you want to use; a palette of custom shapes appears. Click a shape. You can now click and drag the mouse pointer on the document until the shape reaches the size you want. Release the mouse button, and the complete shape appears.

Draw Perfect Shapes

To draw a perfect shape every time, hold down the **Shift** key while you drag. This keeps the proportions intact as you drag.

How to Move and Resize an Object

You can resize and move any visual object that you add to your Word document. This includes graphic images, clip art, WordArt, and any other drawing or shape you create. After you select an object, selection handles surround it. You can drag these handles in any direction to resize the object. You can also drag the object to a new location. The tricky part is knowing exactly where to click to perform either action. In this task, you will learn how to move and resize any object.

1 Select the Object

Select the object you want to move or resize. Notice as soon as you select it, tiny boxes called *selection handles* surround it.

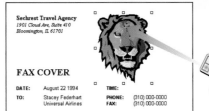

Click

2 Drag to Move

Hover your mouse pointer over the selected object until you see a four-headed arrow. Drag the object to a new location and release the mouse button. Notice the black dotted lines show you exactly where you're moving the object.

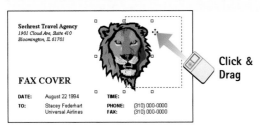

Click & Drag

3 Resize in One Dimension

To resize a selected object in one dimension—that is, to stretch or shrink the object—use only the resizing handles along the sides of the object. To stretch the object, for example, hover your mouse pointer over the handle on the right side and drag the handle. Release the mouse button when the object is stretched the way you want it.

Click & Drag

Release

4 Resize in Two Dimensions

To resize the object in two dimensions, use any of the corner handles. This will enable you to resize both the object's height and width at the same time. Hover your mouse pointer over a corner handle and drag. When the size is right, release the mouse button.

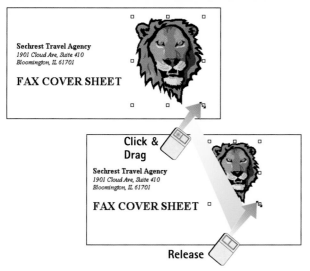

Click & Drag

Release

5 Use the Ctrl Key

To resize in two dimensions at once, from the center of the object outward, hold down the **Ctrl** key and drag any corner selection handle. Release the mouse button and **Ctrl** key when the object is sized the way you want it.

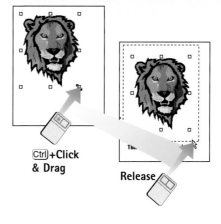

Ctrl +Click & Drag

Release

End

How-To Hints

Copy and Paste

You can easily copy and paste objects that you draw or insert with the graphics tools. Select the object and use the **Cut**, **Copy**, and **Paste** commands to move the object to a new location. You can also copy the object and place it in a new location. Use the **Cut**, **Copy**, and **Paste** buttons on the toolbar, or use these commands on the **Edit** menu.

Rotate Your WordArt

In addition to resizing WordArt objects, you can also rotate them. Use the **Free Rotate** button on the WordArt toolbar to rotate your WordArt object. To rotate, drag any rotation handle, and the WordArt object is rotated in the direction you drag.

My Text Won't Fit Around the Object!

If you move an object near or over text, you may find the text moves out of the way to make room for the object. This is Word's text wrap controls in action. If the text wrap controls are set to the in-line setting, you may experience some frustration when trying to reposition graphic objects. You can always change the text wrap settings for the object. Flip to Task 6 to learn how.

How to Wrap Text Around Graphics

If you're placing a visual object in a document with lots of text, you may want to define how the text wraps around the object. For example, you might prefer the text to appear right up to the edge of the object, or you may like the look of a small amount of space between the object and the text. Word's text wrap controls can help you determine how the text and object appear together.

1 Select the Object

Select the object you want to position text around (place the object where you want it to go if you haven't already done so).

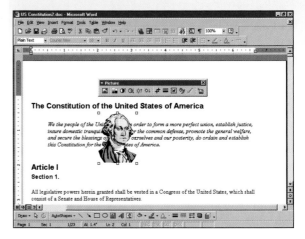

2 Click the Text Wrapping Button

From the Picture toolbar, click the **Text Wrapping** button. (If the toolbar is not displayed, right-click over any displayed toolbar and select **Picture** from the shortcut menu.)

Click

3 Choose a Wrap Option

From the drop-down menu, select the type of text wrapping you want to apply.

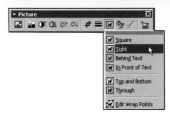

4 The Text Wraps

Depending on the selection you made in step 3, Word wraps any text around the object as directed. In this example, a **Tight** wrap is applied.

5 Or Create Your Own Wrap

For complete control over how text wraps around the object, use the **Edit Wrap Points** command from the Text Wrapping menu on the Picture toolbar.

6 Drag the Points

Edit points are placed around the object. Click and drag a point to move its wrap boundary. Depending on the object, there may be many edit points you can reposition (as shown in this example), or only a few.

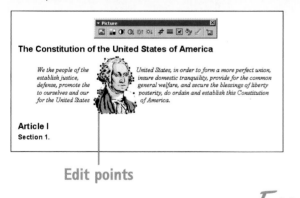

Edit points

End

How-To Hints

Experiment

Be sure to experiment with the various types of wraps to see their effects. You can always change the wrap to a new effect by reselecting from the Text Wrapping drop-down list.

How to Add a Callout to an Object

Some documents you create in Word, such as reports, may require labels, also known as callouts, to the visual objects you insert. For example, you may insert a chart you created in Excel and need to label different areas of importance. It's easy to add callouts by using the drawing tools. There is a variety of callout styles, and you create them by using the same techniques used to make basic shapes (see Task 4, "How to Draw Basic Shapes").

1 Open AutoShapes

From the Drawing toolbar, click the **AutoShapes** button. (If the toolbar is not displayed, right-click over any displayed toolbar and choose **Drawing**.)

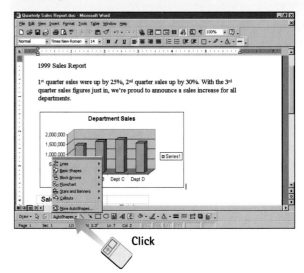

Click

2 Choose a Callout

From the AutoShapes menu, click **Callouts**, and then click a callout style from the palette to use in your document. In this example, I'm selecting **Line Callout 3**.

Click

3 Click to Start Drawing

As soon as you select a callout style, the mouse pointer becomes a crosshair icon. Move to the graphic or other object you want to draw a callout to and click in place.

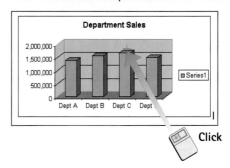

Click

4 Drag the Shape

Drag the shape and position of the callout. As you drag, the callout style you selected appears in outline.

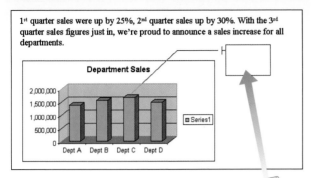

Click & Drag

5 Release the Mouse Button

When the callout is sized and positioned as you want it, release the mouse button. A Text Box toolbar appears and the callout is selected on the page.

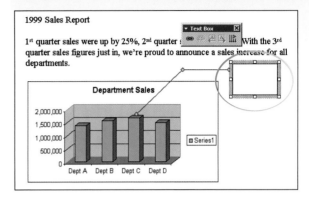

6 Type In Callout Text

Click inside the callout text box and enter the text for the callout.

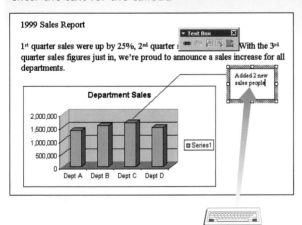

7 Deselect to View

To see how the callout looks, deselect the callout by clicking anywhere outside the callout area. You can edit the callout just like you edit any other shape or object you add to the document, including resizing or moving the callout.

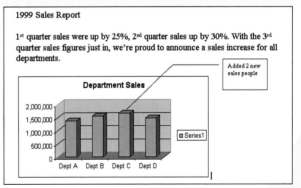

End

How to Add a Text Box

Although Word is a word processing program that automatically lets you enter text on a page, you may encounter documents that require separate text boxes. Text boxes, like clip art and shapes, are considered objects. They hold text, but can also be resized, moved, and formatted like any other visual object. You might use text boxes along with graphics. For example, you may create a text box to appear on top of a shape you've drawn.

Begin

1 Click the Text Box Tool

From the Drawing toolbar, click the **Text Box** tool. (If the Drawing toolbar isn't displayed, right-click over a displayed toolbar and choose **Drawing**.)

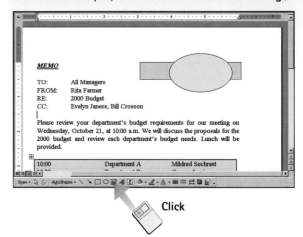

Click

2 Click in Place

The mouse pointer becomes a crosshair icon. Move the icon to the area where you want to draw a text box, and click.

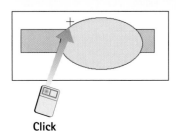

Click

3 Drag the Text Box

Drag the text box to the size you want.

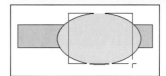

4 The Text Box Is Created

Release the mouse button and the text box appears on the document page.

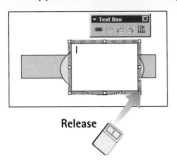

Release

5 Enter the Text

Enter the text you want inside the text box. If you make any mistakes, use the **Backspace** or **Delete** keys to correct them.

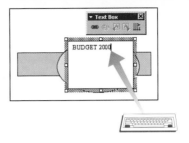

6 Format the Text

To format the text, select it and then apply any of Word's formatting commands to change the font, alignment, and so on.

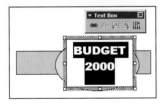

7 View the Text Box

When finished adding and formatting text, click outside the text box to deselect it. To make any adjustments to the text box, such as move or resize it or edit the text, click the text box to select it again.

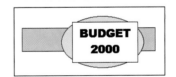

End

How to Change Image Formatting

Many of the visual objects you add can be enhanced with formatting tools. For example, you can format the shapes you draw by changing the fill color or line style. Adjusting your image's formatting can completely change the look of the object. You can tone down an object's loud primary colors by using pastel colors instead. You can also change the importance of the line you have drawn by making its line weight thicker. Be sure to experiment with all of the options to create different kinds of visual effects. In this task, you learn how to use the Format dialog box.

Begin

1 Select the Object

First select the object whose formatting you want to change.

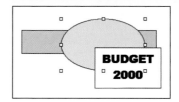

2 Choose the Format Command

Right-click the object to display the shortcut menu and select the **Format** command at the bottom of the menu. Depending on the type of visual object you select, the name of the command will vary. If you right-click a shape, for example, it appears as **Format AutoShape**. If you right-click a text box, it says **Format Text Box**.

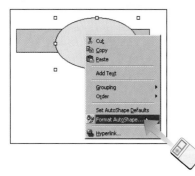

Click

3 The Format Dialog Box

The Format dialog box appears, based on the type of visual object you selected. Click the **Colors and Lines** tab to find options for changing the color or line style of the object.

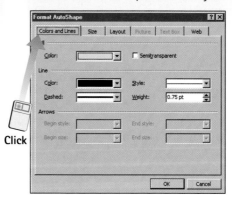

Click

4 Change the Fill Color

To change the fill color, click the **Fill Color** drop-down list and choose another color from the palette.

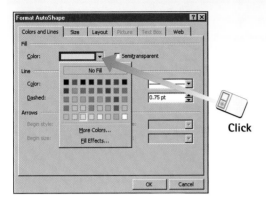

Click

5 Change the Line Weight

If your object contains an outline or border, or if it is a line or arc, use the **Line** options in the **Colors and Lines** tab to change the line's color, style, or weight (set an exact thickness). Click the **Style** drop-down arrow, for example, to display a list of line styles.

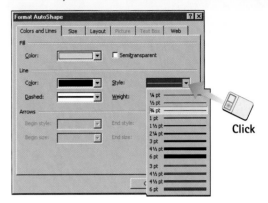

Click

6 Wrapping Text Around Objects

If you want the visual object to sit in the middle of text, you can apply wrapping commands to designate how the text flows around (or through) the object. Click the **Layout** tab and choose a wrapping style to apply. Click **OK** to exit the dialog box and apply any new formatting settings.

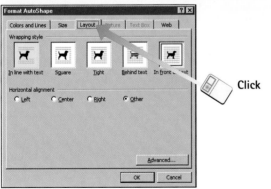

Click

How-To Hints

Other Formatting Options

Be sure to check out the other tabs in the Format dialog box. You can apply numerous other options, depending on the visual object you selected.

Or Use the Drawing Toolbar

The Drawing toolbar contains formatting tools that you can apply directly to the objects you select. To fill an object with a color, for example, click the **Fill Color** button. To choose another line style to use, click the **Line Style** button.

End

How to Add Shadow Effects

Another way to spruce up visual objects is to add shadow effects. A shadow can give a 3D effect to any text box, shape, clip art picture, line, WordArt design, or other visual object. With the drawing tool's Shadow Settings toolbar, you can control exactly where the shadow appears, you can set its color, and you can turn the shadow off if you don't like it anymore.

Begin

1 Select the Object

To add a shadow effect to any object, first select the object.

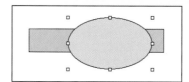

2 Click the Shadow Button

Click the **Shadow** button on the Drawing toolbar to display a palette of shadow effects. To apply an effect, click the one you want.

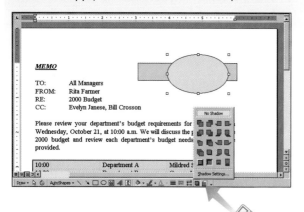

Click

3 Shadow Applied

The shadow effect is immediately applied to the object.

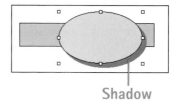

Shadow

4 Open the Shadow Settings Toolbar

For more control over the shadow, display the Shadow Settings toolbar. Click the **Shadow** button and select **Shadow Settings** from the palette.

Click

5 Nudge the Shadow

Use the Shadow Settings toolbar buttons to nudge your shadow and position it exactly where you want it to fall. Use the **Nudge** buttons to nudge the shadow effect in the direction you want it to go.

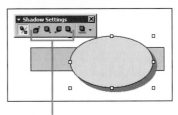

Nudge controls

6 Choose a Shadow Color

To change the shadow's color, click the **Shadow Color** drop-down arrow and click a new color to use. As soon as you select a new color, it is applied to the visual object. To close the Shadow Settings toolbar, click its **Close** button.

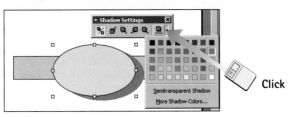

Click

End

How-To Hints

Instant 3D Effects

You can give your visual objects instant 3D effects with the **3D** button on the Drawing toolbar. Click the button to display a palette of 3D effects you can apply. To open the 3D Settings floating toolbar, click **3-D Settings** on the palette. Now you can fine-tune the effects until you find just the right effect for your object.

Removing a Text Box Border

If you prefer your text box not to include a default border, right-click over the text box frame and select **Format Text Box**. Click the **Colors and Lines** tab, click the **Line Color** drop-down arrow, and choose **No Line**. Click **OK** to exit the dialog box.

How to Select Several Graphics As a Group

You can use the layering and grouping commands to change the way objects appear on the document. You can stack objects one on top of another to create interesting effects, such as positioning a WordArt effect over a shape object to create a logo.

You can also group objects together so you can treat them as a single object. Perhaps you have several objects stacked in place, for example, but find you need to move them over a bit. Rather than move each object separately and layer them again, use the Grouping command. This enables you to move the entire group as one object. After you have moved the group, you can break apart the objects again to edit them separately.

Begin

1 Layer the Objects

To layer objects, start by moving them one on top of another to create an effect. You might place a WordArt object on top of a shape you have drawn, or stack a clip art object onto a larger shape to act as a background.

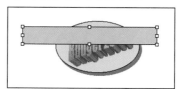

2 Move the Object to Front or Back

To change the layered order of the object, first display the Order options. Right-click over the object you want to layer, and then choose **Order** to display the layering options. To move an object to the back of the stack, for example, choose **Send to Back**.

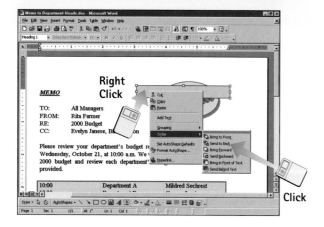

3 The Object Changes Order

The object immediately changes the order in which it was layered. In this example, I moved a rectangle shape to the back of the stack of objects.

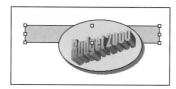

4 Select the Objects to Group

To group several objects together, select each object by clicking the object and holding down the **Shift** key. (Notice that each object's selection handles are active.)

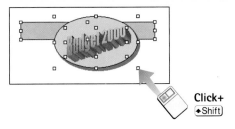

Click+
◆Shift)

5 Use the Group Command

Right-click any of the selected objects, choose **Grouping**, and then select **Group** from the shortcut menu.

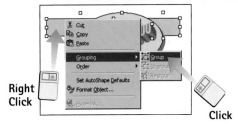

Right
Click

Click

6 A Single Group

The objects are now grouped and surrounded by one set of selection handles. To break apart the objects again, right-click and select **Grouping**, and then select **Ungroup**.

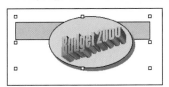

How-To Hints

Layer by Layer
To move layers forward or backward one layer at a time, use the **Bring Forward** or **Send Backward** commands on the shortcut menu.

End

Task

CHAPTER 12

How to Print Files

Once you have created and formatted a Word document, you're ready to print it out or distribute it to others. Before you do, you need to check it over and make sure everything is in order. Use Word's Print Preview mode to examine how your document will look before you print it out. When you are finally ready to print, Word has numerous printing options you can apply. For example, you can change the paper size you want the document printed on, or specify which pages to print. This chapter covers all the basic printing features you can apply to your own documents, including how to print envelopes and labels.

How to Preview a File

Before you print out a document, take a moment to preview how it looks by using the Preview window. Print Preview lets you examine exactly how your file will print, and you can make any last-minute changes before printing. When working on the file, for example, you can't always see how all the page elements—such as page numbers or graphics—look, or tell whether the page layout is pleasing to the eye. With the Preview feature, you can get an overall look at your file, page by page. The Preview window has a toolbar you can use to adjust your preview.

Begin

1 Open Print Preview

Open the **File** menu and select **Print Preview** (alternatively, you can click the **Print Preview** button—the button that looks like a sheet of paper under a magnifying glass—on the Standard toolbar).

Click

2 View the Preview Window

The file opens in a full-page preview. Use the toolbar buttons on the Preview toolbar to adjust your view of the page or pages. For example, you can use the **Magnifier** tool (which is selected by default), and then click anywhere on a page to zoom in for a closer look.

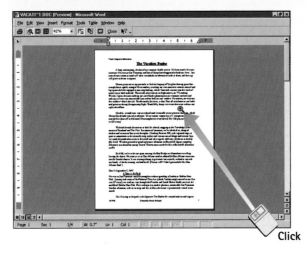

Click

3 Zoom In

Preview zooms in on the area you clicked. To return to full-page view, click again.

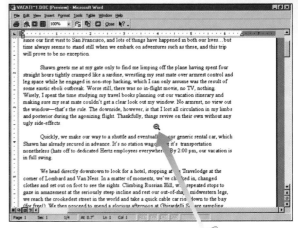

Click

4 Making Changes

To edit while in the Preview window, use the Magnifier tool to zoom in on the area you want to edit, and then deselect the **Magnifier** button on the toolbar by clicking the button to turn it off. The mouse pointer becomes a cursor you can click in the text and make changes to the data.

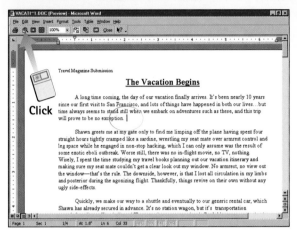

Click

5 Print the File

If your file is exactly as you want it to print, click the **Print** button on the toolbar to send it immediately to your printer.

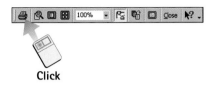

Click

6 Close the Preview Window

To exit the Preview window, click the **Close** button.

Click

End

Page or Pages?

Use the **One Page** button on the Preview toolbar to view a single page. Use the **Multiple Pages** button to view several pages at once; click the button and drag over the number of pages you want onscreen.

TASK *2*

How to Print a File

Printing a Word file requires that you have a printer connected to your computer, the appropriate printer driver (printer software) installed, and the printer turned on and online (ready to print). When you're ready to print, you can send the file immediately to the printer by using the default printer settings, or set specific printing options first by using the Print dialog box. In this task, you learn how to do both.

Begin

1 Open the Print Dialog Box

To set printing options, open the **File** menu and select **Print**.

Click

2 Choose a Printer

The Print dialog box reveals several options you can choose. If you have access to more than one printer, use the **Name** drop-down list to choose another printer.

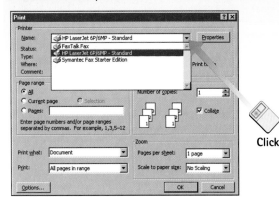

Click

3 Choose What to Print

If your document has user comments, styles, or other special features, you can choose to print only those items by clicking the **Print what** drop-down arrow and making a selection from the list.

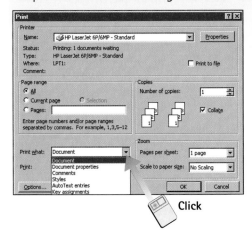

Click

4 Odd or Even

If you're printing a lengthy document that you will later bind as a book, you can use the **Print** drop-down list to choose to print just the odd or even pages.

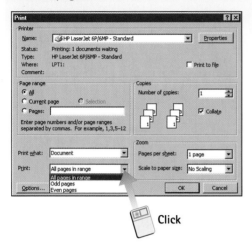

Click

5 Print

Click **OK** to print the file.

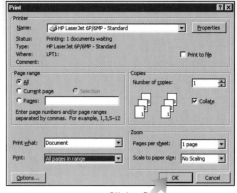

Click

6 Use the Print Toolbar Button

To print the file without selecting any new options, click the **Print** button on the Standard toolbar.

Click

End

How-To Hints

Printing Certain Pages

The Print dialog box also has options for choosing which pages to print. Learn more about using page options in Task 4, "How to Print Single Pages, Groups of Pages, and Multiple Copies."

Change the Paper Size

Some documents may require a different paper size. Learn all about changing paper size and orientation in Task 3, "How to Designate a New Paper Size and Orientation."

How to Designate a New Paper Size and Orientation

By default, Word assumes your document is a standard 8 1/2" by 11" page. If you need to create a document that uses a different paper size, open the Page Setup dialog box and change the settings. From the Paper Size tab, you can change the paper size or page orientation or enter the measurements for a custom paper size. It's best to select a paper size and orientation before building your document. If you change the settings after your document is created, you may have to adjust the text to fit the new size or orientation.

Begin

1 Open Page Setup

Open the **File** menu and select **Page Setup**. This opens the Page Setup dialog box.

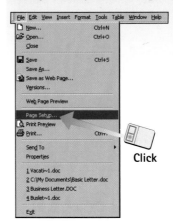

Click

2 Select the Paper Size Tab

Click the **Paper Size** tab to view the options associated with paper sizes and orientation.

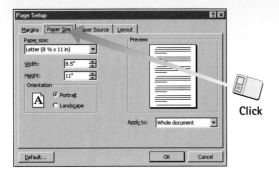

Click

3 Change the Paper Size

Use the **Paper Size** drop-down list to select another paper size. As you scroll through the list, you may notice Word is ready to handle legal-size paper and a variety of envelope sizes. (To create a custom size, select **Custom** from the list and enter the parameters of the paper in the **Width** and **Height** text boxes.)

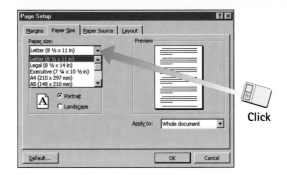

Click

4 Change the Page Orientation

With some documents, you may need to change the way the text is printed on the page—the **Orientation** settings. By default, Word prints the document "shortways" (across the width of the 8 1/2" page). This is called *Portrait*. You can switch to *Landscape* to print across the length of the page ("longways" across the width of the 11" page). The Preview area lets you see how the orientation looks.

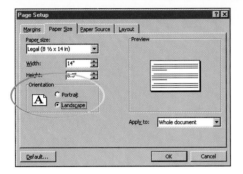

5 Change the Paper Source

Depending on your printer, you may have to change the paper source option before printing. To do so, click the **Paper Source** tab, and then select the appropriate tray.

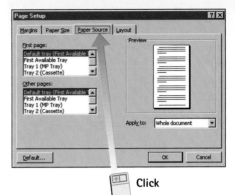

Click

6 Exit the Dialog Box

After you have set your paper size and source options, click **OK** to exit the Page Setup dialog box and start creating the document. When you're ready to print, click the **Print** button on the Standard toolbar.

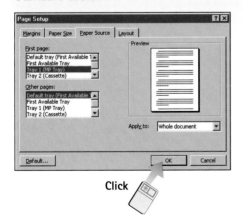

Click

End

How-To Hints

Caution!

If you choose to set a new paper size after you have already designed and created the document, you may need to make a few adjustments to the document. Be sure to check the document in Print Preview (click the **Print Preview** button on the Standard toolbar) to see whether everything still fits properly or whether it needs adjusting.

Changing the Default

If you find yourself using a different paper size over and over again, you can select it from the **Paper Size** tab and click the **Default** button to make it the new default paper size.

How to Print Single Pages, Groups of Pages, and Multiple Copies

The Print options available in the Print dialog box offer you a variety of ways to print document pages. For example, if you have a particularly long report, you can choose to print out only certain pages or just a single page. You can also choose to print a group of related pages, and you can even print multiple copies of a page. In this task, you learn ways to designate which pages of your document you want to print.

Begin

1 Open the Print Dialog Box

Open the **File** menu and choose **Print**. This opens the Print dialog box.

Click

2 Print Only the Current Page

To print only the page where the cursor is currently located, click the **Current page** option under the **Page range** heading in the Print dialog box and proceed to step 6.

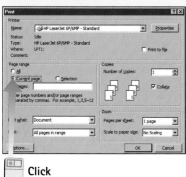

Click

3 Print Only the Selected Text

If you select a block of text before opening the Print dialog box, you can click the **Selection** option and choose to print only the text you've highlighted on the document page. (Skip to step 6 to print.)

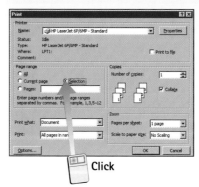

Click

4 Print Only Certain Pages

To designate specific pages, use the **Pages** text box to indicate exactly which pages to print. Click the **Pages** option, and then type in a single page number or a range, such as 2–4. If you're printing noncontiguous pages, such as pages 2, 6, and 10, separate the page numbers with commas.

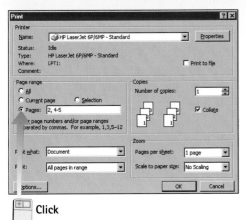

Click

5 Print Multiple Copies

To print multiple copies of the file or pages, indicate a number in the **Number of copies** box.

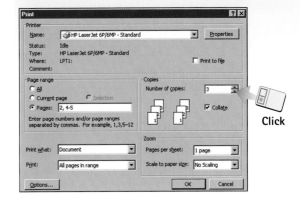

Click

6 Print the Page or Pages

To print the pages you designated, click **OK**.

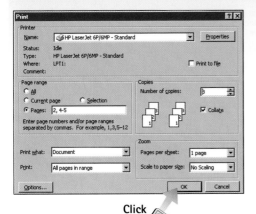

Click

How-To Hints

Zoom Your Printed Pages

Use the **Zoom** options in the Print dialog box to shrink several document pages to fit onto one printed page. Click the **Pages per Sheet** drop-down arrow and designate how many document pages to fit per sheet, and then use the **Scale to Paper Size** drop-down arrow and choose the paper size to print to.

End

How to Print an Envelope

Some Word projects you tackle may involve some special printing needs, such as envelopes. When you create letters in Word, you can create envelopes to go with them. Use Word's Envelopes and Labels dialog box to enter addresses and select from a variety of envelope sizes.

Begin

1 Open the Envelope and Labels

If you have created a letter with an address you want to print on an envelope, open the letter document. If not, you can open the Envelope feature from any document and create a quick envelope. Open the **Tools** menu and select **Envelopes and Labels**.

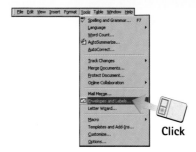

Click

2 Display the Envelopes Tab

Click the **Envelopes** tab. If needed, type in the delivery address and the return address in the appropriate text boxes. If you're using this feature with a letter file, Word borrows the addresses you entered in the letter document.

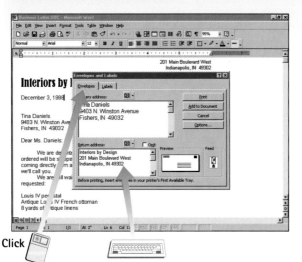

Click

3 Open the Envelope Options

To choose an envelope size other than the default size, click the **Options** button to open the Envelope Options dialog box.

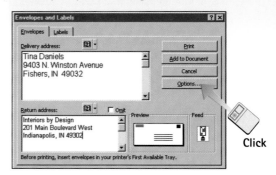

Click

4 Choose an Envelope Size

Select another size from the **Envelope Size** drop-down list.

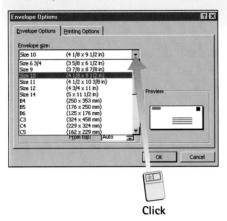

Click

5 Exit Envelope Options

You can also change the font used for the addresses and control the spacing between the addresses and the edges of the envelope. Click **OK** to return to the Envelopes and Labels dialog box after you're finished setting envelope options.

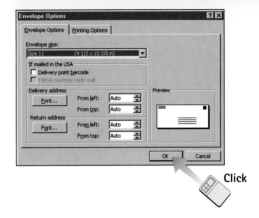

Click

6 Print

To print the envelope, click the **Print** button. Be sure to feed the envelope into your printer correctly. Depending on your printer setup, the Feed area in the dialog box gives you a clue as to how to feed the envelope.

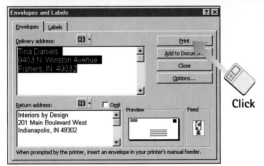

Click

End

How-To Hints

Omit

Select the **Omit** check box in the Envelopes and Labels dialog box if you have preprinted envelopes that already have a return address or company logo.

Add to Document

Select the **Add to Document** button in the Envelopes and Labels dialog box to add the envelope style and contents to the document to save it for later use.

How to Print a Label

Word makes it easy to print labels as well as envelopes. You can choose to print a single label or a full page of labels. Word supports a variety of Avery sizes (a popular label brand). You can even import addresses from your Outlook Address Book or another address database to use as labels.

Be sure to set up your printer to handle the labels first, and then follow the steps in this task to create and print the labels.

Begin

1 Open the Dialog Box

Open the **Tools** menu and select **Envelopes and Labels** to open the Envelopes and Labels dialog box.

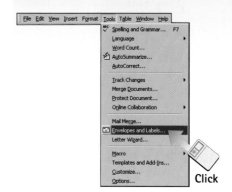

Click

2 Display the Labels Tab

Click the **Labels** tab. If needed, type in the address in the **Address** text box. To import an address, click the **Address Book** icon and open the address database you want to use, such as Outlook's Personal Address Book, and select the address to use as label.

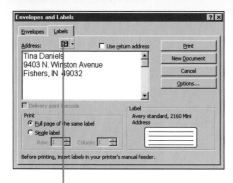

Address Book button

3 Choose a Print Option

Under Print options, select to print a single label or a page of labels. To print a return address label, select the **Use return address** check box.

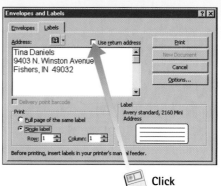

Click

4 Open Label Options Dialog Box

Click the **Options** button to open the Label Options dialog box where you can select a label product and size.

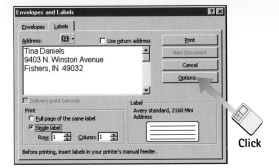

Click

5 Choose a Label Size

Use the **Label products** drop-down list to choose a product, and then select the product number from the **Product** number list box. The **Label information** area displays the dimensions of the label and label page. Click **OK** to return to the Envelopes and Labels dialog box.

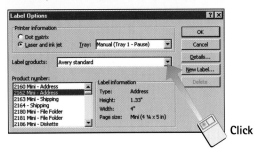

Click

6 Print

To print the label, click the **Print** button.

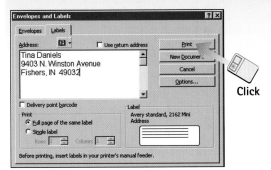

Click

End

How-To Hints

Print a Particular Label

To print a specific label on your label sheet, select the **Single Label** option in the Labels tab and use the **Row** and **Column** settings to specify the label's location on the sheet.

Project

To put more of your newly acquired formatting skills to work, try your hand at creating a report document. In this task, I'll walk you through the steps necessary to lay out a report, including a title page. You can follow this task with your own report text, or you can copy the text used in the example to practice these skills on your own.

Reports often include manual page breaks, headers and footers, and page numbers, so you'll find steps detailing how to insert these items into a report as well. If your report doesn't include such items, simply skip those steps. I'll also show you how to print the report after completing the document.

1 Start a New File

To begin the report, start with a new, blank document page. Click the **New** button on the Standard toolbar. This opens a blank document.

Click

2 Open the Page Setup Dialog Box

Before you begin entering the report text, first set up the page size and margins. To do so, open the Page Setup dialog box. Display the **File** menu and choose **Page Setup**.

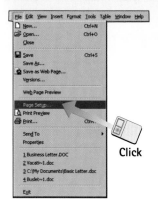

Click

3 Change the Paper Size

To change the paper size for the paper on which you want to print the report, click the **Paper Size** tab. Choose a new size from the **Paper size** drop-down list. If necessary, change the page orientation.

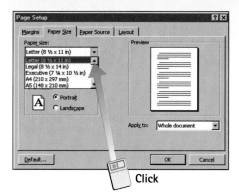

Click

4 Display the Margins Tab

To change the page margins for the report, click the **Margins** tab.

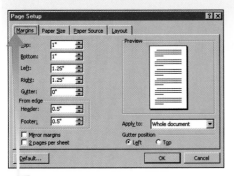

⌨ Click

5 Set New Margins

Set the top and bottom margins to .5 inch and the left and right margins to one inch. Click **OK** to exit the dialog box.

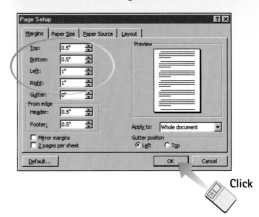

Click

6 Type In a Title Page

To start the report, begin with typing in text to create a title page. To use the new Click-and-Type feature, switch to Print Layout View, double-click in the center of the page somewhere, and enter a title for the report. Make sure center alignment is applied; if it's not, click the **Center** button on the Formatting toolbar.

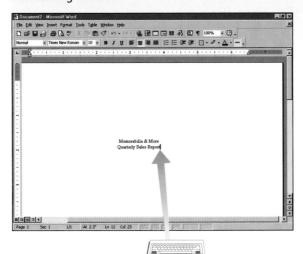

7 Apply a Page Break

Press **Enter** at the end of the title text, and then press **Ctrl+Enter** to create a page break. The next figure shows the page break as it appears in Normal View. Now you're ready to enter the report text.

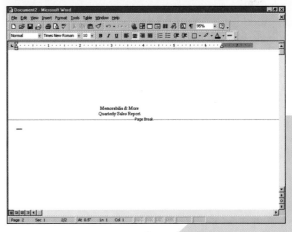

Continues

8 Enter Your Report Text

Enter the text for your report. Use as many pages as you need. If you're just practicing, enter some placeholder text for a single report page.

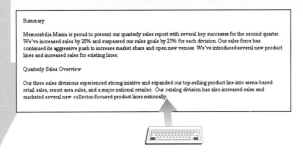

9 Use a Style

You can apply formatting as you want. For example, if your report includes headings throughout, use a style to quickly format each one. Select one heading and format it to suit your needs, and then select the heading and click inside the **Style** text box on the Formatting toolbar. Enter a name for the style and press **Enter**.

10 Apply a Style

To apply the heading style to another heading, select the heading, and then click the **Style** drop-down arrow and choose the style you named in step 9.

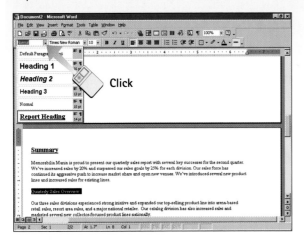

11 Add a Simple Table

Does your report need a table? To quickly add a table to your report, click in the document where you want the table to appear, click the **Insert Table** button on the Standard toolbar, and drag the number of columns and rows you want to use in your table.

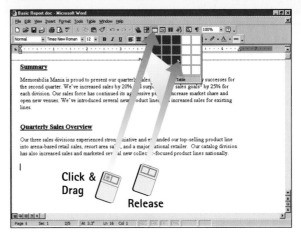

12 Enter Table Text

A table is immediately inserted into your document. Click inside the first table cell and enter the text you want to use. Press **Tab** to move from cell to cell and enter table text.

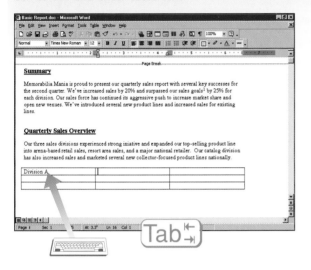

13 Set Vertical Alignment

To set vertical alignment for your report, such as the title page, use Word's Vertical Alignment controls. For example, scroll up to the title page to set vertical alignment for the title text. Open the **File** menu and select **Page Setup**.

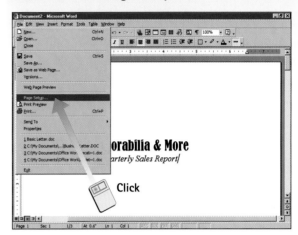

14 Choose Center Alignment

From the Page Setup dialog box, click the Layout tab, and then click the **Vertical alignment** drop-down arrow and choose **Center** alignment. Click **OK** to exit the dialog box and apply the alignment.

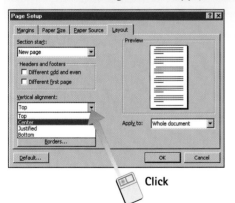

15 Add Page Numbers

To add page numbers to the report, open the **Insert** menu and choose **Page Numbers**. This opens the Page Numbers dialog box.

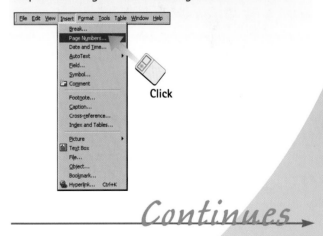

Continues

Project Continued

16 Choose a Position and Alignment

Use the **Position** drop-down list to choose where you want the page numbers positioned. Use the **Alignment** drop-down list to select an alignment. To customize the page numbers, click the **Format** button.

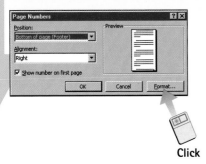

Click

17 Change the Number Format

Click the **Number format** drop-down arrow and choose another number style from the list. Click **OK** to return to the Page Numbers dialog box, and then click **OK** again to apply the page numbers to your document.

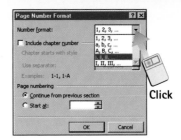

Click

18 Add Headers and Footers

To add headers or footers to your report, open the **View** menu and select **Header and Footer**. This opens the header and footer panes along with the Header and Footer toolbar.

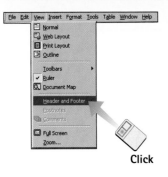

Click

19 Enter Header Text

Type any header or footer text you want to include on every page. Use the **Switch Between Header and Footer** button on the Header and Footer toolbar to move back and forth between header and footer panes.

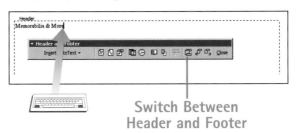

Switch Between Header and Footer

20 Add a Date Field

To add the current date to the header or footer, click the **Insert Date** button on the Header and Footer toolbar. This immediately places the current date in the header or footer pane where the insertion point is located.

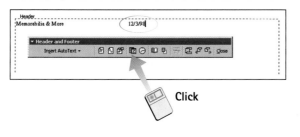

Click

21 Add an AutoText Field

To add an AutoText entry to your header or footer, click the **AutoText** drop-down arrow and choose an entry from the list. It's immediately placed in your header or footer at the location of the insertion point. To exit the header or footer panes, click the **Close** button on the toolbar.

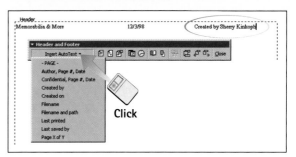

Click

22 Insert a Footnote

To add any footnotes to your report document, click where you want the reference number inserted, and then open the **Insert** menu and choose **Footnote**. This opens the Footnote and Endnote dialog box.

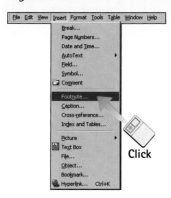

Click

23 Select Footnote

Click the **Footnote** option and click **OK**.

Click

Continues

24 Type the Reference

Type in the footnote you want to reference. If you're just practicing, make up some text for the footnote.

Memorabilia Mania is proud to present our quarterly sales report with several key successes for the second quarter. We've increased sales by 20% and surpassed our sales goals by 25% for each division. Our sales force has continued its aggressive push to increase market share and open new venues. We've introduced several new product lines and increased sales for existing lines. Memorabilia Mania is proud to present our quarterly sales report with several key successes for the second quarter. We've increased sales by 20% and surpassed our sales goals by 25% for each division. Our sales force has continued its aggressive push to increase market share and open new venues. We've introduced several new product lines and increased sales for existing lines.

¹ Based on sales goals set in January 1999

25 Click Print Preview

When finished compiling and formatting your report, switch to Print Preview to see how everything looks. Click the **Print Preview** button on the Standard toolbar.

Click

26 Zoom In

To zoom in and out, use the Magnifier tool. Click to zoom in for a closer look at any area of the page. Click again to zoom back out.

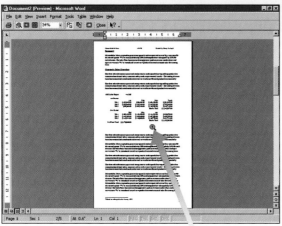

Click

27 Exit Print Preview

To close the Print Preview window, click the **Close** button. This returns you to the document page.

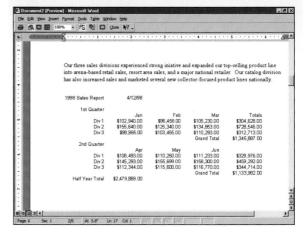

28 Open the Print Dialog Box

When you're ready to print the report, open the **File** menu and choose **Print**. This opens the Print dialog box.

Click

29 Print Only the Title Page

To print only the title page of the report, click the **Pages** option and type a **1** in the text box. (To print the entire report, click the **All** option.)

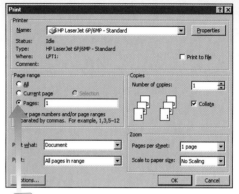

Click

30 Print the Page

To print the page, click **OK**.

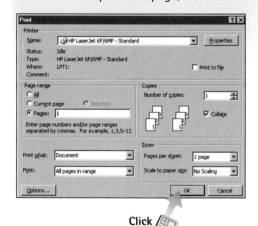

Click

End

How-To Hints

Don't Forget to Save!

Be sure to save your report at some point; click the **Save** button on the Standard toolbar. From the **Save As** dialog box, designate a folder to which to save the file, and then enter a name for the report in the **File Name** text box. Click **Save**.

Task

13

How to Start and Complete a Mail-Merge Document

*O*ne of the more complicated tasks you can do in Word is perform a mail-merge to create *mass mailings*—duplicate letters you want to send out to different people. Mass mailings are a popular way of advertising your goods or services. You can use them to send out new product information to a list of your favorite clients or solicit new ones. You can also use Word's mail-merge functions to generate a Christmas letter to send to friends and family.

You can merge your address book from Outlook or an address database created in Access with a form letter document you create in Word. If you don't currently have an address database, you can even create one by using Word's mail-merge feature.

The mail-merge process borrows information from a database source, such as an address list you've created in another program, and pulls in information from specific fields to insert into your letter. If you're new to the lingo used in databases, each person's address is called a *record*. A record is broken down into pieces, called *fields*, that represent each type of data that comprises the record, such as name, address, or city.

In this chapter, each task covers a particular aspect of setting up and performing a mail-merge. To complete the entire procedure, be sure to follow the steps in each task. ●

How to Create a Form Letter

The first step in using Word's mail-merge features is to create a form letter. This is the actual letter text that each person will receive. When you finish the letter, add any necessary formatting to the text and save the file.

Begin

1 Type the Form Letter

To begin, open a new file and start entering the text that will comprise the letter.

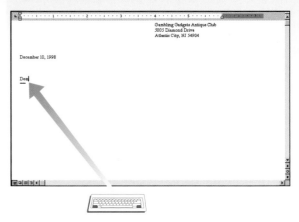

2 Complete the Letter

As you're entering text, leave out any information that can be inserted from the data source (such as name and address). When you're finished with the letter, you're ready to apply any formatting.

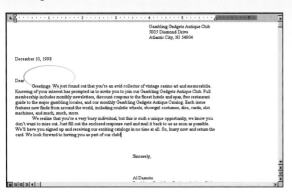

3 Format the Letter

If you like, add any special formatting to the letter. For example, you may want to change the font and size or apply a new alignment. Take a moment and put the finishing touches on the text.

4 Save the Letter

Click the **Save** button on the Standard toolbar to open the Save As dialog box, give the form letter a name, and then click **Save**. You can now leave the form letter open.

Click

5 Open Mail-Merge Helper

Open the **Tools** menu and select **Mail–Merge**. This opens the Mail Merge Helper dialog box.

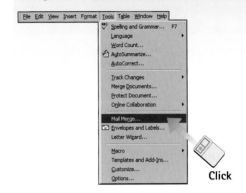

Click

6 Designate the Main Document

Under the **Main Document** heading, click the **Create** button, and then choose **Form Letters.**

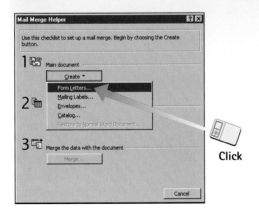

Click

7 Active Window Prompt

A prompt box appears, asking whether you want to use the active window as the main document or create a new main document. Click **Active Window**. This tells Word to use the open document you created in the previous steps as your main document for the mail-merge.

Click

End

How to Create the Data Source

The second step in performing a mail-merge is to specify what address database you want to use. If you keep a record of clients, friends, or family in a program such as Outlook, you can use the existing address book you have already created. If you have an address database you've created in Microsoft Access, you can use it as well.

If you don't have an address database of any kind, you can create your own by using the mail-merge feature. Keep in mind that this will slow you down a bit because you have to enter a record for each person to whom you want to send the form letter.

Begin

1 Click Get Data

After completing step 7 in the previous task, you're returned to the Mail-merge Helper dialog box. Under the **Data source** heading, click the **Get Data** button.

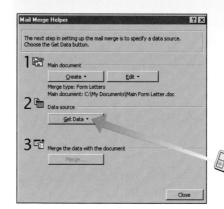

Click

2 Specify the Data Source

From the drop-down list, choose a data source option. If you're using Outlook's address book, choose **Use Address Book**. If you're using an Access database, choose **Open Data Source**. If you need to create a new list of addresses, choose **Create Data Source**.

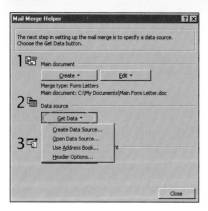

3 Choose an Address Book

If you selected **Use Address Book** in step 2, you will be prompted to select the Outlook address book you want to use. After making your selection, click **OK**. You will also be prompted to choose a profile; select a profile and skip to Task 3.

Click

4 Choose a Database File

If you selected **Open Data Source** in step 2, you must locate the Access database file (or any other file you want to use as your database). Select the file from the list box and click **Open** (you may have to change the **Files of type** field to list the type of database you're looking for; click the drop-down arrow to change the file type displayed). Skip to Task 3.

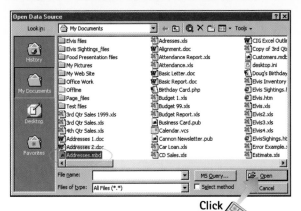

Click

5 Or Create Your Own Address List

If you selected Create Data Source in step 2, the Create Data Source dialog box opens. Word displays common field names in the list box. Fields represent different parts of the address record (such as name, city, state). You can choose which fields you don't want to use in your data source or add new ones.

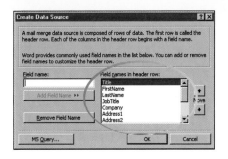

6 Edit the Field Names

To remove a field from the list, such as **Title**, select it and then click the **Remove Field Name** button. To add a field, enter it in the **Field name** text box and click the **Add Field Name** button.

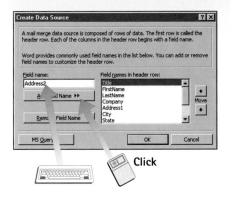

Click

7 Check the List

Use the **Move** buttons to reposition a field in the list box. Click the field you move, and then click the appropriate **Move** arrow button (click **Up** to move the item up in the list, click **Down** to move it down). When you have edited the list to contain all the fields you want to use in the database and positioned them just as you want them, click **OK**.

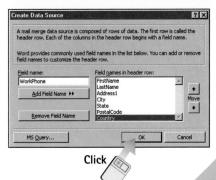

Click

Continues

How to Create the Data Source Continued

8 Give the Data Source a Name

The Save As dialog box opens so you can give the data source a name. Type in a name for the address list in the **File name** text box and click **Save**.

Click

Click

9 Edit the Data Source

A prompt box appears telling you there are no data records. To add some, click the **Edit Data Source** button.

Click

10 Enter the First Record

A Data Form opens onscreen and you can enter the first record. The fields shown are based on those you specified in steps 6 and 7. To start entering the text for the first field, just start typing.

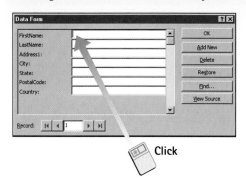

Click

11 Click OK

Use the Tab key to move from field to field and enter text. When you have completed the first record, click **OK** or click the **Add New** button.

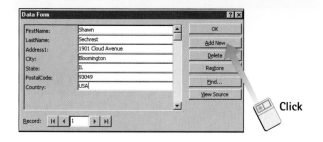

Click

12 Enter the Next Record

The data form clears and you can now enter another record. The Record box at the bottom of the form keeps track of record numbers. Keep entering records for every person in your address list to whom you want to mail a form letter.

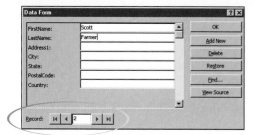

13 Move Between Records

To move back and forth between records you've previously entered, click the arrow buttons at the bottom of the form. You can edit the text within each field just like you edit document text; use the Backspace and Delete keys to fix mistakes.

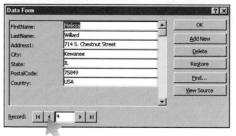

Click

14 Click OK

When finished entering all your records, click **OK**. Now you're ready for Task 3.

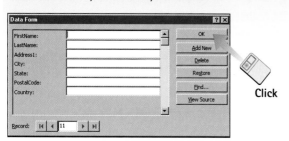

Click

End

How-To Hints

Oops!

If you make changes to an existing record and decide you don't want to keep the changes, click the **Restore** button.

Adding to the Data Source

If you need to add more records to the data source after you've closed the Data Form dialog box, you can open it again. Click the **Edit Data Source** button on the Mail-Merge toolbar. You can also open the **Tools** menu, choose **Mail-Merge**, click the **Edit** button under the **Data Source** heading, and select your data source from the drop-down list.

How to Enter Field Codes

The next phase in performing a mail-merge is to designate where you want to insert pieces of information from your data source into the form letter. For example, you must tell Word where to place the name and address in the form. You do this by inserting field codes. Field codes represent parts of your data source records. When you perform the actual mail-merge, Word inserts data from each record into the field codes, creating a letter for each person in the data source.

Begin

1 Another Message Prompt

Depending on what data source you specified, another prompt box may appear, telling you that your form letter has no merge fields yet. Click **Edit Main Document**.

Click

2 The Mail-Merge Toolbar Appears

The Mail-Merge toolbar appears onscreen along with your form letter. The tools on the Mail-Merge toolbar will help you enter and edit fields, perform the merge, and view records.

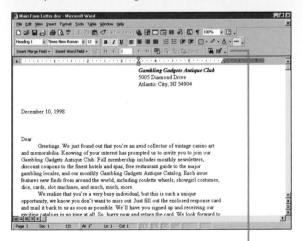

Mail-Merge toolbar

3 Click to Insert the First Field

Begin inserting data fields into your form letter where you want to place data from the address book or database. Click where you want a field inserted, and then click the **Insert Merge Field** drop-down list on the Mail-Merge toolbar.

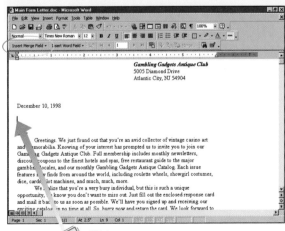

Click

4 Choose a Field

From the drop-down list, choose a field to insert. For example, to insert a name, select the **FirstName** field.

Click

5 The Field Code Appears

Word immediately inserts the field code, surrounded by brackets, into the document. In this example, I've inserted the field code for the person's first name.

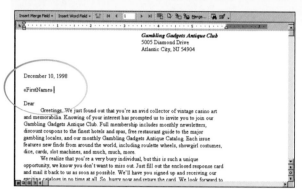

6 Viewing Field Codes

Continue entering field codes representing the data you want to see in the form letter. Be sure to include punctuation or spacing between field codes, if needed.

End

How-To Hints

Editing Field Codes

To remove a field code from your document, select the code, including the brackets, and press **Delete**.

Preview the Data

To get a glimpse at what the actual data will look like in place of the field code, click the **View Merged Data** button on the Mail-Merge toolbar. The codes will show the data from record one in your data source. To view the codes again, click the **View Merged Data** button to turn the preview off.

How to Run a Mail-Merge

When you've completed your form letter, picked a data source, and inserted all the necessary field codes into the document, you're ready to run a mail-merge. When you complete the merge, Word displays an individual document for each person in your data source and the field codes fill to reflect data from that person's record.

Begin

1 Merge the Data

When you're ready to merge the data from your data source with the form letter, click the **Start Mail-Merge** button on the Mail-merge toolbar.

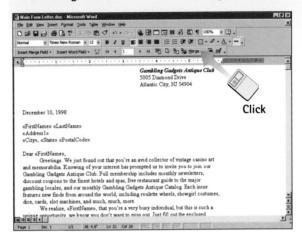

Click

2 Choose a Merge

When the Merge dialog box appears, select how you want the merge to occur. You can choose to merge to a new document, printer, or email program. Click the **Merge to** drop-down arrow and choose an option.

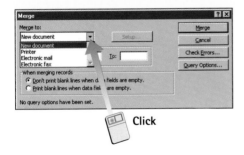

Click

3 Select Which Records

Use the **Records to be merged** options to choose exactly which records you want to use with the mail-merge. You can choose a range of records, for example, or choose to merge all the records. To use all the records in your data source, click **All**.

Click

4 What About Blanks?

You can also designate how the mail-merge should handle blank fields in your records. Select the options you want to use, and then click **Merge**.

Click

5 Word Merges the Data

Word merges your form letter with the fields you specified from the data source and creates an individual letter for each record in your data source. Scroll through the pages to see the results.

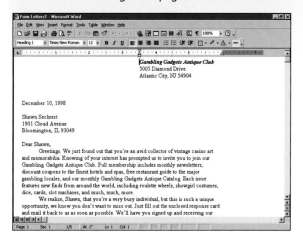

6 Save It

You can print the letters now or save them to print later. To save the merge, open the **File** menu and select **Save As**. From the Save As dialog box, enter a filename for the form letters and click **Save**.

End

How-To Hints

Or Use the Mail-Merge Helper Box

Another way to complete the mail-merge is to use the Mail-Merge Helper dialog box. Click the **Mail-Merge Helper** button on the Mail-Merge toolbar to open the dialog box. Next, click the **Merge** button to display the Merge dialog box and use as described in steps 2–4.

Create Mailing Labels

You can also make address labels to go along with the form letters you created with the mail-merge. Learn how in the next task, "How to Create Envelopes and Labels with a Mail-Merge."

How to Create Envelopes and Labels with a Mail-Merge

It's easy to create quick envelopes or labels based on your data source, whether it's the data source you just created yourself in Task 2 or you're using an address book from Outlook. The steps in this task will walk you through the entire procedure, focusing on envelopes. You can use the same steps, with slight variations, to create labels as well.

Begin

1 Select the Mail-Merge Command

Open the **Tools** menu and choose **Mail-Merge**. You can start the procedure for making envelopes or labels with the merged document from Task 4 still open onscreen.

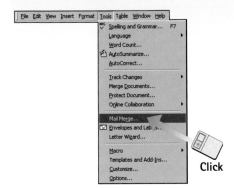

Click

2 Select Envelopes or Labels

From the Mail-Merge Helper dialog box, click the **Create** button and choose **Envelopes** or **Mailing Labels** from the list. The remainder of this task will focus on envelopes.

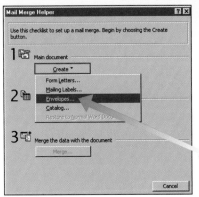

Click

3 Choose a New Document

From the prompt box that appears, click **New Main Document** to start the merge in a new file.

Click

4 Select a Data Source

Click the **Get Data** button and choose your data source. To use an existing data source, such as an Access database or a data source you created using Task 2, select **Open Data Source**.

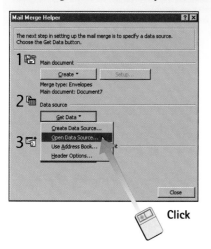

Click

5 Select the File

From the Open Data Source dialog box, select the data source file you want to use and click **Open**.

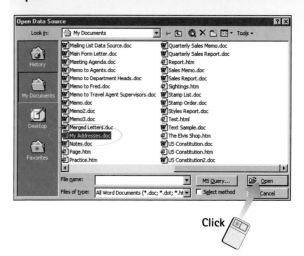

Click

6 Another Prompt Box

Yet another prompt box appears, this one telling you to set up your main document. Click **Set Up Main Document**.

Click

7 Choose an Envelope Size

From the Envelope Options dialog box, select the envelope size you want to use. Click the **Envelope size** drop-down arrow and change the size, if needed. Click **OK** to continue.

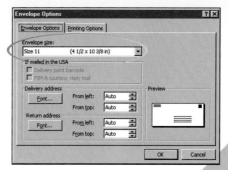

Continues

8 Enter Address Fields

Click the **Insert Merge Field** button to begin building the field codes you want to include on each envelope in the merge.

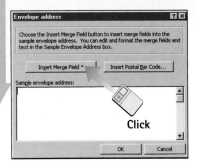

9 Choose a Field

From the list that appears, select the first field to appear on the envelope, such as **FirstName**.

10 Start a New Line

Continue entering fields, inserting punctuation or spaces where needed. To start a new line, press **Enter**.

11 Click OK

When finished entering all the necessary fields, click **OK**.

12 Open the Merge Dialog Box

From the Mail-Merge Helper dialog box, click the **Merge** button.

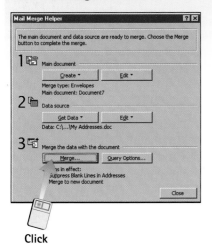

Click

13 Choose the Records

To merge to a different source, such as your printer, click the **Merge to** drop-down arrow and choose the source. To merge the envelopes to a new file so you can check them over before printing, leave **New Document** selected. You can also specify which records to merge; click **All** to create envelopes for every person in the data source or specify which records to create.

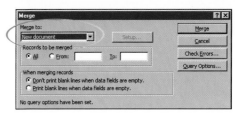

14 Start the Merge

When you're ready to perform the merge, click the **Merge** button.

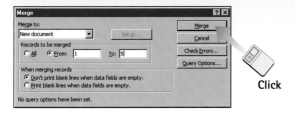

Click

15 The Envelopes Are Created

Word creates a file with envelopes for each person in your data source (or for the specific records you specified in step 13). You can now save and print the file as needed.

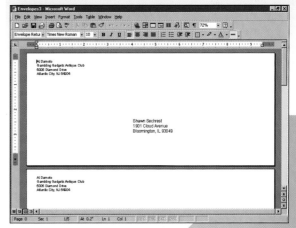

End

Project

If you created a basic letter back in Chapter 8, you can use the same project to generate a mass mailing. For example, if you created a sample letter to send to a stockholder, you can use that same letter as a form letter to send out to every stockholder in your data source list. This project will show you how to turn the basic letter from Chapter 8 into a form letter and then perform a mail-merge by using the data source you created in Task 2 of this chapter.

1 Open the Basic Letter

Open the basic letter project you created in Chapter 8.

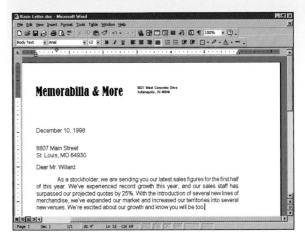

2 Delete Text

Scan the document and delete any text that refers to a specific person or address.

3 Open Mail-Merge Helper

Open the **Tools** menu and select **Mail-Merge**. This opens the mail-merge Helper dialog box.

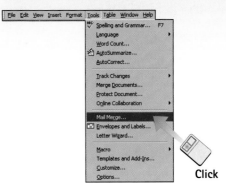

Click

4 Choose Form Letters

Click the **Create** button and select **Form Letters**.

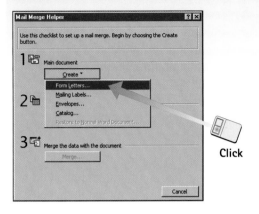

Click

5 Use the Active Window

Because we're using the current document as the form letter, click the **Active Window** button in the prompt box that appears.

Click

6 Select the Data Source

Click the **Get Data** button and choose the data source you want to use. If you created a new data source back in Task 2 of this chapter, you can use it with this project. Select **Open Data Source**.

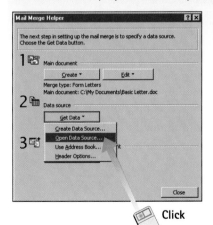

Click

7 Locate the Data Source File

Locate the data source file you want to work with, select it, and click **Open**.

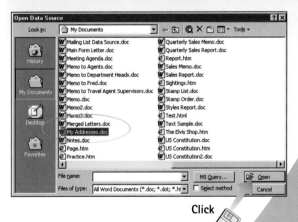

Click

Continues

8 Edit Main Document

Another prompt box appears telling you the main document has no fields; click **Edit Main Document**.

Click

9 Insert Fields

Click in the letter where you want to insert a field, such as the recipient's name and address, and then click the **Insert Merge Field** drop-down arrow and select a field.

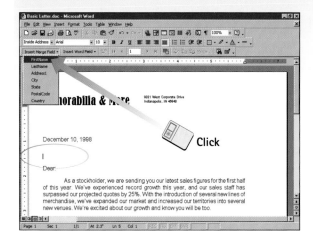

Click

10 Fields Are Added

Each time you select a field from the drop-down list, it's added to the letter, as shown in this example. Be sure to enter any spacing or punctuation as necessary.

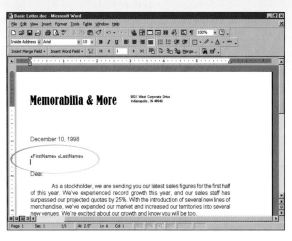

11 Format the Fields

You may need to format the fields so the formatting matches that of the rest of your letter. Select the fields and apply any formatting commands, such as font size.

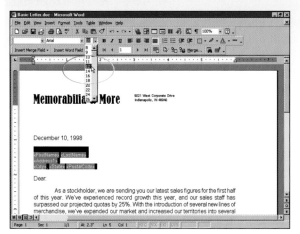

12 Edit the Salutation

If you want to change the salutation to be more general, Word's AutoText list has one that easily fits the stockholder letter. Click in the document where you want to insert the salutation, open the **Insert** menu, choose **AutoText**, and then select **Dear Sir or Madam**.

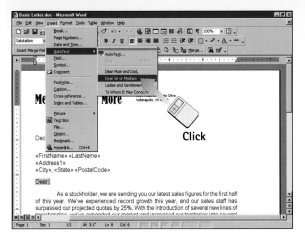

Click

13 Start the Merge

Word inserts the salutation, as shown in this example. To start the merge, click the **Start Mail-Merge** button on the Mail-Merge toolbar.

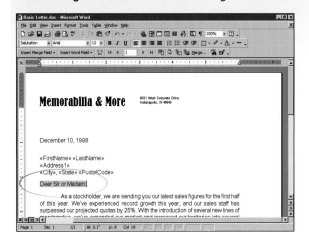

14 Change the Options

Use the Merge dialog box to specify specific records to merge, where to merge to, and how to handle blank fields. When you're ready to merge, click the **Merge** button.

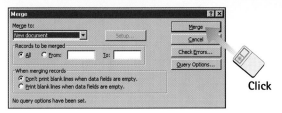

Click

15 The Letter Is Merged

Word merges the form letter with the data source records to create a new document with a letter for each stockholder; scroll through the document to see each letter. You can now save or print the file.

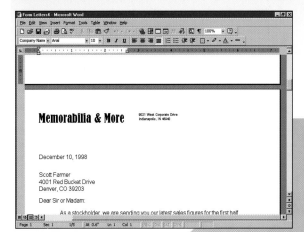

End

Task

14

How to Use Word
on the Web

Microsoft specifically designed Word to utilize the Internet and the World Wide Web. You will find plenty of Web-browsing features in Word. You can access information from the Web without leaving the Word program window. You can also create Web documents by using Word's Web publishing features. Every file you create can be converted to an HTML file to publish on the Web or a corporate intranet. ●

How to Open a Web Document from Word

If a document file has a link or URL, you can open the corresponding Web page without leaving your Word program window or opening your Web browser. Microsoft's programmers have designed Word to access the Web on its own. Using the Web toolbar, you can navigate pages, perform a search, and follow links. You can type in the URLs for pages you want to view or follow links from page to page.

Begin

1 Follow a Link

If you're currently viewing a document that has a link you want to follow, click the link.

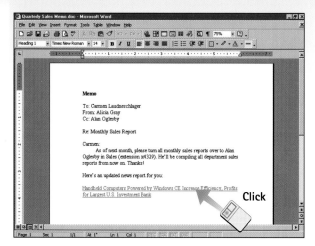

Click

2 Log On

If you're not logged on to your Internet connection, a Dial-up Connection dialog box may appear, depending on how your computer is set up. Click **Connect**.

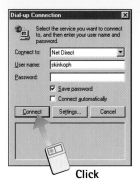

Click

3 Document Displayed

After you have established your connection, Word displays the Web page.

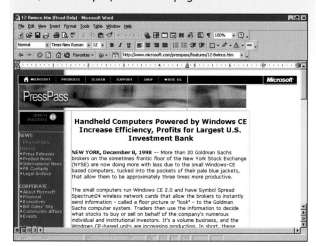

4 Display the Web Toolbar

If the Web toolbar isn't visible, right-click a toolbar area and select **Web** (or open the **View** menu, choose **Toolbars**, and then select **Web**).

Right Click

5 Navigate Pages

You can use the Web toolbar to navigate the Web from within the program window. Use the **Back** and **Forward** buttons to view pages you have loaded. You can enter new URLs or click links to see other pages.

Back   Forward

End

How-To Hints

Saving Web Pages

You can save Web pages by using the Save As dialog box. Open the **File** menu and select **Save As**. You can assign the page a name and choose to save it as an HTML document or another file type.

Using the Web Toolbar

The toolbar buttons on the Web toolbar work the same way they do in Internet Explorer. You can stop a page from downloading, return to your home page, visit pages you've marked as favorites, and even conduct a Web search.

How to Save a Word File for the Web

Web pages are formatted in *HTML code*, which stands for HyperText Markup Language—coding that Web browser programs can interpret. You can easily save any document file as an HTML document to be posted on the Web. If you have a document you would like to post on the Internet or add to your Web site, save the file in HTML format. This converts the formatting into codes that can be interpreted by Web browsers.

Begin

1 Open the File

Open the file you want to save as an HTML document.

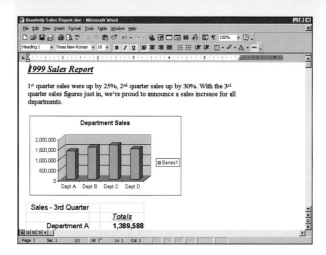

2 Open the Save As Dialog Box

Display the **File** menu and select **Save as Web Page**. This opens the Save As dialog box.

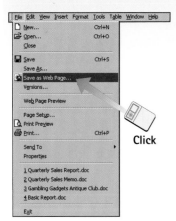

Click

3 Enter a Filename

Designate a folder to save the file to, and assign a name to the file, if needed. Notice that the **Save as type** box lists the file type as a Web page.

4 Change the Page Title

If you want other Internet users to see a specific type of title in their browser's title bar when viewing the page, click the **Change Title** button. This opens the Set Page Title dialog box.

Click

5 Enter a New Title

Word assigns a default page title, but you can type in your own title. Click inside the **Page title** text box and enter a title for the page. Click **OK** to return to the Save As dialog box.

6 Click Save

Click the **Save** button.

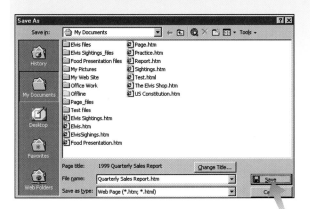

Click

7 File Is Converted

The file is converted to HTML format, Word switches you to Web Layout View, and the file's name on the title bar now reflects a Web page format.

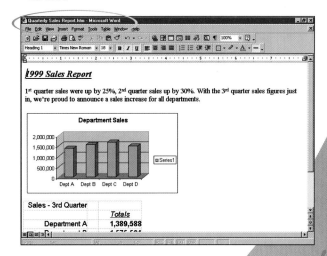

End

How to Use Word's Web Page Wizard

Word comes with an excellent wizard for helping you create professional-looking Web pages. You can save any Word document you create as an HTML file, but the Web Page Wizard offers you preformatted layouts in a variety of styles. All you have to do is fill in your own text. With the Web Page Wizard, you can create several pages that make up your own Web site.

Begin

1 Open the New Dialog Box

From the Word program window, open the **File** menu and select **New**. This opens the New dialog box.

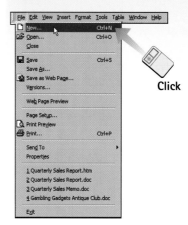

Click

2 Choose the Web Page Wizard

From the Web Pages tab, double-click the **Web Page Wizard**. This opens the wizard and also displays a sample Web page in the background.

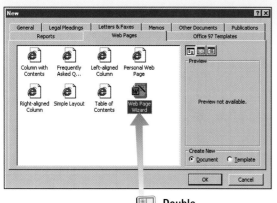

Double Click

3 Start the Wizard

Word switches you to Web Layout View and opens the Web Page Wizard. In the first wizard dialog box that appears, click **Next** to get started.

Click

4 Name Your Web Site

Click inside the **Web site title** text box and enter a name for your Web site. To save the pages in the default location, click **Next** to continue. To save the pages in another location besides the default location, click the **Browse** button and locate the folder where you want to save the pages.

Click

5 Choose a Navigation

Most Web pages use frames for navigation so you can see parts of the site from one page. Choose the type of frame navigation you prefer to use for your site and click **Next** to continue.

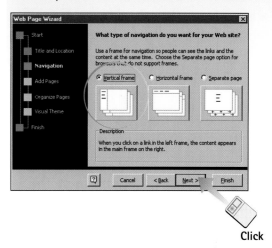

Click

6 Choose Pages

Use the next Wizard box to designate how many pages you want to create for your Web site. You can use one page or many pages, depending on how much information you want to present. By default, the Wizard starts you with three pages. To add another page, click the **Add New Blank Page** button. To remove a page, select it in the list box and click **Remove Page**. Click **Next** to continue.

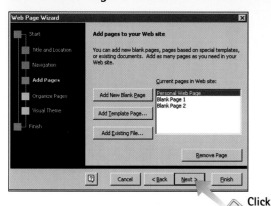

Click

7 Order the Pages

Use the next box to organize how you want the pages to appear. To rearrange the order, select a page in the list box and click the **Move Up** or **Move Down** buttons. Use the **Rename** button to rename a page. Click **Next** to continue.

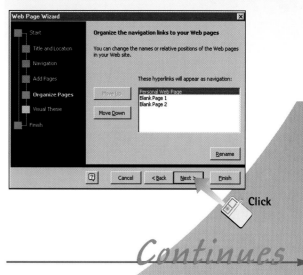

Click

Continues

8 Set a Theme

To add some pizzazz to your Web page(s), consider adding a theme—a preset background format. Click the **Add a visual theme** option, and then click the **Browse Themes** button.

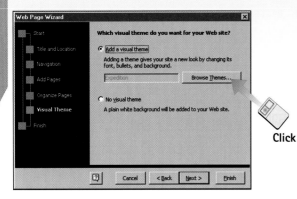

Click

9 Choose a Theme

From the Theme dialog box, select a theme and the sample area shows you what it looks like. When you find a theme you like, select it and click **OK**.

Click

10 Continue

You're returned to the wizard dialog box. Click **Next** to continue.

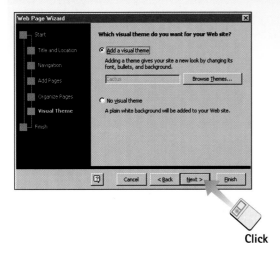

Click

11 Finish

At the final wizard dialog box, click **Finish**.

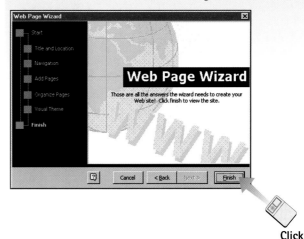

Click

12 The Web Page Opens

The Web page (or pages) opens in Word along with the floating Frames toolbar. From here, you can start filling in the placeholder text with your own.

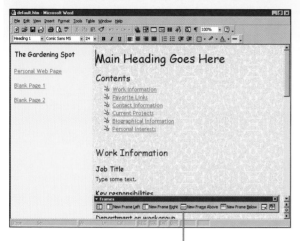

Frames toolbar

13 Enter Your Own Text

Select the text and type in your own text.

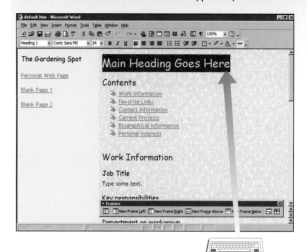

14 The New Text Appears

The selected placeholder text is immediately replaced with new text you type. You won't have to worry about formatting because the template has already assigned compatible formatting throughout.

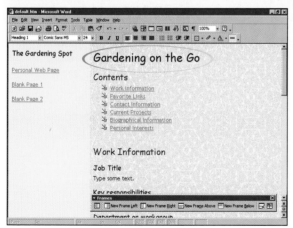

End

How-To Hints

Not Installed?

Some of the themes you may select in the Theme dialog box aren't installed. Insert your Word CD-ROM and click the **Install** button to install the theme to your hard disk drive.

Publish to the Web

Use Microsoft's Web Publishing Wizard to help you post your Web page to a server. If you're posting to a network server in your company, you will need to check with the system administrator for assistance. If you're posting the Web page to your Internet service provider's server, be sure to check the guidelines. When you're ready to post, click the **Start** menu and choose **Programs, Accessories, Internet Tools, Web Publishing Wizard**.

Save Your Work

Don't forget to save your work when finished. Word will save your Web page or pages as an HTML document when you click the **Save** button on the toolbar.

How to Create a Custom Web Page in Word

If you prefer to design your own Web page without help from Word's Web Page Wizard, you can use Word's formatting tools to assign styles and create headings and body text for your page. You can easily add lists and graphics (see Task 9, "How to Add a Graphic to Your Web Page," to learn how). When you're finished, save your page to post on the Web.

Begin

1 Open the New Dialog Box

Display the **File** menu and select **New**. This opens the New dialog box.

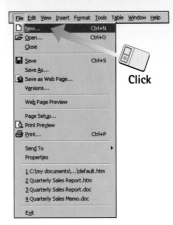

Click

2 Select the Blank Web Page

From the **General** tab, double-click the **Web Page** icon.

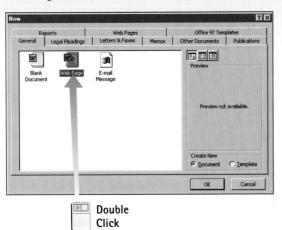

Double Click

3 It's Blank

Word switches the view to Web Layout View and opens a blank Web page in your program window.

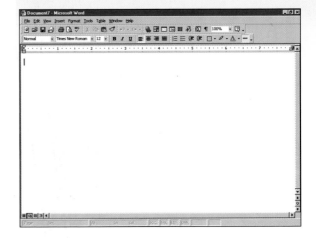

4 Select a Heading Style

To enter a heading for the Web page, click the **Style** drop-down list on the Formatting toolbar and choose a heading style, such as **Heading 1**. Heading styles range in sizes from large to small.

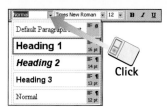

Click

5 Type In the Heading Text

Type in the heading text. If you're creating a personal Web page, for example, you might type **Welcome to Ralph's Page**. If you're creating a company Web page, type in the company name. If your page has a particular focus, such as gardening, include the focus in the heading.

6 Keep Adding Text

Continue selecting styles to use and typing in your own text. You can format the text any way you like, changing fonts, increasing font sizes, and more. When you're finished, be sure to save your work. Check out Tasks 5–9 to learn how to add links, graphics, and other effects to your Web page.

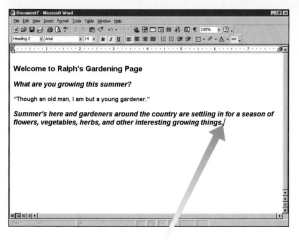

How-To Hints

Use the Web Tools Box

To help you format and build your Web page, display the floating Web Tools toolbar. Right-click over any toolbar and select **Web Tools**. To learn what a button does, hover your mouse pointer over the button to reveal a ScreenTip.

End

How to Insert a Hyperlink

You can quickly insert a hyperlink into your document. Word recognizes *URLs*—Uniform Resource Locators—as links as soon as you type them. However, you must be careful about spelling the URL correctly.

When you're creating Web pages, you can turn any text into a link by using the Insert Hyperlink dialog box. The dialog box enables you to create links to other Web pages or other files on your computer. If your Web page is exceptionally long, you can even link to other areas on the page. Learn how to insert hyperlinks in this task.

Begin

1 Select the Text

Start by entering the text you want to use as a link. If you created a Web page by using the Web Page Wizard, for example, you can select a pre-underlined link and type in your own text. If you created a Web page from scratch, you can select any word or phrase to turn into a link.

Click

2 Open Insert Hyperlink Dialog Box

Open the **Insert** menu and select **Hyperlink** or click the **Create Hyperlink** button on the Standard toolbar. This opens the Insert Hyperlink dialog box.

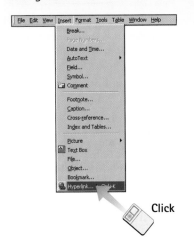

Click

3 Enter the URL

Click inside the **Type the file or Web page name** text box and enter the URL of the Web page to which you want to link. If the URL you want to use is listed in the list box, you can select it instead of typing it.

4 Exit the Dialog Box

Click **OK** to close the dialog box.

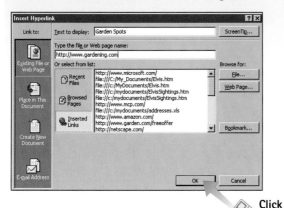

Click

5 The Text Appears as a Link

The text you worked with appears in blue and has an underline to indicate it's a hyperlink. You can repeat these steps to add as many links as you want to the page.

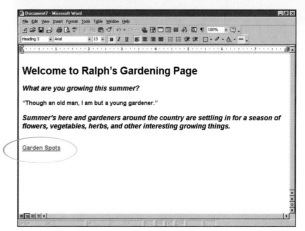

End

How-To Hints

Check Them Out

Be sure to check your URLs to make sure they're correct. It's frustrating to a Web surfer to encounter URLs that aren't up-to-date or that take the user to the wrong information.

Look Up a Page

If you don't know the exact URL you want to use as a hyperlink, click the **Web Page** button to open your Web browser and locate the page. When you find the page, close the browser window to return to the Insert Hyperlink dialog box. The URL will now appear in the list box (you may have to click **Browsed Pages**). Select the URL from the list and click **OK**.

How to Add Pizzazz to a Web Document with Word's Web Page Themes

If you created a Web page with the Web Page Wizard in Task 3, you briefly saw how to add a theme to your page. Themes are preformatted backgrounds, fonts, and sizes you can apply to your Web page, similar to styles you apply to Word text. You can change the theme of your Web document at any time to create new looks or make your Web page seem more up-to-date. If you created a Web page from scratch, as demonstrated in Task 4, you can add a theme to jazz up the appearance of your page.

Begin

1 Open the Web Page

Start by opening the Web page you want to use in Word.

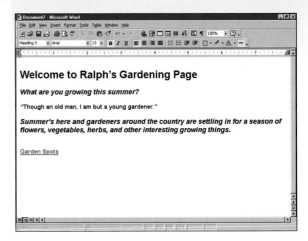

2 Select the Theme Command

Open the **Format** menu and select **Theme**. This opens the Theme dialog box.

Click

3 Preview a Theme

Select a theme from the list box. As soon as you do, a sample of the theme appears in the sample box. Use the scrollbar to scroll through the list of available themes and preview each one.

4 Select a Theme

When you find a theme you like, select it and click **OK** to close the dialog box.

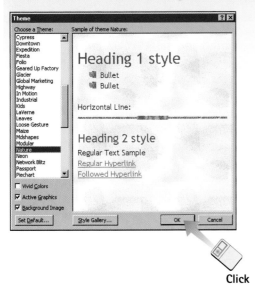

Click

5 Theme Applied

Word applies the theme to your Web page. If you decide you don't like it after all, click the **Undo** button or return to the Theme dialog box and choose another.

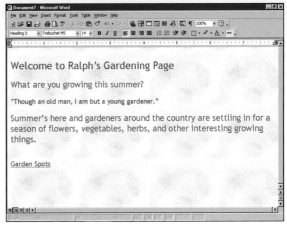

End

How-To Hints

Not Installed?

Some of the themes you may select in the Theme dialog box aren't installed. Insert your Office CD-ROM and click the **Install** button to install the theme to your hard disk drive.

Check It Out

It's a good idea to check how your page appears in the Web browser after choosing a theme. Open the **File** menu and select **Web Page Preview**. This opens the page in your browser. Now you can check to see whether the background is too busy or whether the text is legible.

How to Create Scrolling Text

You can apply any of Word's formatting commands to Web page text. For example, you can add color to text, or turn a list into a snazzy bulleted list with graphics as bullet symbols. In addition to the regular formatting commands, the Web Tools toolbar offers a variety of options you can apply. One of the most interesting effects you can add to your Web page is to create scrolling text, animated text that seemingly moves across the page. In this task, you learn how to animate your own text.

Begin

1 Click in Place

Start by clicking in the Web page where you want to insert scrolling text.

Click

2 Display the Web Tools Toolbar

If the Web Tools toolbar is not displayed, right-click over a displayed toolbar and choose **Web Tools** from the shortcut menu.

Right Click

Click

3 Click the Scrolling Text Button

On the Web Tools toolbar, click the **Scrolling Text** button. This opens the Scrolling Text dialog box.

Click

4 Choose a Scroll and Enter Text

Click the **Behavior** drop-down arrow to display a list of scroll behaviors and select the one you want. Click inside the **Type the scrolling text here** box and enter your own text.

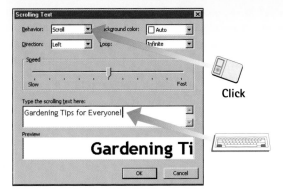

Click

5 Adjust the Speed

Drag the **Speed** control to adjust how fast or slow you want the text to scroll.

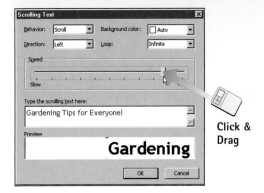

Click & Drag

6 Exit the Dialog Box

Click the **Loop** drop-down list and set how often you want the text to scroll. To set the scroll effect to scroll continuously, leave the **Infinite** option selected. Click **OK** to exit the dialog box.

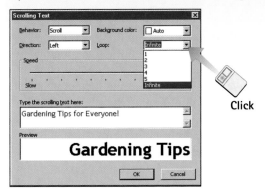

Click

7 View the Effect

Word adds the scrolling text box to your Web page. You won't be able to see the animation unless you switch to Web Page Preview. Learn how to do this in Task 10, "How to Check Your Page's Appearance in Internet Explorer."

End

How to Add Backgrounds and Frames

If you're creating a Web page from scratch or fine-tuning one created with the Web Page Wizard, you may want to change the background. This is particularly true if you don't like the current background or can't find a theme background that looks right. Instead, try a simple color background, or choose from the many effects available in the Fill Effects dialog box.

Frames are used to help the Web user navigate a site or page. You can apply frames to your current page to make the site contents more manageable. In this task, you learn how to change the background and add frames.

Begin

1 Open the Background Dialog Box

Open the **Format** menu and select **Background**. This displays a palette of alternate colors you can apply. To assign a plain color background, select a color from the palette.

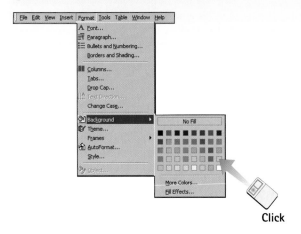

Click

2 View More Colors

For more color choices, click the **More Colors** option in the Background palette to open the Colors dialog box. Click a color from the palette and click **OK** to apply it to your Web page.

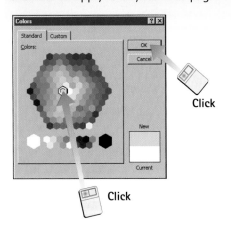

Click

Click

3 Try a Fill Effect

Click the **Fill Effects** option on the Background palette to open the Fill Effects dialog box. This dialog box has tabs for selecting a gradient effect, a pattern, or a texture. Explore each tab to see the various effects you can create. For example, click the **Texture** tab and select a texture; click **OK** to exit the dialog box and apply the effect.

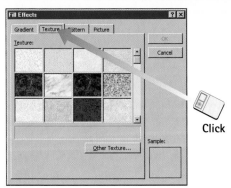

Click

4 Add a Frame

To add a frame to your Web page, open the **Format** menu, select **Frames**, and then choose the type of frame. For example, select the **Table of Contents in Frame** to create a frame that holds a table of contents to items in your Web site. To create a blank frame, select **New Frames Page**.

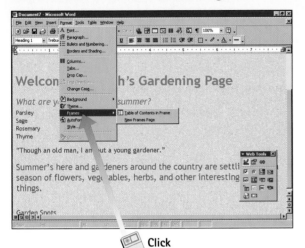

Click

5 The Page Is Broken into Frames

If you selected the Table of Contents, Word opens a table of contents frame to the left and a floating Frames toolbar appears; edit the contents frame to suit your needs. If you selected a blank frame, the floating Frames toolbar appears and you can begin adding as many frames as you need.

Contents frame   Floating toolbar

6 Add a New Frame

Click at the bottom of the Web page and then click the **New Frame Below** button on the Frames toolbar. This adds an empty frame below, as shown in this figure. You can add and edit text to frames, assign backgrounds, or add links inside the frame just like another Web page.

New empty frame   Click

How-To Hints

Delete a Frame

To remove a frame from your Web page, click inside the frame and then click the **Delete Frame** button on the Frames toolbar.

Working with Frames

Each frame is a separate document, so you can add and edit text and add any other item to the document, such as graphics, backgrounds, and more. You must also save the document as part of your Web site.

End

How to Add a Graphic to Your Web Page

You can also add graphics to your Web page, including clip art, ruled lines, tables, control buttons, multimedia clips, and more. This task will focus on adding images, which are easy to add to a page. Images can spruce up a drab Web page and add visual interest. For example, you can use company logos, photos, and clip art, or graphic objects you draw yourself.

Most Web browsers can display only GIF, JPEG, and XBM image files, so it's best to stick with these file types when inserting images into your own pages.

Begin

1 Click in Place

Click the insertion point where you want to insert the image. It's a good idea to put an image at the top of the Web page so the person viewing your page immediately sees your nice graphic.

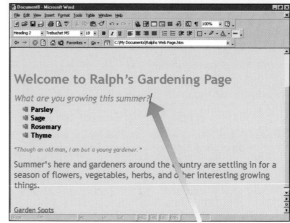

Click

2 Use the Insert Command

Open the **Insert** menu, select **Picture**, and then choose **From File**. This opens the Insert Picture dialog box. (To learn how to insert clip art, see Chapter 11, "How to Work with Graphics," Task 1, "How to Insert Clip Art.")

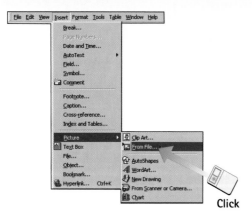

Click

3 Locate the Image

Find and select the image file you want to use in your Web page and click the **Insert** button.

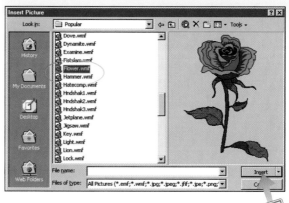

Click

4 Resize the Image

The image is inserted into your page. You can resize it by selecting it and dragging any of the resizing handles.

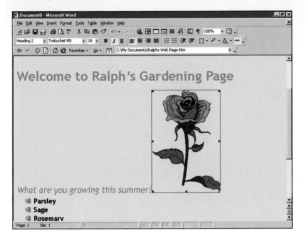

5 Open the Format Picture Box

To better position the image next to text, right-click and select **Format Picture** from the short-cut menu. This opens the Format Picture dialog box.

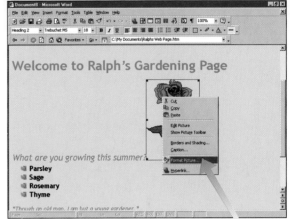

Click

6 Change the Wrap Settings

Use the Format Picture dialog box to fine-tune the wrapping and positioning controls for the image by using the various tabs. For example, click the **Layout** tab and select a wrapping style, such as **Square**, to fit the text around the picture.

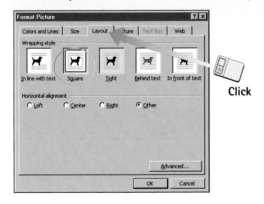

Click

7 Enter Placeholder Text

Finally, click the **Web** tab and enter a description of the image or alternative text in the **Alternative text** box. This text will describe the image in case it doesn't display properly in the Web browser window. Some users choose to browse the Web without viewing graphics to speed up their downloading time. Click **OK** to save your new settings.

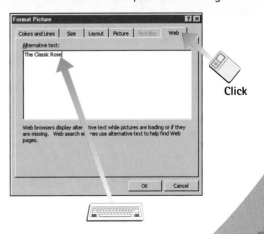

Click

End

How to Check Your Page's Appearance in Internet Explorer

Viewing your Web page in Web Layout view doesn't always give you a good perspective as to how everything looks for the person browsing the page. To check out how things really appear in a browser window, use Word's Web Page Preview command.

Begin

1 Open the Web Page

Open the Web page you want to view.

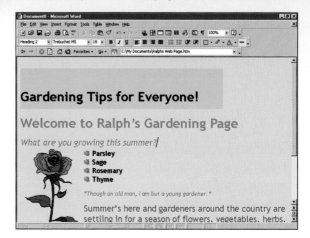

2 Select Web Page Preview

Display the **File** menu and choose **Web Page Preview**.

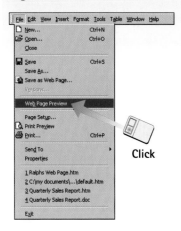

Click

3 Check Out the Page

Your Web browser window opens and displays your Web page exactly as other users will see it. Scroll through and check out your page.

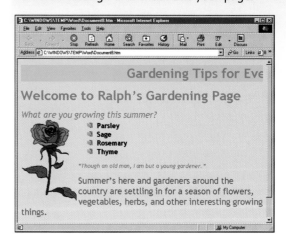

4 Exit the Browser Window

To close the browser window and return to Word, click the **Close** button in the upper-right corner of the program window.

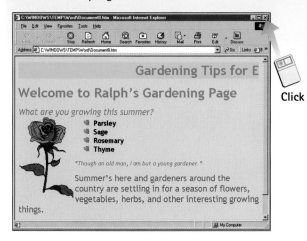

Click

5 Return to the Word Window

Now you're back in the Word window where you can make any corrections to the Web page elements.

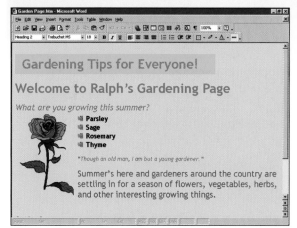

End

How-To Hints

Verify Those Links

Be sure to verify that every hyperlink you insert into your Web page works properly and links to the correct page. You can do this from Web Page Preview. Simply click the link to view the corresponding page.

Watch Those Color Combinations

When applying different themes and color backgrounds to your Web page, make sure your text remains legible and check to make sure the colors are easy on the eyes. If your page has too many conflicting visual elements, someone viewing your page may miss your message.

Open Your Page in Internet Explorer

You don't have to be using Word to view a Word Web page. You can open your document from the Internet Explorer browser window. Display the **File** menu and select **Open**. Then click the **Browse** button and locate the Word Web page you want to view and click **Open**, and then click **OK**.

Project

Project

If you've been following along with the various projects in this book, you have learned to create a basic letter and a report, and turn them into a mass mailing. In this project, I'll show you how to turn the report you created back in Chapter 12, "How to Print Files," into a Web page document.

When the Web page is complete, there are various ways to post it to a Web server, depending on your account. Check your Internet service or system administrator for additional guidance for posting the page.

1 Open the Report

Open the report document you created back in Chapter 12.

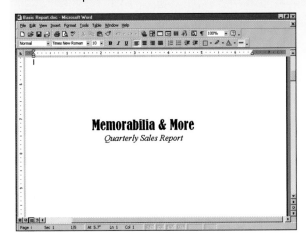

2 Save As a Web Page

Open the **File** menu and select **Save as Web Page**. This opens the Save As dialog box.

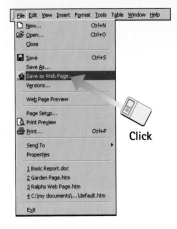

Click

3 Name the File

Click inside the **File name** text box and enter a name for the file. Notice the file format is already set to Web Page.

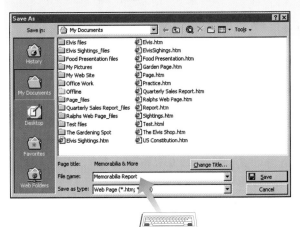

4 Enter a Page Title

Word assigns a default page title for the Web page based on the first line of text and displays the title in the Save As dialog box. To enter a different title, click the **Page title** button and type in a new title. Click **OK** to return to the Save As dialog box.

5 Click Save

You may get a message indicating that some features may be lost. To save the file, click the **Save** button.

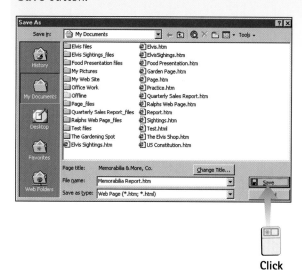

Click

6 Add a Theme

To add a theme to your report, open the **Format** menu and choose **Theme**.

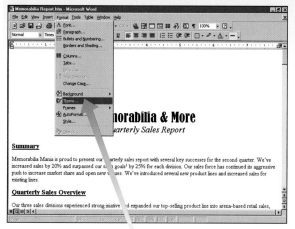

 Click

7 Select a Theme

Scroll through the list of themes and click a theme to preview it.

End

8 Apply the Theme

When you find a theme you like, click **OK** and it's immediately applied to the Web page.

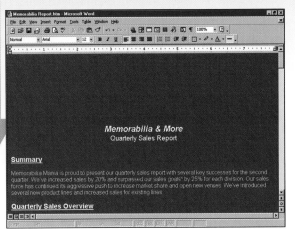

9 Add Some Artwork

To add clip art to your page, click where you want it inserted, open the **Insert** menu, select **Picture**, and then choose **Clip Art**. This opens the Insert ClipArt dialog box.

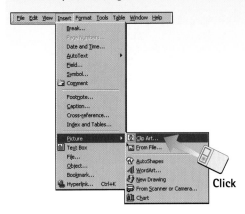

Click

10 Select a Category

Click the category you want to view.

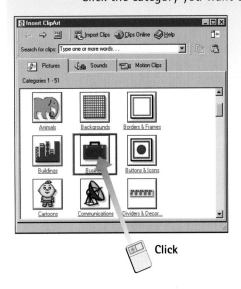

Click

11 Select Clip Art

Scroll through the clip art, click the one you want to insert, and then click the **Insert Clip** button on the balloon menu.

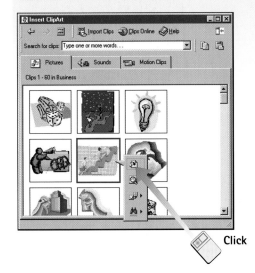

Click

12 Change the Text Wrap

You may need to resize the clip art to fit properly, or change how the text wraps around the graphic object. Right-click over the object and choose **Format Picture**.

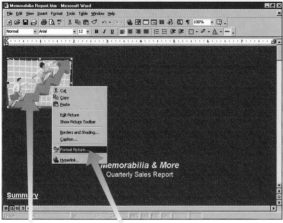

 Right Click

 Click

13 Click the Layout Tab

From the Format Picture dialog box, click the **Layout** tab, and then select the wrap style you want to apply. Click **OK** to exit the dialog box and apply the setting.

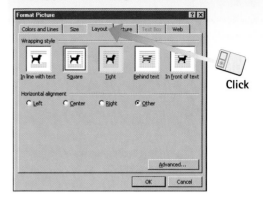

Click

14 Preview the Page

When the Web page looks exactly how you want it, use the Web Page Preview command to check out how it appears in the browser window. Open the **File** menu and choose **Web Page Preview**.

Click

15 Check Over the Page

Check over your Web page, and then click the **Close (X)** button to return to the Word window. Make any additional changes to the page and then save your work. Now you're ready to post the page.

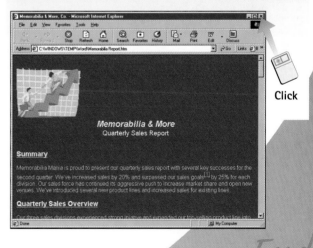

Click

End

Task

CHAPTER 15

How to Customize Word to Suit Your Work Needs

*I*n this final chapter of the book, I'll show you some basic ways you can customize Word to suit the way you work. For example, you can change many of Word's default settings to match the way documents are produced in your company, or you can change them to suit your own preferences. You can create your own custom toolbars and even create macros to speed up common tasks you perform daily with Word.

Don't worry about making changes to these types of settings. If you decide you don't like the new customized settings, you can always change them back. Feel free to experiment with the available options and see how they can enhance your productivity. ●

How to Create a New Toolbar

One way you can customize Word is to create your own toolbar. You can tailor-make a toolbar that contains only the buttons you want, regardless of with which toolbar the buttons are normally associated. This is particularly useful if you find yourself performing the same type of document tasks over and over; a toolbar would provide you quick access to all the commands you use frequently rather than those the Word programmers think you might need. In this task, you learn how to create and add buttons to a brand-new toolbar.

Begin

1 Open the Customize Dialog Box

Open the **Tools** menu and select **Customize**. This opens the Customize dialog box.

Click

2 Display the Toolbars Tab

Click the Toolbars tab, and then click the New button. This opens the New Toolbar dialog box.

 Click

3 Enter a Name

Click inside the **Toolbar name** text box and type in a name for the new toolbar. Click **OK** to return to the Customize dialog box.

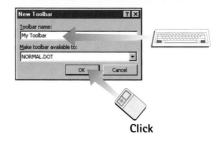

Click

4 Display the Commands Tab

A new, empty toolbar immediately appears onscreen. Click the **Commands** tab.

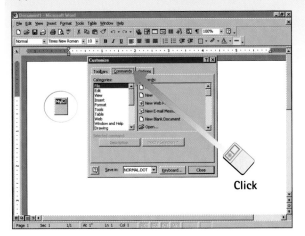

Click

5 Add a Button

Highlight a category in the left list box, and then locate the command you want to add to the toolbar in the right list box. To add the command to the new toolbar, click and drag it from the list over to the toolbar.

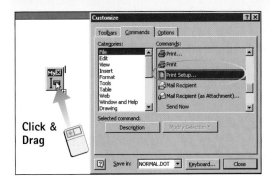

Click & Drag

6 Drop It in Place

Drop the command on the toolbar by releasing the mouse button. The command now appears as a button on the toolbar.

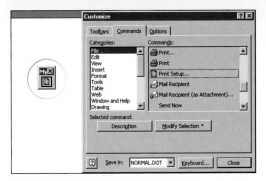

7 Add More Buttons

Continue dragging commands from the Customize dialog box onto the toolbar. Be sure to scroll through all the available categories and commands to see what's available.

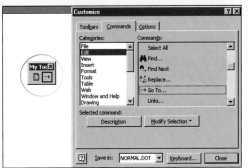

Continues

8 Group Your Buttons

If you add two or more similar command buttons to the toolbar, you may want to separate them from the other buttons with a divider line, called a group line. Right-click over the button you want to add a group line to the left of, and then choose **Begin a Group** from the shortcut menu.

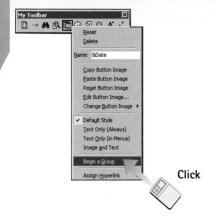

Click

9 A Group Line Is Added

A faint group line immediately appears on the toolbar.

Group line

10 Add Another Line

Repeat step 8 to add another group line to the other side of the group, as shown in this example.

Group lines

11 Change the Button Image

You can also customize the button image that appears on a button. Right-click a button to display the shortcut menu, and then select **Change Button Image** to display a palette of buttons from which you can choose.

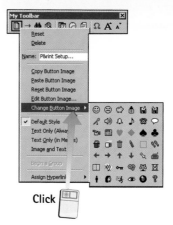

Click

12 The Button Changes

Word immediately replaces the button icon with the icon you selected from the palette, as shown in this figure.

new button

13 Move a Button

To move a button to another position on the toolbar, click and drag the button.

Click & Drag

14 Drop in Place

Drop the button where you want it to appear on the toolbar. To remove a button entirely, drag it off the toolbar.

new position

15 Close the Customize Dialog Box

When the toolbar is exactly as you want it, click the Close button in the Customize dialog box. You can now drag the toolbar's title bar to move the toolbar; double-click the title bar to anchor the toolbar at the top of the program window.

Click

End

How to Change the User Preference Settings

The Options dialog box has 10 different tabs of options you can change to suit your own work needs. Peruse these tabs to find options for controlling what items appear in the program window, where files are stored, editing features, and all kinds of other user preferences. In this task, you find an overview of the Options dialog box and learn how to set several useful options to help you with your own Word productivity.

Begin

1 Open the Options Dialog Box

Display the **Tools** menu and select **Options**. This opens the Options dialog box.

Click

2 Turn Off Onscreen Elements

Use the View tab to turn on or off onscreen items such as the Status bar, scroll bars, and ScreenTips. The tab also has check boxes for showing tab characters, spaces, paragraph marks, and other nonprinting characters.

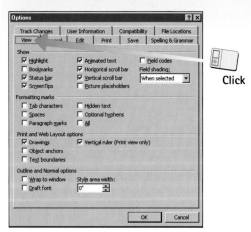

Click

3 Change Measurement Units

By default, Word uses the inch as its measurement unit, but you can change this setting. Click the **General** tab and click the **Measurement units** drop-down arrow and choose another measurement.

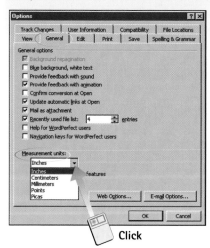

Click

4 Change the Used File List

Whenever you open the File menu, Word lists the last four files you worked on at the very bottom of the menu; to open a file, just click on its name in the list. You can change the number of files listed by adjusting the **Recently used file list** setting in the **General** tab. Click the spin arrows to set a new number or type in a number.

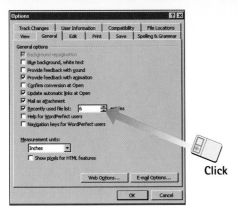

Click

5 Change Edit Options

Click the **Edit** tab to find a slew of edit options you can turn on or off. For example, if you prefer not to use the Click-and-Type feature, deselect the **Enable click and type** text box. Check over the edit options and see whether there are others you'd like to turn on or off.

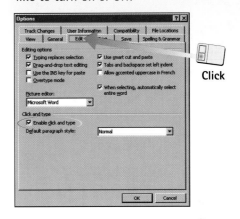

Click

6 Change the Print Options

The Print tab has options for determining how your documents print, including items such as field codes or user comments. Look through the options on this tab to find any preferences you want to set regarding printing.

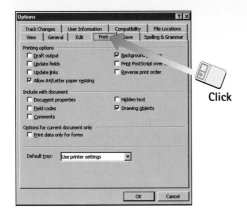

Click

7 Save Automatically

The **Save** tab has options pertaining to how Word saves files. If you want Word to automatically save your document every few minutes in case of power failure (or other dreaded computer glitches), make sure the **Save AutoRecover info every** check box is selected, and then use the spin arrows to set the number of minutes between saves.

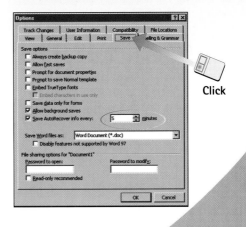

Click

End

8 Save Files As Other File Types

To save all your Word files in another file format, click the **Save Word files as** drop-down arrow and select another file type from the list box.

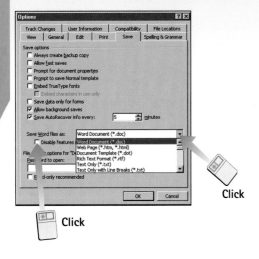

Click

Click

9 Change Spelling & Grammar Options

Click the **Spelling & Grammar** tab to view options for Word's spelling and grammar check features. Here you can turn the feature on or off, or specify variables to ignore or check.

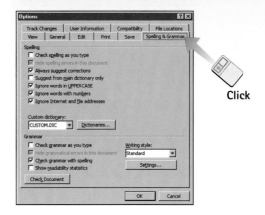

Click

10 Save to a Different Folder

By default, Word always saves to the My Documents folder on your computer unless you specify another location in the Save As dialog box. If you prefer to save all your files to another folder, click the **File Locations** tab, select **Documents**, and then click the **Modify** button.

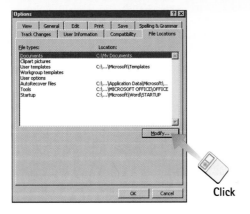

Click

11 Choose Another Location

Use the Modify Location dialog box to change to another folder. Select the folder and click **OK** to return to the File Locations tab.

Click

12 View Compatibility Options

Click the **Compatibility** tab to view a list of options for viewing the current file. This tab is useful if you're viewing files from other programs. You can turn options on or off with a click.

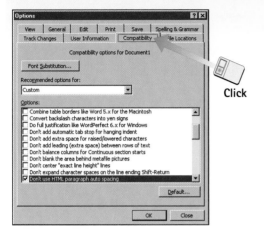

Click

13 Change User Information

Click the **User Information** tab to find several areas for changing your user initials, name, and creating a mailing address to appear on letters and envelopes you create with Word. Click inside a box and type any changes.

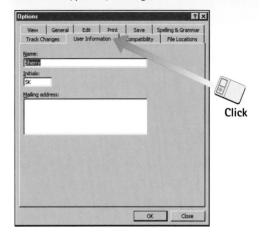

Click

14 View Track Change Options

Click the **Track Changes** tab to view options for changing how users share documents and how Word tracks changes between different users. To learn more about tracking changes, see Chapter 6, "How to Check Your Document for Errors," Task 6, "How to Track Document Changes Between Users."

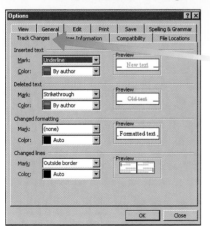

Click

15 Exit the Dialog Box

To apply any changes you make to the options in the Options dialog box, click **OK** to exit from the dialog box.

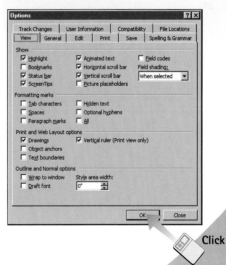

Click

End

How to Change the Default Font and Size

When you first install and open Word, it starts each new file with a default font and size. You may prefer to use a different font or a larger size for every document. This is particularly true if your company has a set standard for memos, letters, and other printed communications materials. Rather than change the font and size manually each time you start a new file, you can easily change the default settings by using the Font dialog box.

Begin

1 Open the Font Dialog Box

Open the **Format** menu and choose **Font**. This opens the Font dialog box with the **Font** tab displayed.

Click

2 Or Use the Shortcut Menu

Another way to open the Font dialog box is to right-click in the document page and choose **Font** from the shortcut menu.

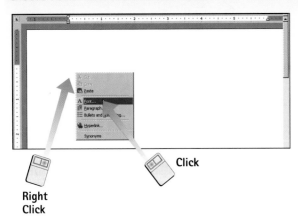

Right Click

Click

3 Change the Font

To change the font, scroll through the **Font** list and select the font you want to use.

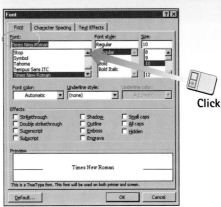

Click

4 Change the Size

To change the font size, scroll through the **Size** list and select a new size.

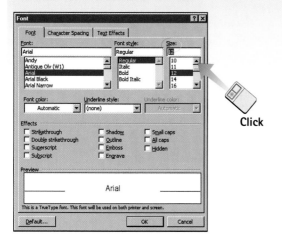

Click

5 Click Default

Change any other formatting you want to make the default setting, and then click the **Default** button.

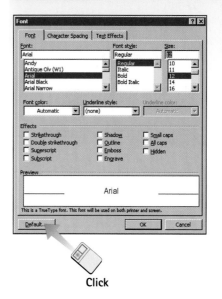

Click

6 Click Yes

A prompt box appears warning you that you're about to change the default font. Click **Yes**.

Click

7 The New Settings Are Applied

Word's Formatting toolbar now reflects the new defaults in place; in this example, the font is now Arial and the size is 12 point.

End

How to Create a Simple Macro to Speed Up Text Entry and Formatting

A macro is a set of recorded instructions you use to automate a common Word task. Use macros to speed up repetitive tasks such as selecting menu commands, formatting text, and other tedious operations. You can record a macro, for example, that opens the Font dialog box and assigns superscript, which saves you the time of using the keyboard or mouse methods to access the dialog box. In this task, I'll show you how to create a macro for opening the Font dialog box and assigning superscript formatting. Follow these same steps to create other useful macros.

Begin

1 Start a Macro

Open the **Tools** menu, select **Macro**, and then select **Record New Macro**.

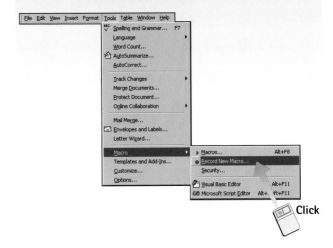

Click

2 Enter a Macro Name

Click inside the **Macro name** text box and type in a one-word name for the macro.

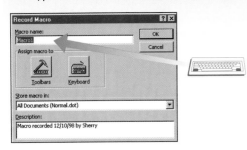

3 Define a Shortcut Key

Click the Keyboard button to open a dialog box for defining a shortcut key combination to use to run the macro.

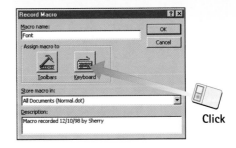

Click

4 Enter a Shortcut Key

Enter a shortcut key in the **Press new shortcut key** text box. Try using the Alt or Ctrl keys along with other keyboard characters, such as **Alt+I**. You may have to try several combinations until you find a combination that's not currently assigned to another Word function. Click **Assign** to assign the shortcut key to your macro.

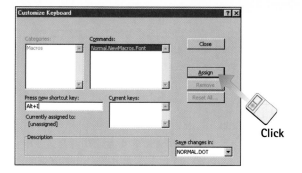

Click

5 Close the Dialog Box

Click **Close** to exit the dialog box and start recording the macro.

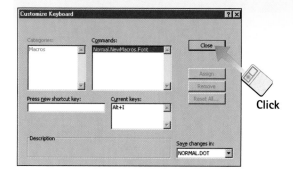

Click

6 Record the Macro

The Macro toolbar appears onscreen in record mode. Carefully follow all the steps necessary to perform the task for which you're creating a macro; use the mouse or keyboard to open menus and dialog boxes and select commands. In this example, I'm opening the Font dialog box to select superscript formatting.

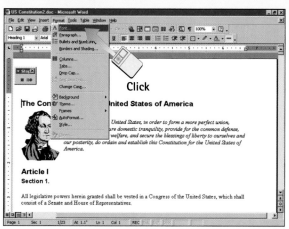

Click

7 Stop Recording

To stop recording the macro, complete the task and click the **Stop** button on the Macro toolbar. The next time you want to perform the task, type in the keyboard shortcut key you assigned.

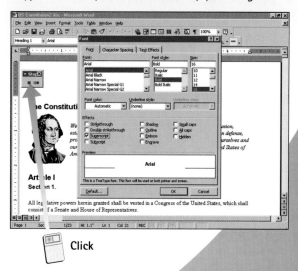

Click

End

5

How to Build a Custom Template

In Chapter 2, "How to Save, Close, Open, and Create New Files," Task 2, "How to Build a New File with a Wizard," you learned how to build a Word document based on a template. You can also turn any document you create into a template file that can be used over and over again. For example, perhaps you find yourself repeatedly producing the same type of letter. Rather than rebuild it each time, turn the letter into a template. The key to creating a template is to save the document in Word's template file format rather than as a document file. This task will show you how.

Begin

1 Create the File

Start a new blank file, and then enter all the text necessary to comprise the file.

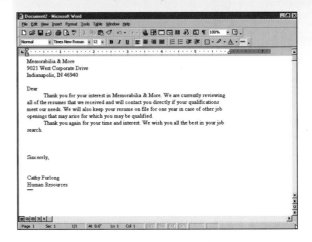

2 Format the Document

Add the necessary formatting commands to make the document look just the way you want it. You can even insert fields, such as date and salutation fields.

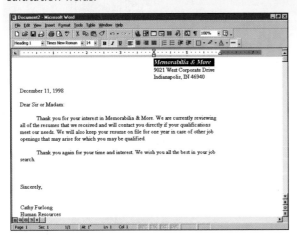

3 Save the Document

Open the **File** menu and select **Save As**. This opens the Save As dialog box.

Click

4 Enter a Filename

Click inside the **File name** text box and type in a name for the template.

5 Select the Template File Type

Click the **Save as type** drop-down arrow and select **Document Template (*.dot)** from the list box. This saves the file as a template rather than a regular document. Templates are stored with other Word template files in the Templates folder. Click **Save**.

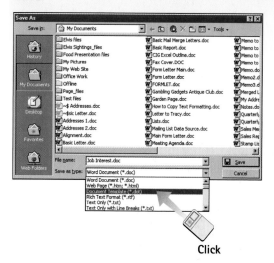

Click

6 Start a New File

To use the template at another time, open the **File** menu and select **New**. This opens the New dialog box.

Click

7 Choose the Template

Click the **General** tab and double-click the template file. This starts a new document based on the template you created.

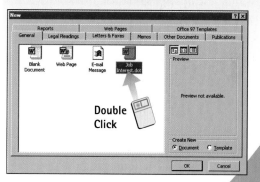

Double
Click

End

Project

Macros are a great way to speed up your work. For example, you can create macros to quickly format text or perform repetitive program tasks for you. In this project, I'll show you how to create a macro for quickly applying a style throughout your document. You can use these steps to apply an existing Word style or a style you created yourself by using the steps in Chapter 8, "How to Change Paragraph Formatting," Task 9, "How to Change a Style."

1 Open the Macro Feature

Select the text to which you want to apply a style, open the **Tools** menu, choose **Macro**, and then select **Record New Macro**. This opens the Record Macro dialog box.

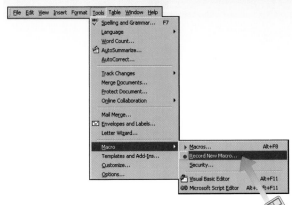

Click

2 Enter a Macro Name

Click inside the Macro name text box and type in a name for the new macro, and then click the **Keyboard** button.

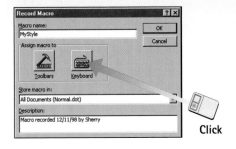

Click

3 Type a Shortcut Key

In the Customize Keyboard dialog box, click inside the **Press new shortcut key** text box and enter a key combination to assign as the shortcut for your new macro. In this example, I'm using Alt+O. Click **Assign**.

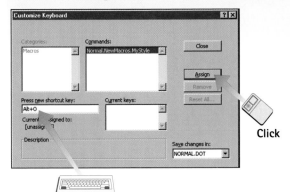

Click

4 Click Close

Exit the Customize Keyboard dialog box by clicking **Close**. This returns you to the document with the Macro toolbar onscreen.

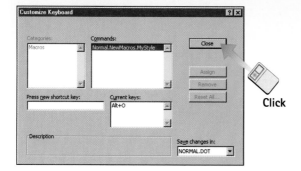

Click

5 Record the Macro

To record the macro for selecting a style, click the **Style** drop-down arrow on the Formatting toolbar.

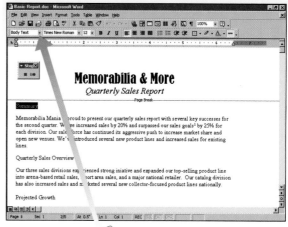

Click

6 Select a Style

Click the style you want to apply.

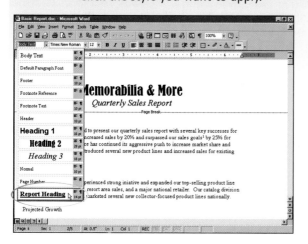

7 Stop Recording

Click the **Stop** button on the Macro toolbar to stop recording the macro. The next time you want to run the macro to apply the style, select the text and then press the shortcut key you assigned.

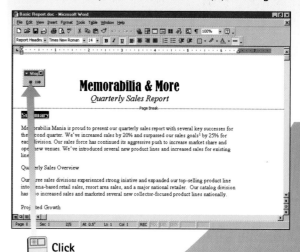

Click

End

Glossary

A–B

active document   The *document* currently selected in your Word window.

active window   In a multiple-window environment, the window that you are currently using or that is currently selected. Only one window can be active at a time, and keystrokes and commands affect the active window.

alignment   The way text lines up against the margins of a page, within the width of a *column*, or against tab stops.

AutoCorrect   A *Word* feature that corrects text or changes a string of characters to a word or phrase automatically.

AutoText   A formatted block of boilerplate text that you can insert wherever you need it.

browser   A program for surfing the *Internet* (such as Internet Explorer or Netscape Navigator).

C

cell   The intersection of a *column* and a *row* in a table.

Click-and-Type   A new feature in Word 2000 that lets you double-click anywhere on the document page and start typing. You can use this feature only in Print Layout or Web Layout view.

clip art   A predrawn illustration or *graphics object* you can insert into a Word file. Microsoft Word comes with a collection of clip art files you can use to illustrate your documents.

Clipboard   See *Windows Clipboard.*

Clipboard toolbar   A feature that's new to Word 2000, the Clipboard toolbar lets you paste multiple items in random order. The Clipboard can hold up to 12 cut or copied items.

close box   A small box with an X in it that's located in the upper-right corner of every Windows window and many dialog boxes; click it to close the program file, dialog box, or floating toolbar.

command   An instruction that tells the computer to carry out a task or perform an action.

comment   Extra information you can insert regarding your *Word* text. A comment can be a note to yourself or someone else who will read the file. The comment remains hidden until you point to the Comment indicator symbol.

cursor   The flashing vertical line that shows where text is entered. Also referred to as the *insertion point.*

D

data source   In a mail-merge procedure, the data source is the database list containing all the records you want to use with the mail-merge file.

database   A computer program that specializes in organizing, storing, and retrieving data. The term also describes a collection of data.

document   A file you create with a program such as Word. A document can be saved with a unique file name by which it can be retrieved.

document window   A rectangular portion of the screen in which you view and edit a *document.* A document window is typically located inside a program window.

download   To transfer a file from the *Internet* to your computer through telephone lines and a modem.

drag-and-drop   A technique for moving or copying data from one location to another. Select the item to move or copy, hold down the left mouse button, drag the item to a new location, and release the mouse button to drop it in place.

E

email   Electronic mail; a system that uses the *Internet* to send messages electronically over telephone wires instead of on paper.

Excel   A popular spreadsheet program designed for organizing and working with numbers, performing calculations, and other mathematical operations.

export   The process of converting and saving a file to be used in another program. See also *import*.

F

field   In a mail-merge document, a field indicates a piece of data from a data source that contains a particular type of information, such as Last Name, Phone Number, or Quantity.

file   A document you create and save in Word.

file format   When you save a file, it's saved in a format that tells the program how to display the file. To open the file in another program, you must convert the file into a format the other program can read. With Word, you can save your document files in different file formats so other users can read the files. For example, you can save a Word document as a WordPerfect file.

floating palette   A *palette* that can be dragged away from its *toolbar*.

floating toolbar   A *toolbar* that is not docked at the edges of the application window. A floating toolbar stays on top of other windows within the application window.

font   A typeface, such as Arial or Times New Roman, distinguished by a set of similarly styled characters.

footer   Text that appears at the bottom of every printed page. See also *header*.

formatting   Characteristics you can apply to text, paragraphs, or pages to change the way the data looks; formatting commands include bold, italic, color, fonts, and alignment.

G–H

graphics object   A picture you paste into a file or a line or shape (text box, rectangle, arc, picture) that you draw by using the tools on the Drawing toolbar.

handles   Small black squares located around the perimeter of selected *graphics objects*. By dragging the handles, you can move, copy, or size the selected object.

header   Text that appears at the top of every printed page. See also *footer*.

hyperlink   Colored, underlined text that you can click to open another file or go to a *Web* address.

I–L

import   The process of converting and opening a file that was stored or created in another program. See also *export*.

insertion point   A flashing vertical line that shows the text entry point. Also referred to as the *cursor*.

Internet   A global network of connected computers that lets people connect to others via email, Web pages, and more. Most users connect to the Internet by using a service provider (see *Internet service provider*).

Internet service provider (ISP)   A private enterprise that provides a *server* through which you can connect to the Internet, usually for a small fee (also called *local service provider*).

intranet   A miniature Internet that operates within a company or organization.

landscape   The horizontal orientation of a page; opposite of *portrait*, or vertical, orientation.

local service provider   See *Internet service provider*.

M–O

mail merge   The process of creating several identical *documents* (such as form letters or mailing labels) that each pull a different set of information (such as addresses) out of a *database* (also called a data source).

merge fields   The placeholder text in a mail-merge document where database information is inserted in each finished, or merged, copy of the document.

object   A table, chart, or graphic you create and edit. An object can be inserted, pasted, or copied into any file.

Office Assistant   Animated Office help system that provides interactive help, tips, and other online assistance.

P–R

palette   A box containing choices for color and other special effects that you use when working with objects and text. A palette appears when you click a *toolbar* button, such as Border or Fill Color. See also *floating palette*.

portrait   The vertical orientation of a page; opposite of *landscape*, or horizontal, orientation.

Preview   A view that displays your document as it will appear when you print it. Items such as text and graphics appear in their actual positions.

record   A single row in a *database* or list. The first row of a database usually contains *field* names, and each additional row in the database is a record.

S

ScreenTips   Helpful notes that appear on your screen to explain a function or feature.

server   A computer used on the *Internet* or a network environment that stores email messages, *Web* pages, and other data.

split bar   The horizontal or vertical line dividing a split *document*. You can change the position of the split bar by dragging it, or you can remove the split bar by double-clicking it.

style   A collection of formatting settings you can apply to text.

T

table   Data about a specific topic that is stored in *records* (rows) and *fields* (columns).

taskbar   The horizontal bar across the bottom of the Windows desktop; it includes the Start button and buttons for any programs, documents, or items that are open.

template   Available in all Office programs, including *Word*, templates provide predesigned patterns on which files can be based.

toolbar   A collection of frequently used *commands* that appear as icon buttons you can click to activate.

U–Z

URL (Uniform Resource Locator)   A *Web* site address.

Web   See *World Wide Web*.

Windows Clipboard   A temporary holding area in computer memory that stores information that was cut or copied (such as text or graphics). You transfer data from the Clipboard by using the Paste *command*.

wizards   A set of dialog boxes that ask questions to walk you through processes such as creating a file or an *object* based on your answers.

Word   A popular word processing program used to create text-based *documents*.

World Wide Web (WWW)   The part of the *Internet* where *Web* sites are posted and available to Web *browsers*.

Index